JOHN
the twenty-third

LEONE ALGISI

JOHN

the twenty-third

Translated by
PETER RYDE

WESTMINSTER, MD   LONDON

THE NEWMAN PRESS   DARTON, LONGMAN & TODD

DARTON, LONGMAN & TODD LTD
29a Gloucester Road
London, SW7

THE NEWMAN PRESS
Westminster, Md

*Originally published by Marietti Editori under the title of
'Giovanni XXIII'*

*This English translation is © 1963, Darton, Longman & Todd Ltd
and is made from the revised French edition published by
P. Léthielleux (Paris) and with ecclesiastical permission of the
archdiocese of Paris.*

First published 1963

Printed in Great Britain by the Villafield Press, Bishopbriggs, Glasgow

CONTENTS

CONTENTS

LIST OF ILLUSTRATIONS

(All illustrations are placed between pages 56 and 57)

Chapter One

CHILDHOOD

Angelo Giuseppe Roncalli was born on November 25, 1881, at Sotto il Monte, a little town in the province of Bergamo, lying at the very foot of the first slopes which rise slowly from the plain of the Po towards the foothills of the Alps east of Lake Como. Like many market towns, it is an attractive place. During the winter months the sides of the hills undulate gently beneath a thick layer of snow, through which the tops of rows of poles and vine-plants can be seen, while in spring the fruit trees are magically bedecked in a thousand colours. In summer the still and scorching air is heavy with the fragrance of clover and thatch. Even today peacefulness reigns there and the inhabitants are noted for their great gentleness. To the north, where the lake lies, there is a brighter and more languid atmosphere; to the west the landscape melts away towards the course of the nearby River Adda where a little mist always hangs.

Behind the first range of mountains lies the village of Pontida, which figures prominently in the communal history of Lombardy. Behind the second range stretches the Imagna valley, inhabited by a people who, finding themselves too cramped in the narrow limits of their birth-place, have spread across the world, always alert and hard-working wherever they have gone. From that valley several centuries ago, perhaps from Roncaglia di Copin, members of a virile stock came down into the plain to cultivate more fertile land; to this day that family still has vigorous branches in some of the noblest Bergamesque and Italian houses.

The parents of little Angelo, who were married in 1877, already had two daughters. The father, Giovanni Battista, worked the land and must surely have given thanks to the Lord when the first boy was born. But in this family every child, boy or girl, was welcomed as a gift from God. After the first three, born at intervals of about one year, there followed ten others.

Giovanni Battista was of the same stamp as his forebears, hard-working and affectionate. A natural tranquillity, an uprightness in adversity, and an understanding and conciliatory nature, all these qualities no doubt aided his nomination as Justice of the Peace for the region. To have such a large family was nothing new for the Roncallis. The grandfather had seven children and the great-grand-father nine. In the Bergamesque country such fertility was common, especially among rural families. Even today it is not unusual to find families of ten, in spite of the depopulation which made its influence felt in Bergamo about 1900. In those days people generally married young. On his return from military service Giovanni Battista had already chosen his life companion and was not long in bringing her to his home.

Marriage did not mean leaving the paternal home. New generations would group themselves round the original vine-stock. Thus there grew up a feeling of economic security for the aged, the sick, and young married couples alike. Thanks to a tacit but effective contribution from all the members of the family, young married couples were helped through the critical phase of 'mouths that consume and arms that bring in nothing', until they were ready to take their place in the productive cycle and to bring fresh energy to the support of the older generation. In this way a kind of primitive insurance on a family scale was established.

The head of the family, thrifty and experienced, pooled

all the proceeds that were to be had from the sale of agricultural produce, from cattle-raising and manual labour. Members of the household would receive what they needed for immediate consumption and a little pocket money besides. In principle nothing came in which was not earmarked for the family coffers. The children began work at an early age, staying at school only a few years. By the time the last ones were born the elder ones had already been contributing to the prosperity of the house for some time. A large family would preserve its dignity by working loyally together, thereby encouraging the growth of affection and forming strong bonds.

Angelo's family, like any other, grew up in this atmosphere. It was not wealthy, for it owned no property and rented the land from which it earned its living. The farming family of Roncalli was nevertheless able to lead an honourable and quiet existence, and keep itself from extreme poverty. They knew nothing of that obsession for an ever greater degree of comfort which turns a rich man into a kind of miser who never has enough money; nor did they know anything of those anxieties concerning the future which the arrival of a number of children can inspire in others. Providence was their supreme stay and to it the prosperity of the house was entrusted. There was a feeling that everything was ordered by it, and in that belief lay comfort and hope. Making no attempt to evade his responsibility to the family, each member of the household lived not for himself, but in harmony with the others. Each one's character was modelled on acts of self-denial and kindheartedness, for which the variety of temperaments provided the opportunity. It was not a life of isolation; even if contact with the outside world was unusual, family life in all its different aspects developed in each one the qualities which create a feeling of trust. Egotism did not exist; they lived together in harmony, sharing the same sorrows and joys.

In this sanctuary the mother, Marianna Giulia Mazzola, occupied a place of honour. Always busy, as she grew older she became more and more silent, without being any the less attentive to the needs of everyone and everything. She was undemonstrative yet ever ready to console, to preach harmony, to give good advice. Without neglecting her duties as a wife, she became more and more a mother absorbed in a task which hardly ever released her from the house and which shut her up in an intimate world of cares and preoccupations that sometimes caused her anxiety.

The life of the Church played its part in instilling into the children strong feelings of piety. They babbled their prayers even before they had learned to speak properly. At the end of the day the whole family gathered round the great kitchen table to recite the rosary. In the long winter evenings uncle Zaverio, the grandfather's brother, the old bachelor of the household, would read the Bible or the meditations of Da Ponte. These were brief interludes during which the devout and thoughtful attitude of the grown-ups made a more vivid impression on the young ones than the words of the text. Early in the morning, winter or summer, they got up for first Mass. Often it would still be dark, but the keen fragrant air must have been invigorating for, at a time of terrible infant mortality, ten of Giovanni-Battista's thirteen children grew up strong and vigorous.

On Sundays, dressed in their best clothes which were replaced every two or three years, they attended their second Mass of the day, High Mass. After lunch they retraced their steps in procession to the church for religious instruction by the priest. The church was not far from the house, as it served the Brusico district. A little distance away on the hillside stood the fine old church of San Giovanni, the real mother church of the parish where the faithful still went on pilgrimage at the time of the main Church festivals.

The priest was the real head of the locality. Made

welcome in every home, he knew its history and its secrets and he knew how to get the best out of its members. When he spoke from the pulpit, expressing himself easily in the local dialect, his words were received like manna from heaven. His sermon in a sense took the place of the news-paper; he announced births, gave notice of illnesses and deaths, and created an atmosphere of unity in the village. He explained the Gospel simply, insisting on fundamental and simple truths; in this way he opened the hearts of his parishioners, who were by nature extremely thoughtful, to the blessings of life, detachment from vanities, an unfailing sense of God, and resignation in the face of death. Angelo grew up in these surroundings, absorbing for all time that helpful, trusting, and natural atmosphere. He was like any other child, slightly more sensitive perhaps, but physically robust. He took in his stride the normal phases of child-hood: first communion and primary school, which at that time did not go beyond the third grade in most areas of Italy. He was studious; his detachment from material things made him enjoy the charm of books, especially the missal and even the breviary, which he often saw in the hands of the priest. Sometimes he would take refuge and remain alone in a little upstairs room where he had stored some of his books. Those around him had already taken note of his inclinations and he was given the less arduous work to do in the fields. They knew, although he had never spoken of it to anyone, that he had chosen another way. It was not without some anxiety that the father thought about this child who was already isolating himself in his own secret world, but finding that the boy had calmly made up his mind he was reassured, the more so because he felt that his mother, so silent and gentle, also approved the choice that their son had made.

The path Angelo took was not only the path of study but also that of the priesthood. Looking back in later years, he thought that he had been drawn towards this ideal more by the atmosphere of faith in which he lived than by any inner voice or call from outside. And so he spoke of it early both to his mother and to the priest. At the age of eight Angelo was sent to school at the house of the priest of the neighbouring district, Carvico. The worthy but fiery Don Pietro Bolis agreed to take him and nearly every day for a year he sat him down at the end of his long kitchen table and initiated him into the rudiments of Latin and logical analysis. This introduction was rather crude. For a child of that age preparation for so difficult a language should have lasted much longer. They set to work on declensions at once. The priest certainly expected too much intelligence from his pupil and had great faith in his system of education which sometimes included a box on the ears. On this last matter, Angelo's father had left him complete freedom, but he clearly went too far. Sometimes he would keep the child kneeling on the flagstones of the little corridor close to the entrance to the house, and the small boy used to be particularly upset to see the father of the priest, looking on, stern and silent, at all this physical punishment. At last, when the school year came to an end, his temporary teacher considered that the pupil was good enough to go to college and study for the third grade. Perhaps he did not feel up to going on with his teaching, or perhaps he no longer had the time to do it.

The best solution at that time would have been to go to the seminary. But the fees, reasonable though they were, meant too heavy a sacrifice when set against the family's modest income. Since there was a flourishing comprehensive college at Celana, about five miles from Sotto il Monte, it was decided to send the young boy there to follow the third grade. The school had a reputation for learning, whereas Angelo, apart from a few scraps of Latin, knew nothing. There is still some doubt about how the college was able to take this pupil who had had such a hasty ground-work when his classmates were two or three years ahead of him. Perhaps the rector, Mgr Benedetti, gave way before the recommendations of the neighbouring priest of San Gregorio, who was a friend of the Roncalli family.

In order to shorten the journey that he would have to make every day, the boy used to climb the hill of San Giovanni and go to Cà de Rizzi, near Pontida, to the home of relatives of his father, where he spent the week. From there he would walk the mile or two to school with a friend, Pietro Donizetti, who was a year older than himself but in a lower class. So it went on right through the winter. In the early spring a breath of scandal affecting the family with whom the young student was staying, but of which he was completely ignorant, made his mother decide to bring him home. The journey to college thus became longer. Sometimes the kind doctor from Pontida, rounding a bend in the hill, would come upon the young student and his friend walking to Celana and would offer them a lift in his carriage.

What with school and the journeys to and from it, little time was left for extra study. Angelo also had the misfortune to be under a teacher who was not up to his job. At the end of the second term this state of affairs was brought to an abrupt end, for his father, realizing that the reports indicated gaps too big either to be attributed to the pupil or to be made good by him with the best will in the world, decided to take Angelo away and keep him at home. However, the thought of how the boy had stood up to the long, tiring journeys throughout the winter so moved his parents that they now undertook the heavy responsibility of sending him to the seminary.

Angelo's brief stay at Celana had not been wasted. It was the first place where he was to be remembered with affection. In spite of disappointment as far as his education was concerned, the young pupil had observed and taken in much; people and things had opened up for him a world that was different from the one he had known at home. His character, too, was given the chance to test itself. One day, some boarders had asked him to procure certain articles for them in spite of the fact that it was forbidden. Angelo had refused, but a day boy had undertaken to do it. The affair was discovered and his friends, knowing his meekness, had put the blame on him. He was reprimanded and forced to go to the parish priest of San Gregorio with a letter telling of the affair. The young boy, whose protestations of innocence had not been believed, asked himself whether it was really fair that he should be the carrier of this undeserved accusation, and on the way he tore it up. He did not even mind when the priest promptly boxed his ears on learning of the incident. His conscience was clear.

Chapter Two

THE SEMINARY

ANGELO first went to the seminary at Bergamo in October 1893, when he was twelve, after an entrance examination which placed him in the third class. To become a seminarist is to bid an emphatic farewell to one's childhood. After one year of this new life he was already beginning to show signs of a maturity which marked him out at once from other boys of his age. Life in a seminary has been described too often to need retelling, but comparison with life in a barracks should be resisted, for it has neither its robot-like discipline, its barren emptiness, nor its vulgarity. The two institutions have, perhaps, only one point in common—external orderliness, in the case of the seminary freely accepted and arising not from strict regulations but from well co-ordinated activities.

The seminary at Bergamo has a reputation dating back to the early years of its existence—a fact which we owe to the historical studies of the person who, on that far-off day in 1893, arrived at the seminary little conscious of the long road that lay before him.* It has a strong character of its own. This arises on the one hand from the Bergamesque character which cares little for material things, is restrained in its feelings, opposed to every kind of double dealing, which clings instinctively to what is solid and substantial, and is conscientious in its work. On the other hand it is also the product of a fruitful tradition which can be traced

* Cf. Angelo Giuseppe Roncalli, *Ili inizi del seminario di Bergamo e S Carlo Borromeo*, Bergamo, 1939.

back to the time of Saint Charles Borromeo, and which is
handed on by teachers notable both for their holiness and
for the realism of their thinking.

The vice-rector of the seminary was Don David Re.
Angelo was to become his most intimate confidant and to
share more than any other his anxieties and joys. He was
a distinguished servant of the Church, open-minded and
generous-hearted, endowed with a spirit that was first and
foremost priestly; one of those men who, in the hands of an
eminent bishop, are a treasure and a support to be counted
on in any circumstances. His frail body concealed a formidable inner vitality. Those who have passed through the
seminary have not always been equally brilliant, but on
the other hand they have given proof of an ardent apostolate, a love of humanity, a spirit of sacrifice, devotion,
disinterestedness and detachment from wealth which have
surrounded the priesthood with a halo of respect. The
clergy have resisted every scandal and every storm raised
by impiety. Gradually as the years of study pass, the
seminarist is so to speak immersed in the life of the diocese,
with its practical problems and with its peculiar environ-
ment less discernible in its outward appearance than in the
style, fervour, and strictness of its sacerdotal code. When
the young priest leaves the seminary he feels equipped and
prepared by the words of his teachers and by their methods
of instruction, but even more by the quiet influence of the
seminary and its traditions.

At that time the seminary at Bergamo was passing
through one of the most active periods of its history. This
forms part of the wider history of Italian Catholicism and
covers a period stretching from 1870, the date of the uni-
fication of Italy and the disappearance of the Papal
State, to the years of the first World War. Throughout this
time the Catholics had on the one hand to solve a difficult
matter of conscience in the political sphere before they
could take a full part in the life of the nation and bring to

an end the conflict between their patriotism and their
faith, and on the other hand they were obliged to tackle
in the social sphere not only the opposition of the liberals
but also the challenge of a nascent socialism.

The Roman Question to an increasing extent set the
Catholics apart from political life. At the elections the *non
expedit* order of Pius IX and of Leo XIII was observed. All
the same, more enlightened minds gave warning of the dis-
advantages and pleaded for freedom of political action, in
spite of the opposition of some strictly conservative elements. From the foundation of Italian unity until the end
of the century, the world of Italian Catholicism appeared
to be torn by a continuous struggle, at times very petty,
between two trends which often gave the appearance of
factions. On one side there were those in favour of compromise with what was called the revolution; on the other
were those against compromise, determined to destroy
every bridge between themselves and the revolution. Both
sides sincerely believed they were defending the fundamental values of Catholicism, but each refused to allow to
the other honest motives in the struggle which confronted
them. Those who opposed a compromise were not sufficiently aware of the dangers to which this isolation of the
Catholics in face of the revolution might lead, while those
in favour failed to realize the gravity and complexity of the
Roman Question, reducing it simply to the resentment of a
dispossessed sovereign.

To this political division was added another in the social
sphere. Here and there in different dioceses the first signs
of organized Christian Democracy were beginning to
appear; control was in the hands of laymen, who, conscious
of the headstrong march of the masses towards social
advancement, wished to draw close to them and to enrol
them in organizations inspired by the Gospel. By a strange
contrast the progressives of the political front, in their
desire to participate in the defence of the monarchy, were

not always able to distinguish it from the established social order and often fought the policy of Christian Democracy, which was in their opinion subversive and underhand. That is why several of the best bishops in Italy were to be seen running the risk of defending conservative positions in the social sphere while at the same time their political opinions were completely open and extremely liberal.

It was altogether a sad story involving much wastage of effort which would probably have been better employed in the defence of the common heritage of the Faith, already under attack from the fashionable anti-clerical propaganda of the time. Bergamo was one of the most sensitive thermo-meters of the situation during the closing decades of the century. Its bishop, a man of zealous faith, an active fighter but at the same time stubborn, inflexible, and jealous of his episcopal authority, had died in 1879, leaving the succes-sion to Mgr Camillo Guindani, well known already for his learning and his moderation, and a close friend of Mgr Bonomelli, the apostle and the prophet of harmony between Church and State.

The activities of the Catholics were already considerable. The fourth Congress of Italian Catholics, held in the seminary at Bergamo in 1877, had opened up splendid prospects to those men and institutions who wished to throw their energies into the work of bringing the Church closer to the people and to the country itself. A group of laymen, headed by Count Medolago-Albani and Professor Nicolò Rezzara, directed its energies towards the realization of a whole network of social institutions. These affected the interests of working people; growers, farmers, casual labourers and farm-workers, in the most difficult stages of their working lives. Rural banks were set up for small and medium-sized loans; communal kitchens and food depôts to restrict the prices of essential commodities and to break the monopoly of commercial firms; communal milk shops, societies of wine growers, publicly owned mills, lodgings at cheap rents and different forms of insurance for cattle and harvests. These various organizations placed the diocese of Bergamo in the forefront of the Italian social movement and put it on the same level as such countries as France, Belgium and Germany where works of that kind had been in progress upwards of ten years.

Nicolò Rezzara, the tireless apostle to whom most of the credit for these undertakings was due, placed before Mgr Guindani in 1895 the first statistical record of the achievements of social action. This record referred, in its conclusions, to the existence of fifty-four Catholic associations of mutual help and different forms of assistance, of forty-four organizations for credit, production, consumption, and insurance. Altogether the number was 200 associations and more than 42,000 members. A large-scale conference held at the seminary in October demonstrated the strict discipline of the movement and the astonishing success that had already been achieved. It was a vast phenomenon of Catholic penetration into the world of working men, pursuing its course slowly and silently like all great natural phenomena. Whereas in other regions of Italy socialism was being planted deep in the masses, here it was forestalled and eliminated by Catholic enterprise The language in which Mgr Guindani addressed his clergy in 1893, during a speech in which he was commenting on the directives of the encyclical *Rerum Novarum*, is so astonishingly up to date that a number of present-day orators appear, by comparison, behind the times. Then, as now, too many Italian Catholics, while proclaiming themselves to be 'progressives' were only 'conservatives', hiding their profound lack of social sense beneath a more or less sincere varnish of 'paternalism'. At Bergamo, on the other hand, the watchword was 'not words but actions', 'active Catholics or museum-piece Catholics.'

It is interesting to read the appeal made by a genuine radical freemason, Engel, to the Minister of the Interior in

1891 concerning the government's attitude with regard to
'the action of the anti-national party in the province of
Bergamo'—'in the land of Garibaldi's Thousand,* a party
has come to the fore with the utmost boldness and with a
formidable organization. That party is the clerical party';
or the reports sent to Rome in 1895, 1896, and 1898, by the
prefect Fiorentini, who was a liberal.

> I was most disagreeably surprised by the large-scale expansion
> and the very strong organization of the clerical party (Feb. 22,
> 1895).
>
> In every parish in town and country there have been set up
> clerical associations simply pursuing religious and political ends,
> or engaged in mutual help. It is no exaggeration to say that the
> entire province is covered with a network which hinders or
> inspires the activity of the greater part of the population (Aug.
> 25, 1896).
>
> The organization of the clerical party . . . is becoming
> increasingly powerful and irresistible . . . Even from outside,
> this province gives such an impression of being ultramontane
> that the French supporters of clericalism here christened it—a
> kind of honorific title for their Bergamesque colleagues—the
> Vendée of Italy (March 1, 1898).

In 1898, the black year of the barricades in Milan and law-
suits against Socialists and Catholics, Nicolò Rezzara said:

> In action there is a need to be neither timid nor foolhardy;
> never like potentates . . . but equally never like rabbits . . . I
> remind all good Christians that faith, prayer, and self-denial are
> not enough to save us . . . to these must be added good works . . .
> it is not enough to hurl anathemas against socialism and
> anarchy . . . it is necessary to have, once and for all, the courage
> to admit each his own social faults. Eyes must be opened wide
> and as this century draws to a close a good programme must be
> drawn up for the enterprises of the next . . . We have, all of us,
> fostered the growth of socialism by our slothfulness, by our bad
> examples, by absenteeism, by sordid economies on the one
> hand and by senseless extravagance on the other . . . The
> conservatives, even our own, have remained, up to now

---

* It is known that there were 170 Bergamesques among Garibaldi's
legendary band.

together with the governing class, aloof from any idea or any activity designed to hinder the march of socialism. Furthermore, there were many who, putting Socialists and zealous Catholics on the same footing, were actively engaged . . . in refusing to allow either group any form of propaganda or initiative and even calling in aid against them the full power, penalties and wrath of the law . . . If such people really wish to lose all influence over others, that is their business . . . as for us, the militant Catholics, there will be nothing left for us to do except recite the *De Profundis* over the grave of a class of citizens who neither wished nor knew how to save themselves.

Meanwhile an even more important phenomenon was observed at Bergamo about that time: the entry of Catholics into the life of the nation. It was realized there that stable and positive reforms could only be achieved through legal channels. The old refrain: 'No politics!' was becoming less fashionable every day and it was also realized that the formulae *non expedit* and 'neither elected nor electors' had achieved their object, which was to define the action of the Church and to make it independent of all legitimism. But now it was necessary to replace these worn-out formulae by a new impulse which would, at this crucial hour for the nation, make it possible to repudiate the slogan of 'Catholics hostile to the fatherland' and forestall the socialists in their rise to power.

That was the path taken by a province which had been among the most faithful to the *non expedit*. At the time of the legislative elections in 1890 more than four-fifths of the electors had deserted the poll. Bergamo maintained that of all the Italian provinces it had had the smallest number of voters; in twelve communes it had not even been possible to find a candidate; at one centre not a single person had turned up on polling day to set up the electoral office, and out of 400 voters the mayor alone had gone to the poll. In several constituencies a candidate had only been found with difficulty, in spite of the ambitions and appetites which usually come to light in such circumstances. Yet in that

province which was so obedient to the directives of the
Catholic hierarchy the time was nearly ripe for the
Catholics to go over to political action. Abstention from
voting was not considered by them to be a definite renunciation of the exercise of civic rights, but rather as paving
the way for deliberate and organized intervention. It was,
in fact, a kind of active abstentionism.

If this trend of public opinion in Bergamo had an
influence on Italian public opinion and contributed to the
national revival, the credit for it must largely go to the two
influential organs of the local Catholic press: the daily
L'Eco di Bergamo started in 1880, and the weekly Il
Campanone dating from 1885; the first run by Gian Battista
Caironi and the second by Nicolò Rezzara. This advance
first became apparent with the wholesale participation of
the Catholics in the administrative elections, as a result of
which almost every single one of the Bergamesque communes passed into their hands. This first step was taken
before any intervention of a political nature; although they
were aware that obedience to the Pope required for the
time being abstention from the national elections, the
temporary character of that abstention was beginning to
emerge: it was a question of observing a simple disciplinary
rule in order to avoid the danger of a premature intervention.

> Our watchword—said the *Eco* in 1880—is absolute submission
> to the Pope. The general instructions regarding the attitude of
> Italian Catholics towards political elections is clear and precise:
> *Non expedit*. It is not at the moment permissible to intervene in
> the political sphere . . . therefore abstention . . . It is our belief
> that some really useful contribution to the country's welfare
> will only be made in complete harmony with the Pope . . .
> premature intervention would do more harm than good.

But at the same time, well before the famous declaration
of Filippo Meda in October 1894 (namely: 'I belong to the
school which has chosen for its banner preparation for

abstention') and well before the significant advance of Don Albertario (1896) towards the formula of waiting, which stirred up so much scandal among conservative Catholics, *L'Eco di Bergamo* published on June 9, 1880 a revealing article entitled 'Abstention and preparation' in which, abandoning an 'entirely passive' abstention, it announced: 'Thus was born the idea of active abstention, an abstention which has nothing in common with laziness, but which is vigorously preparing for action.' The same paper concluded in more explicit language on May 29, 1886, when congratulating the Catholics on their exemplary obedience to the *non expedit*: 'Italians, in their devotion to the Pope, are abstaining at the present time from taking part in the political elections; they are ready to play a large part in them when the Pope considers that the time has come.'

This idea of active preparation put out by the newspapers was taken up by lecturers, and from the central associations it passed to the outside groups with the full support of the bishop, Mgr Guindani, and of a Bergamesque prelate, the future Cardinal Antonio Agliardi, who was held in high esteem by Leo XIII. Slowly but surely there grew up a movement which 'like an army ready for action' was prepared to launch itself into the struggle at the first word of command. The prefect Fiorentini was perfectly well aware of the tremendous possibilities of this discipline, and he wrote to the Minister of the Interior about it on February 28, 1886. This report contains a very fine eulogy intended for the people of the province of Bergamo:

> The activities of the clerical organization are making themselves felt especially in the administrative elections, in accordance with its statutes. In the town it has as mouthpieces the daily paper *L'Eco di Bergamo* and the weekly *Il Campano*, both at the disposal of that section of the clerical party which is rightly called 'intransigent'. The influence of the clerical party is such that in the event of the Pontifical Sovereign giving orders to take part in the political elections, there might emerge, provided the present legislation still existed which allows the unthinking

masses to have a vote, a real danger for the central administration of the State, at least in this province which is nevertheless
fundamentally extremely patriotic . . . The population of this
province is basically serious and hard-working. In any event, if
ever the destiny of this country were in danger, it would be the
first to rise, contemptuous of long speeches, and plunge into
action.

Contrary to what the liberal-monarchist prefect feared,
no order came from the Pope. The directives from Rome
remained, generally speaking, the same as before. Cardinal
Agliardi, appealed to from Bergamo for advance information, declared that in the Vatican it was not considered
prudent to make innovations in that direction. Nevertheless
events were moving so rapidly that those who were beginning to feel sure of the advantages of political action were
made to feel uneasy.

It was the eve of the elections of 1904. The stormy 19th
Congress of Catholics at Bologna produced some unfortunate disturbances: the resignation of President Grosoli and
the dissolution, on the orders of Pius X, of the *Opera dei
Congressi* themselves. By virtue of a papal concession, only
the second group of that organization, the one concerned
with social welfare, remained. It operated from Bergamo
and was directed by Count Medolago-Albani with Rezzara
as secretary.

As a result of repeated clumsy interventions by the
government authorities, socialist pressure was becoming
more intense every day. In September a general strike
paralysed the whole of Italy. The Giolitti Government
was thinking of the elections at the time, intending to
exploit the fears which they had roused and to extract
stronger support from the country. The only unknown
element was the attitude of the Catholics; their abstention
would certainly not favour the forces of order. In reply to a
memorandum on October 2 from Mgr Bonomelli,
Bishop of Cremona, the Pope wrote that adherence to the

traditional orders was required. For his part the head of
the government, Giolitti, had declared some months
before: 'Church and State are two parallel lines which will
never meet.'

Meanwhile, at Bergamo, they were thinking of making
one last great effort. It was known that the government
was looking hopefully to 'the centre in which was to be
found the most complete Catholic organization.' After an
agreement had been reached at Milan between the
Minister for Foreign Affairs, Tittoni, and Count Gianforte
Suardi, the moderate liberal member for the constituency
of Trescore Balneario (Bergamo), a lawyer, Paolo Bonomi,
was dispatched to the Vatican with instructions to make
known the desire of Mgr Guindani and of Nicolò Rezzara
that Catholics should take part in the coming elections.
The historic audience of October 17 had one positive result
that had not been anticipated. Pius X, who had followed
the lawyer's peroration with his elbow on the table and his
head resting on the palm of his hand, remained in silent
thought for a moment; then raising his eyes to heaven, he
declared in a slow serious voice: 'Go, follow the dictates of
your conscience.' 'Did we understand you correctly, your
Holiness? Can we say that the answer is "yes"?' 'I repeat,
follow the dictates of your conscience.' 'Thank you, thank
you, your Holiness.' The Holy Father accompanied the
man from Bergamo as far as the door, and as he bade him
good-bye he added: 'Repeat to Rezzara the reply that I
have given you and tell him that the Pope will remain
silent.'

A long-felt dream had come true. For the first time
Catholics would go to the poll. Some days later at the
elections Bergamo gave Italy her first Catholic deputy, the
honourable Agostino Cameroni: their first difficult step
into public life which was, within a few decades, to place
them at the key-point of the nation. The events we have
been describing correspond roughly to the dates of Angelo

Roncalli's stay in the seminary and indicate the world he looked out on from there.

While following the strict programme of prayer, study, and discipline, young seminarists do not lose sight of what is going on outside the seminary in the sphere of their future ministry. Already their minds turn outwards to where the priests who directed them to the seminary are at work. Each year the older students are launched into the world and many of these often return to the seminary and pass on to their former fellow students their experiences and their problems.

In perhaps no other Italian seminary is the seminarist attracted so much by the ideal of the pastoral ministry as he is at Bergamo. Any priestly duty which does not give him contact with the parish, whether it be in curial administration or in teaching, is looked on as a sort of deviation from the real objective: the care of souls. Wherever the priests and bishops who have been trained in the seminary at Bergamo may be sent, their characteristic feature is the facility with which they work themselves, by means of a many-sided activity, into the stream of public life; they will not rest until they can take part in all the activities, even if they do not organize them.

The bishop, Mgr Guindani, was anxious that his clergy should take part in the widespread movement which was galvanizing the diocese. He set up for the young priests a union of social studies, intended to give them doctrinal preparation and to make them ready for modern pastoral practice. Later he created at the seminary a chair of law and political economy which is coveted to this day by a large number of seminaries in Italy.

Not all the clergy, it is true, shared their bishop's clear vision. His predecessor's ideas, unyielding and somewhat narrow, still exerted an influence on some of the priests. Rumours found their way into the seminary concerning the opposition that would be encountered by Catholic Action in certain areas of the diocese. Stories of the lively resistance put up by the highly respected Canon Cossali, archdeacon of the cathedral, by the priest at Almenno, Don Teanini, and by others, round whom there grew in course of time a kind of legend, finally infiltrated into the seminary despite the discreet veil that was drawn over anything that might upset the bishop. It was a case of ignorant individuals having taken as their motto the *Frangar non flectar* of Ciceronian times, to such an extent that, merely from an excess of religious zeal, they brought an action against their superior in the Vatican; unfortunately a great Catholic paper in Milan assured them of its support. These were to a certain extent dark and troubled years, a time of differences between men who, although in full agreement on the fundamental principles of religious doctrine, were unable to admit their variety in application and gave battle, out of sheer short-sightedness, in the very camp of their most faithful allies.

Meanwhile, the bishop had his seminary very much at heart. Intelligent men at the top supported his projects and formed teams of priests who came to swell the ranks of those workers in the parishes who were more alive to modern needs. Angelo Roncalli the seminarist followed this development of the times closely. At this time he was learning the advantages of obedience, agreement, patience, restraint, silence and sitting still. Thus he was learning to know men whom he esteemed for all their faults. He was enthusiastic at the sight of all the energy springing forth from the body of the Church at the very moment when anti-clerical rhetoric was predicting that it would dry up in a short time.

When he entered the seminary he had at once felt at his ease and at peace with himself. His studies no longer caused him doubts and uncertainties; he followed them not only without difficulty, but joyously even, figuring prominently in his class. His future intellectual tendencies were already beginning to appear: a taste for humanistic culture, a passionate love of history, an optimistic vision of his time, the conviction that events follow a Christian pattern and work together for good under the guidance of providence. He was as it were lulled by the rhythm of the daily round. The life of the seminary, a veritable bee-hive hard at work, where each day his soul made some important fresh discovery, breathed an air of profound peace. For the young boy from Sotto il Monte already renowned in his family for reflection, it created an atmosphere of happiness.

The years slipped by; after college, the *lycée*; after the *lycée*, the study of theology. And it was at that moment that the seminarist became an ordinand and tackled priestly studies, the sacred sciences: dogmatic, biblical, patristic, juridical, moral, ascetic. At that time—in 1899—his companions recognized that he was already more poised, more mature than they. He had outgrown that adventurous, headstrong temperament which in the case of so many only disappears when they first come up against the harsh experiences of the priesthood. His superiors thought highly of him; they entrusted him with responsibility for the youngest pupils. His strong and well-modulated voice, together with a certain knowledge of music, led to his being put forward as choir-master. Everything seemed to combine to make a happy ending to his long apprenticeship at the seminary of Bergamo. Angelo already imagined himself as a priest in some little parish in the diocese; however, he was too far advanced. Towards the end of 1900, just before he was nineteen, he began his third year in theology, the last subject but one of the course. But the rules of Canon Law held the door to the priesthood closed until the age of 24; he would therefore have had to wait.

In the midst of all this an important change took place. Flaminio Cerasoli, the highly esteemed canon of a Roman basilica and a native of Bergamo, had left his fortune, which dated back to 1640, for the building of a college in

Rome to house a certain number of Bergamesque students with ecclesiastical leanings who wanted to complete their studies in the academic surroundings of Rome. Eventually that charitable institution had been embodied in the pontifical seminary at Rome. It retained its title of the Noble Cerasoli College and it also retained a certain autonomy which, however, tended to grow less as the years went by, but it was entirely dependent on the material and spiritual life of the larger community.

The advantages which the diocese of Bergamo derives from the long period spent by its best students in the heart of Christianity, are incalculable. The Bergamesque character and temperament cannot always be said to blend easily with the Roman mentality. Bergamo has got to know Rome and the atmosphere of her Curia through long years of familiarity and tradition. Like the rest of northern Italy, but perhaps with better reason, it used to resent Rome's lack of academic spirit, her emphasis on administration, and the fact that her attitude towards Church problems was diplomatic rather than pastoral. On their arrival in Rome, therefore, students from Bergamo are not immune from a certain prejudice and their first meeting with their fellow students does not take place without friction; nevertheless the Roman seminary encourages fusion and conciliation. Without losing the cachet of distinction and refinement which Rome confers and which befits a pontifical institution, it maintains a tradition of education linked, in its origins, with that of the Lombard seminaries. Its programme embraces a very solid tradition of piety and an advanced curriculum designed to make the most of the students and to protect them from the temptations that beset them in their career. Thus the way is open for a meeting with all that is best in Rome: the Pope, university life, supra-nationalism, classical splendour. On their return to their dioceses those priests who have been educated in Rome have discarded the parish-pump outlook and that feeling of self-sufficiency which pervades any provincial town that is proud of its traditions. They combine zest and realism in action with a more catholic outlook and an open-mindedness better suited to the broad horizons of the Church. Sometimes they do not go back to the province of their birth, but hardly ever does love of their diocese fail to win the day over the charm of Rome; and it takes the explicit intervention of some Roman authority to force them to stay.

For the past ten years Bergamo had been unable to send seminarists to Rome. A lawsuit was in progress between the bishop and the Roman administrators of the college. It was not until the end of 1900 that the case was won and the bursaries for students came into operation again. Thus it was that on January 3, 1901, three ordinands, Angelo Roncalli, Guglielmo Carozzi, and Achille Ballini, chosen from among the best, set off for Rome. Angelo was the youngest, but he had already begun his third year of theology while the other two were about to begin their second. Yet all three preferred to revert to the beginning of the academic course. For Angelo it provided an excellent way of filling in time.

Nine years of concentrated hard work followed. Anyone who has studied at the Roman seminary knows all about the achievements and defects of the pupils of the Noble Cesaroli College. They bear the marks of the ruggedness of their native earth and give the impression at first of being slightly rustic and uncouth. But their distinctive personalities, dogged determination, and the brilliance of their intelligence soon make themselves felt. The ease with which they settle down to their studies and win the hearts of their professors earns them the nickname among their fellow students of 'swotters'. A certain inner detachment is apparent in their attitude to their surroundings; but they clearly see the path ahead and go their way confidently and without pretence. A sense of discipline suppresses in them any temptation to rebel.

Angelo soon adapted himself to his new life. The stern lines of the Apollinaris at that time reminded him a little of a cage. In his narrow cell with its small window barred like a convent he felt cut off from air and light. But he was of a mild and reasonable disposition. He calmly endured the impact of the new life. His friendly nature enabled him to enter completely into the life of the community. The rector, Mgr Bugarini, a saintly man but somewhat hidebound by the traditions of Rome, was not slow to take note of his quiet and exemplary behaviour. The professor of dogmatic theology, Father Tabarelli, admired him particularly for the answers he gave. They were less brilliant than those of Ballini, but more precise and better thought out; moreover his whole attitude suggested a good balance between the flesh and the spirit.

These were not easy times for Catholic studies. The storm of modernism was already beginning to blow and was soon to make itself felt in the theological schools. Some years before the arrival of Angelo, Bonaiuti, who was to become the father of Italian modernism, had been a student in the same seminary. Copies of his pamphlets on the new doctrines were even circulated there, and passed from hand to hand under the benches or under cover of darkness. One of them, in particular, contained Bonaiuti's defence of Loisy. Although Angelo knew all about it he always politely but firmly refused to read them or to pass them on. Instinctively he mistrusted any teaching which did not conform absolutely to tradition and to the judgement of the hierarchy. This mistrust arose, not from lack of courage but because he was convinced of the weakness of theological theories formed outside the ægis of the Church. His companions liked him and respected him none the less for that. He wished to preserve his world inviolate, but to all outward appearances he remained the soul of affability. His conversation was full of courtesy. The recreation hour used to be spent pleasantly, if not always at games.

The years slipped by, but meantime in Rome important events had taken place. Leo XIII, the great Pope of the encyclical *Rerum Novarum*, had been succeeded by Pius X. Angelo had watched the smoke go up from the conclave and had been present at the coronation. In December of the same year he was ordained deacon and on June 8, 1904, after completing his fourth year of theology, he sought priest's orders. After two months' waiting the longed-for date arrived: on August 10, in the church of Santa Maria in Monte Santo in the Piazza del Popolo, Angelo was ordained priest and the following day he celebrated his first Mass at St. Peter's.

That day, unforgettable in itself, was to be linked in his memory with another happy event. He was one of a crowd of pilgrims who wished to see the Pope. As Pius X went by, Angelo's companion said: 'Your Holiness, here is a young priest from Bergamo who has just celebrated his first Mass this morning.' The Pope stopped and leaned towards him. The emotion of the first sacrifice still fresh in the mind of the young priest was linked with his joy at this personal meeting with the Vicar of Christ, and he began to repeat to the Pope the promises of his newly begun priesthood. 'Very good', the Pope said in a paternal voice, 'I give you my blessing and exhort you to live up to your resolutions.' He straightened himself, walked on a little towards another group of pilgrims, then turned back and asked him: 'And when do you sing your first Mass back at home?' 'At the Feast of the Assumption, Holy Father.' The Pope smiled and looked at him for a moment. Perhaps he was thinking of the Lombard and Venetian villages rejoicing at the thought of having a new priest, for he repeated: 'At the Assumption! What a feast! And how those bells will ring out in Bergamo!'

Chapter Three

AT THE SIDE OF A GREAT BISHOP

A T the beginning of the new academic year, towards the
end of 1904, Don Angelo applied to join the Faculty
of Canon Law at the Apollinaris. It was the custom for
pupils of the Cerasoli College, after obtaining their doctor-
ate of theology, to complete their studies in some special
sacred subject; but this was not to be. In October Mgr
Guindani, Bishop of Bergamo, died there from an illness
which became apparent at the time that Angelo was taking
holy orders. One Sunday afternoon in December, Don
Carozzi, his friend and compatriot, broke the news to Don
Angelo that Count Radini Tedeschi had been nominated
to the bishopric of Bergamo. Mgr Radini, he went on, had
himself confirmed the truth of this to him at St. Peter's,
where Don Carozzi was the youngest canon. Some days
later the two friends visited the official residence of the
newly elected bishop to pay him their respects. Little did
Don Angelo suspect at the time the influence that the
distinguished prelate was to have on his life.

Mgr Radini had been very active: first in the office of
the Secretary of State, then in charge of the pilgrimages
to Lourdes and the Holy Land, and above all in running
the *Opera dei Congressi*. There it was that Italian Catholics
made ready their weapons, sometimes a little too noisily,
for future action. The congress, held at Bologna in November 1903, and the plenary assembly of the general committee, on July 2, 1904, had given rise to outbursts which
degenerated at times into personal attacks. The conflict

between the conservatives and the progressive element (Grosoli, Radini, Meda, Rezzara) was so violent that Pius X had to send an admonitory note. Then on July 15 the Count sent out a circular to the associations of the *Opera dei Congressi*, which he had first submitted to the Pope. But on July 19 a disclaimer appeared in the *Osservatore Romano* which led to the resignation of Grosoli, Radini, and Meda, and which was followed by the dissolution of the movement itself.*

Mgr Radini emerged with his head unbowed from this ordeal, immensely disappointed at seeing the work of so many years brought to nothing but with a feeling of humble submission to the directives of the Pope. The Pope had a personal regard for him, admiring his uprightness and generosity. He had always had him in mind for the see of Bergamo and when he received his acceptance of it, he told him: 'Monsignor, you have treated me with great kindness. You had been proposed for the archbishopric of Palermo; I refused. For Ravenna; I again refused. For Bergamo; this time I agreed. Off you go. As far as it is possible to console a bishop, let me say that Bergamo is the first diocese in all Italy.'

The Pope who, on the face of it, seemed to be restraining the Catholic urge for social action, sent Mgr Radini into 'the capital of social institutions', where he was to find men like Rezzara and Medolago who had collaborated with him until recently in the movement, the second section of which—that of public and social works—still survived elsewhere. Radini was just the bishop needed at Bergamo for he

* In the report sent to Brussels by the embassy, it is stated that Pius X was displeased with some words that had been added to the circular in its final form: 'With the exception of those things which concern the inalienable rights of the Holy See, Catholics look on historical eras and their events as milestones along the path of progress, *determined though they are to see that the work of the moment is not hampered by questions that are now dead as far as the national conscience is concerned.*' That addition gave away too clearly the opinion of the progressive wing. The Pope wanted neither victors nor vanquished, but union between the two wings of Italian Catholics.

was certainly destined to carry on the courageous work of Mgr Guindani; he and his diocese seemed made to be complementary to each other.

As for Don Angelo, his destiny was to be linked with that of the great bishop. During the days that followed his nomination Radini remained in close touch with the two young Bergamesque priests studying at the Apollinaris. Although they did not suspect it, he was in the process of choosing his secretary: 'If I were to choose a lively secretary', he said to the rector of the seminary shortly afterwards, 'I should choose Carozzi. But I prefer Roncalli who has better judgement.' And so Don Angelo had to interrupt his studies to follow his bishop; the first of many unforeseen turning-points in his life. On January 29, 1905, Pius X himself consecrated Radini in the Sistine Chapel; Don Angelo, who had arrived in a carriage with the new bishop, was privileged to serve at Mass and to hand him the Gospel. Radini went to his diocese on April 9 and at the same time Don Angelo undertook his first appointment as a priest, which was to last ten years.

The young priest, firmly resolved to give proof of absolute obedience and absolute devotion, was not slow to discover his bishop's greatness of spirit and to attach himself unreservedly to the man who represented for him the ideal of the sacerdotal life. After Mgr Radini's death, he wrote his biography, which bears the imprint of the master upon the disciple.

> More than once, he was to write in this work, I felt my hand trembling under the pressure of overpowering emotions, so great was the love that I felt for my bishop because of the transcendent purity of his spirit and because of the openness of his heart. I revered him for his humanity, which nobody was in a better position to appreciate than myself ... And I comfort myself with the thought that anyone wishing to evoke his memory, by word of mouth or in writing, could hardly avoid the impression which I gained as I lived at his side of greatness and strength springing rather from his ardent spirit than from his achievements ...

It would be difficult to imagine a deeper intimacy between a secretary and his bishop. The secretary is the shadow that goes with him everywhere, discreet, attentive to his needs, without forgetting for one moment the gulf that divides them. In this way Don Angelo took part in the bishop's activities, sharing his hopes, his anxieties and his joys. The episcopacy began with a pilgrimage to Milan and the tomb of St. Charles Borromeo, followed by a pilgrimage to Ars, Lourdes, and Paray-le-Monial in France, journeys which left the young secretary with unforgettable memories.

The pastoral visitation began at the end of the first year: it was spread over four years and embraced the 352 parishes of the diocese. The vigour and frankness of the bishop and the multiplicity of his projects might have given the impression that he wanted to turn everything upside down. But Don Angelo understood at once, and it gave him great satisfaction that his zeal was prompted by the high opinion which the bishop had formed of the clergy and the faithful in his diocese: he admired his clergy who, even in isolated mountain villages, preserved their faith intact and spent themselves in an untiring apostolate. His priests, who may perhaps have had rough features but whose hearts were as sensitive as that of a mother for the needs of her children, trained Christians who were nourished on a solid doctrine, accustomed to a strict moral discipline and moved by a genuine spirit of sacrifice and obedience to the Church. The uprightness and sincerity of these men commanded admiration even when they differed from their bishop.

On several occasions the bishop could not restrain his enthusiasm in the face of certain demonstrations of faith and Don Angelo, moved by the same feelings of admiration, recognized the cause of this generous impulse of the laymen led by humble priests, workers among workers: by their piety and their holiness they made ready the Lord's harvest. He took advantage of these pastoral visitations to delve still deeper into the history of the diocese. The parish archives or sometimes, more simply, a picture caught sight of in a church or sacristy, provided him with material from which to write about the past in whose treasures he discerned the seeds of the present. Thus he discovered his vocation as an historian. He gathered together with scrupulous care all the various threads which make up the history of the Church, and noted the continuity between the past, the present and the future. In this way he became imbued with that spirit of calm judgement that lends stability to the characteristic enthusiasm of the young.

The bishop was here there and everywhere in the diocese, and all the time his strong personality was asserting itself. It left its mark on countless activities that were beginning to bear fruit in various directions: seminary, clergy, liturgy, social welfare, youth movements, education. The incisiveness and skill which he showed in dealing with matters made a deep impression on his secretary. He studied his bishop's decrees carefully, finding no cause for criticism in them. His natural meekness would in any case have precluded him from doing so.

He was learning all the time. A secretary accustomed to hearing the same words repeated again and again might be expected to become indifferent to the utterances of the bishop he served. Don Angelo, on the contrary, never tired of enjoying his eloquence:

> How well he used to speak, he said. He certainly knew the secret of finding the right thought, tone of voice and gesture: the thought would be simple, even sublime; the voice loud and resonant or soft as the occasion required, but always beautiful and melodious; gestures that were unobtrusive and dignified, and suited to the occasion and to the audience he was addressing . . . One felt happy to belong to a Church that was the trustee and the mistress of such noble teaching.

Mgr Radini was a real driving force, but he did not aspire to centralize everything. His idea was to get all the forces at his disposal to work together and shoulder their own responsibilities. His view was that unless he was prepared to trust people and put up with their short-comings all initiative would be stifled. He would not interfere without good reason, and he showered praise and encouragement; in public no word of blame ever passed his lips. If some serious disorder required firm handling by the Church, the decree would be so full of wisdom and goodness that it amounted to a new proof of his love. Inexhaustible, he worked quietly but without respite: 'The only respite that the bishop ought to ask of God and deserve', he used to say, 'is that of paradise.' Until the end of his life Don Angelo was to remember that axiom.

There were others. 'Good', the prelate used to say, 'must be well done.' By that he was certainly not advocating the exercise of a prudence which, paralysed by too many safeguards, wastes time in delay and comes to nothing in the end. He remembered that not even Christ himself succeeded in pleasing everybody. For him prudence meant above all action, but that action, in order to be good, had to be free, detached from all servitude. Better a smaller degree of good than a greater degree of good obtained to the detriment of love or by means capable of bringing discredit on the Church. Sure of itself, his school was a school of courage.

Catholic and social action had suffered a severe blow from the dissolution of the *Opera dei Congressi*. There were certain actions of Pius X, necessitated by exceptional circumstances, such as the condemnation of modernism, the dismissal of Romolo Murri, leader of the Christian Democratic movement, and other interventions of a disciplinary nature, that appeared quite wrongly to apply the brake rather than give a forward impulse. Even the best among them, who were frequently criticized and attacked by strict partisans of the *status quo*, felt the cold wind of discouragement and even of fear. Something of this atmosphere of mistrust which sapped initiative, was felt even at Bergamo. But the bishop, whom some already regarded as a victim of it, was on the look-out. He was concerned not for himself, but for the general good. He preached obedience to Rome, but an obedience that was intelligent, alert, prudent, one not based on surrender. He did not hesitate to sacrifice a man like Count Medolago-Albani, through whose far-sighted inspiration so much had been achieved, when it seemed to him that his rather conservative ideas were becoming a danger to the good work done by others. He gave the members of his diocese to understand that any inclination to halt or to retreat would not be tolerated. Thus, in the midst of the general upheaval in which the gains of recent years had been lost Bergamo succeeded in preserving intact, and even increasing, the inheritance of good works and ideas accumulated throughout the ages.

Something happened to show just how far-reaching this courage could be. A strike broke out at Ranica, a small place just outside Bergamo. Here is Don Angelo's account of it:

When the strike began in the autumn of 1909, the bishop's name appeared at the head of the list of subscribers, who were anxious to ensure that those on strike should get food. On all sides the cry of scandal was raised; ill-disposed reports were sent to those in authority. Even among right-thinking people several held the view that a cause forfeited the right to be supported if there was any danger of the means employed being carried to extremes.

Mgr Radini was not of this way of thinking. What was at stake at Ranica was not a particular question of wages or of individual right but the fundamental principle of the freedom of the Christian labour organizations in the face of powerfully organized capitalism. And so he let the commotion run its course and calmly continued to take an interest in the strikers. Then when tempers had cooled a little, Pius X wrote to him on October 20 in his own hand, as he usually did, declaring that he could not disapprove of what he had deemed it proper to do with full cognizance of place, persons, and circumstances.

There was still lacking in Italy one of those splendid examples such as had been seen in Belgium, Germany, and England. For this reason there was satisfaction that in Italy also the workers' cause was being stoutly defended, and with dignity, not only from the heights of the episcopal pulpit but even down in the main square when there were clashes between capital and labour.

The bishop's attitude towards events was bold and enlightened, and his principle, which Don Angelo was later to adopt, was not to work only for the present. He sowed for the future, accepting the risk that he might not be understood. In politics he was particularly careful to maintain his independence: 'His conviction was that today as yesterday a bishop is the better fitted to serve religion and society if he keeps to his pastoral function, that is to say if he remains aloof from any political prejudice or intrigue, firmly maintaining the position to which he has been assigned.' Don Angelo was just the man to appreciate this aspect of his bishop. He saw only one difference between them; the bishop's temperament was more fiery, more impulsive; his own was more controlled. But in feelings and natural kindness he felt very close to him.

> This man, this bishop, with his military gait and his lively determination, was really good, good right through. How patient he could be and how forbearing! Others less ardent would have grown tired, but not he. He could be compassionate or he could be silent; he could wait or he could forget. Knowing what he wanted, he was strict and inflexible in matters of discipline, but no-one appealed to his heart in vain.

The secretary happened sometimes to be present at scenes which made a strong impression on him. At one of these the bishop, who had just severely reprimanded a priest accused of doing wrong, realized shortly afterwards that he had been mistaken and threw himself at his feet asking forgiveness. The bishop knew that the secretary was close to him and sometimes he surprised him by his attitude of paternal affection.

Never shall I forget, Don Angelo was to write later, Mgr Radini's delicacy of feeling and his little marks of affection for me; nor shall I forget the amount of time he devoted to his young priest, the patience with which he bore his shortcomings, the trouble he took to instil into him a love of work and sacrifice. And so being with him was not only like attending a great school for the teaching of ecclesiastical duties and virtues, it also meant enjoying a constant happiness and peace, even in the midst of the turmoil of work . . . taking care all the time to keep oneself in his shadow.

In those last words the secretary has borrowed an expression in use by everyone round him to describe his life at Radini's side: 'He is the bishop's shadow.' Those who knew Don Angelo may sometimes have wondered, on reading those lines, whether, in speaking of his bishop, he has not to a large extent described himself. Radini had found at Bergamo a diocese made to measure and a secretary quick to identify himself in thought with his bishop. Those pages hold up a kind of mirror; they reflect a portrait of Mgr Radini which would need only a little touching up and a change of name to be applicable to the future Mgr Roncalli.

Nobody was in a better position than his priests to understand the gentleness and goodness of Mgr Radini. He knew them all personally and was a good judge of the merits of each one . . . He was more ready to take note of their good qualities than to exaggerate their shortcomings. He might sometimes have been open to the criticism of having too high an opinion of someone or of having too much confidence in him, but never of having too little. He treated everyone with the greatest deference . . . He took care not to let a single word or gesture fall which did not express respect and courtesy, even when times were critical and he was tired or worried. More than one person will no doubt remember the complete sincerity of remarks spoken about himself, uttered sometimes by the bishop in the course of an intimate conversation: never will anyone complain of having heard a harsh word.

The following portrait might also bear two names:

Mgr Radini was endowed by nature to a notable degree with that distinctive personality which, according to the Holy

Spirit, makes a man friendly: *Vir amabilis ad societatem*. He could appreciate the charm of good conversation and communicate it to others. He had seen a good deal of churchmen in all parts of the world and had learned much from them . . . he spoke with incomparable geniality . . . and had an infinite capacity for gaiety. And, indeed, his soul had never been exposed to those passions which engender sadness; there was no room in him for weariness or melancholy. Always ready to listen to the voice of conscience he derived a great satisfaction from the feeling of duty performed, and it was this in particular which caused his face to be suffused with pure and perpetual joy . . . It can truly be said that his soul was reflected in his face, that it gave him his dignified manner and his wonderful simplicity. It could also be seen in his attractive appearance, in his expression, in the deep-sounding yet tender voice, and in the benevolent and smiling majesty with which he would greet, open-armed, a friend, a guest, or a colleague. There was a radiant goodness about his whole person. And any man to whom he opened his heart felt able to lean upon him for support, to entrust himself to him with complete confidence and safety: *Amicus fidelis, Protectio fortis* was one of his favourite expressions, as though those words were made for him.

'Shadow of his bishop', and yet Don Angelo did not disappear completely from the orbit of his master, for he had been assigned a sphere of action in which he was able to develop his personal contact with people. From now on the young secretary was going to become a very busy priest. He left the bishopric three days a week to go to the nearby seminary and give lessons there on apologetics and ecclesiastical history; moreover, he was diocesan assistant to the Women's Catholic Action, a member of various diocesan committees, and he also found time to carry out research in libraries and archives, driven by an innate passion that was later to be the cause of his writing a monumental historical work.

Professor Roncalli was neither a pedant nor a rigid adherent to scholastic methods. Very understanding and indulgent in his judgements, he would encourage and set at ease the least gifted and least well prepared of his pupils.

He had only to satisfy himself that a little goodwill, a little application was being shown, and that a degree of understanding existed of the fundamental problems of the subject that was being taught, and his satisfaction and praise were unstinted. He was to be seen arriving for his lessons, often a little late from his last engagement, sometimes slightly out of breath after hurrying up several flights of stairs in the old seminary, but the moment he was among his pupils he would recover his serenity. He spoke eloquently, but what he said was to the point and by no means commonplace. In his lessons his exuberant nature had great difficulty in keeping to simple texts; and he would open up before his pupils the wider horizons of a learning that was hardly academic but very suggestive.

The doctrinal standpoints he adopted were well considered. The two subjects he taught raised questions which, in the uncertain atmosphere of those years of struggle against modernism, needed to be handled with discretion. The seminary of Bergamo was itself passing through a troubled time. Within almost a year of Don Angelo a young professor had taken the same course at Rome, and had subsequently specialized in biblical studies. This Don Giuseppe Moioli, a figure so remote and austere as to make it seem absurd that he would one day be suspected of modernism, had had to be removed from the seminary and had taken with him a colleague guilty of having defended his actions. Don Angelo was upset by the departure of the two friends and by the way the affair ended. Certain forces had intervened to which the bishop had had to yield, though with reluctance. Some went as far—so obscure and confused was the situation at the time—as to accuse Don Angelo of modernism.

The present author must confess to having inspected with an intense interest mingled with curiosity the pages of notes which Professor Roncalli, as he then was, used to dictate to his pupils, and which have been preserved to this day by some of them. They contain the greater part of his lessons in exactly the same form that was given in class. They reveal sound and well-balanced scholarship. A scrupulous respect for the thinking of the Church is apparent on every page together with an attempt to judge the most modern theological conceptions in the light of the teachings of doctrinal authority. Yet his views could hardly be called timid; they take care not to unsettle the pupil's mind in any way, but at the same time they are loyal, balanced, and honest. It is clear that the professor was familiar with the most controversial questions. Sometimes he would not hesitate to give a searching account of problems, leaving the door open, wherever possible, to bolder solutions even when his sympathies lay nearer to a more definite orthodoxy. He found so much to teach that was uncontroversial. The history of the Church, in particular, a sphere in which he felt more at home, provided him with the opportunity for pages of lucid notes worthy of admiration. That militant, miraculous story was so well suited to the development of the idea of providence, and of the mysterious realization of God's plan, and it was to a certain extent through the inspiration of that ancient history that he explained the events of his own time. Current history was not as limited as it appeared to be. It extended beyond the boundaries of a diocese. Even in those years Bergamo remained the inspiration of advanced Catholic movements. The feverish rhythm of these organizations was to sweep Don Angelo himself into their activities.

In the sphere of electoral action, the diocese, which had at the very beginning succeeded in securing a partial abrogation of the *non expedit*, was making progress in its attempt to send devout Catholics to Parliament. This was not, in fact, to Rome's way of thinking. Pius X preferred as a counter to the Socialist and Radical threat, that Catholics should support the moderate Liberals on condition of suitable guarantees. He did not look with approval, in this transition stage, upon the entry of Catholics into Parliament. Catholic candidates, elected as such, ran the risk of compromising themselves. They had to take up a definite attitude over problems on which the Church still reserved its final judgement, such as that of the *non expedit*, which was being enforced less and less, or of the Roman Question, although Pius X had declared: 'If the king ordered me to take over Rome again because he was leaving it and was presenting it to me, I should reply: Let him stay in the Quirinal, we will discuss it another day . . . The Holy See would be in need of other things . . .'

At Bergamo the question was beginning to be asked whether the Catholic vote in support of the Liberals was really unequivocal and without danger.* True to their spirit of obedience the Bergamesque Catholics had, at the time of the general elections in 1907, collaborated in the election of five moderate Liberal deputies. But already at the partial elections of 1907 they had put forward the candidature of a Catholic, Bonomi, who it is true nearly failed in spite of the support of a fairly strong party. Pius X had been content at the time to accept the position. As for Bishop Radini, aware as he was of the delicate position he was in, he had maintained a discreet silence.

The problem cropped up again at the elections of 1913. The old policy of the Holy See was well remembered by the electoral union, formed at Rome under the presidency of Count Gentiloni. At Bergamo the local situation seemed to require different handling. Dissatisfaction was expressed with the attitude of the Liberals who had previously been elected. Some of them had failed to respect the programme they had undertaken to carry out and had made common cause with a group of Social Conservatives which was considered intolerable by the working-class Catholics.

The days that followed, from the beginning of April until

---

* Don Sturzo was later to speak, in too violent terms, of the 'prostitution of a vote.'

the date of the elections (October 26) were full of anxiety
for the diocesan administration whose president was
Professor Rezzara, the indefatigable leader of the entire
Catholic movement, and whose vice-president was Don
Clienze Bortolotti, that militant priest who had succeeded
Caironi at the end of 1903 as the new editor of the *Eco di
Bergamo*. Roncalli was one of its members in his capacity
as president of the fifth section (branch of the Women's
Catholic Action). It would be interesting to reproduce at
this point the minutes of the meetings of the diocesan
administration which were held to consider the elections.
The attendance of the bishop's secretary is recorded at
almost all these meetings, especially those of April 17, 21,
and 29, May 13 and 27, and June 6. At the meeting of
April 17 examination was made, at a local level, of the
difficulties of the electoral situation, and the decision was
made to draw up a memorandum to be presented to Count
Gentiloni at Rome. Catholic support for the moderate
Liberal candidates is considered to be inadmissible in two
electoral colleges: namely Caprino-Ponte S Pietro, where
Crespi had declared his intention of opposing the candidate
from Bergamo, a lawyer called Preda, and Zogno where
there was a desire to put forward a man from the plains
instead of Carugati.

The memorandum was approved by the meeting of
April 21 and taken to Rome by Don Clienze Bortolotti and
the solicitor Volpi. It represented the 'unanimous' opinion
of the diocesan administration and carried the signatures
of all the members. The last but one to sign was Roncalli.
On April 29 the solicitor informed the assembly that the
memorandum had been 'very much praised' in Rome and
that the central administration had full confidence in the
diocesan authority at Bergamo. Even the office of the
Secretary of State expressed no opinion over 'the affairs of
Bergamo'. Rezzara, in his turn, read a letter from Count
Gentiloni which expressed approval and encouragement.

By way of contrast the assembly of May 27 was stormy. Much time had already been wasted and at Caprino Crespi had made good use of the electoral body. The clergy were divided, one section of them apparently inclined to disobey the diocesan directives; the influence of patronage and money was feared. Someone proposed the withdrawal of Preda's candidacy but the point had been reached at which withdrawal would be worse than defeat, it would amount to a reward for indiscipline . . . Don Angelo declared that he was worried over the outcome of the struggle. He deplored the lack of competent workers and the resistance of the clergy: 'The clergy of the electoral college have too often given proof of their instability and of a tendency to lack of discipline', he said. Yet it was impossible to withdraw the candidature in question, and he added: 'We shall be all the more disgraced, if Preda is beaten, for having abandoned him.' Finally the following announcement was proposed: 'The president of the third section . . . announce(s) with pleasure that the discipline of the clergy is assured and consequently that it is necessary to have confidence in the success of the candidate Preda.' The announcement was agreed. Of the nine members present eight voted in favour. A bulletin bears the words: 'We are confident.' Don Angelo wondered if the struggle was really one of principle. He mentioned the matter to the bishop who, seeing the awkward position in which his secretary found himself among the members of the electoral committee, deemed it right that he should remain aloof from the actual electoral activities.

The worst was still to come. Count Medolago-Albani, who had already been in disagreement with Rezzara for several years, had been asked by Rome to express his views in a confidential memorandum. He was severe and denounced the Bergamesque Catholics as ambitious, as 'aspiring to petty honours', as 'unaware of the dangers', 'of creating profound divisions within the Catholic camp, of embittering relations between Catholics and moderate Liberals.' The confidence that Medolago enjoyed at Rome and the fact that he knew Pius X well told against the diocesan administration. Mgr Radini had to hurry to Rome where he was just in time to sign a note, already prepared for the *Osservatore Romano*, repudiating the electoral activity of Rezzara and of the diocesan administration. His secretary was with him. He heard the bishop's 'frank and sincere language' as he wrote to Rezzara on June 29: 'Some have sought to describe the administration as contrary to the papal directives. It is most distressing; but you can be sure that I informed those concerned and that I have straightened matters out.'

Don Angelo saw the suffering that came to these two eminent personalities. In spite of the assurances given by Rome, neither of them could escape the impression of no longer enjoying the Pope's confidence.

There was another cause of distress—Don Angelo wrote—a sharp thorn driven into the heart of Mgr Radini. It drew blood, and although the bleeding was silent and concealed, it was none the less real and painful. This prelate, at the heart of whose purest thoughts stood Rome and the Pope . . . this incomparable bishop who sacrificed a great deal in order to follow unswervingly the directives of the Apostolic See, wondered anxiously whether he still fully deserved the Holy Father's trust. That was his greatest ordeal, and although it is still indelicate to speak of it, it would be failing seriously both in truth and justice to pass over it completely in silence.

This ordeal came to the two men at the end of their lives, at a time when they were beginning to suffer from the cancerous disease from which they were both to die. Bishop Radini died on August 21, 1914, Rezzara on February 8, 1915. The last thoughts of both were for the Pope. The first great European war was already raging. Don Angelo had just gone through one of those trials which bring unexpected enrichment to life.

Chapter Four

SILENT WORK

D ON ANGELO felt very much alone after the disappearance of his bishop. Another chapter in his life had just closed leaving him with vivid and lasting memories. He would like to have remained connected by some function or other to the world he knew. It would have been easy for the new bishop to make use of him and of his rich store of experience. Don Angelo hoped that he would, but he was disappointed. In the new prelate's entourage were influences which had shown themselves hostile to Radini. On his death the impression was that a new line would be taken. The secretary realized that by going elsewhere he would allow everybody greater freedom of action; and so he humbly withdrew and his faithful friend of student days, Don Carozzi, who occupied the post of treasurer at the seminary, set aside a little room for him in his house where he could meditate and work. He still had his teaching at the seminary and his work for Catholic Action. Meanwhile the war was beginning to cause gaps in the theological classes. One after the other, pupils were called up. Some of the professors had already left. Others, not desiring to see all the chairs left vacant, claimed medical exemption or on the grounds of the needs of the parochial ministry. Don Angelo no longer had any special claim for exemption, and so he expected to be recalled to the colours at any moment.

He was already familiar with military life. In 1902 he had completed his national service as a 'volunteer'. That form of engagement shortened the normal period of service from three years to one, on condition of payment of a thousand lire, and allowed him free choice of any branch of the service. He enlisted in the 73rd Infantry Regiment stationed at Bergamo and was thus able to be near the seminary. When the call came—it was Whitsunday—he was not in the least disturbed by it; rather was he happy, at the time of his country's danger, to be among those who contributed their share to the common good. Those were the historic days of May 1915.

One of his pupils, on guard duty at the General Military Hospital in Milan, noticed him one day, a trifle embarrassed by his civilian clothing, in the yard of the building. He was in the middle of a group of conscripts seated round a table in the shade of a chestnut tree which still stands in the main courtyard of the present Catholic University. A billeting officer was checking them in and issuing travel warrants. The pupil, seeing his old professor's embarrassment, took his papers from him and handed them to the sergeant who stamped them and handed over the first day's pay: 1.88 lire. The professor made his pupil a present of it to buy his friends a drink. He was issued with his kit by the sergeant and left for Bergamo again, having been posted to the hospital in that town.

He loved working with soldiers. They would arrive at Bergamo in ambulances, their wounds hastily dressed, their eyes still filled with the immense sadness caused by the sight of so much horror. But in a short space of time as their wounds healed and they grew stronger, the love of life took hold of them again and they emerged more serious, stronger, more mature. First as orderly, then as chaplain, Don Angelo spoke easily about religion to these men in their misfortune. He found just the right note to strike in sympathizing with them in their ordeals and thus paved the way for reconciliation not only with life but with their faith. He understood them all the better because he suffered with them. His suffering was of a different kind from theirs, but it fitted him for bringing Christian comfort to them. The renunciation which he had accepted of the people, places and things that he loved, and the silence which spread over his life after a period of endless activity, all contributed to the deepening of his understanding of the suffering of others.

In other respects humiliations were not lacking for him. Anti-clericalism was fashionable among doctors and senior officers. One lieutenant-colonel, who could not abide soldier-priests, poured sarcasm on him. The contempt with which he treated Don Angelo hurt him deeply, for he saw himself thus deprived of all authority over his subordinates. But after the young chaplain had sent him a report, this officer made some sort of verbal apology: 'Do not be angry, sergeant. I can see that really I am a poor man who must be content to add a new serpent to that of my kepi. You, on the other hand—(was he joking or prophesying?)—you will get on, you will go far, monsignor, bishop, cardinal!' This ordeal also served to hasten the purification of his soul. During the years he had spent with his bishop, the evidence of his great ability had perhaps inspired a suspicion of pride. It was good to step down again: after the pain of it came resignation, giving oneself to God, profound joy.

In the evenings he found comfort in another kind of work. Indeed he had accustomed himself to very little sleep. On the table of the main hospital there were beginning to accumulate the pages of the biography which he dedicated to the memory of Bishop Radini.

Perhaps—he wrote on August 22, 1916, when he sent the manuscript to the publishers—it may not be without interest to recall in the future that these pages were written while the European war was dragging on, that terrible war that cost so much in blood and tears. They were written, not in the peace and quiet of an office but in the midst of every kind of distraction, by a man who, following the teaching and example of

Mgr Radini, gave what he could to his country in her hour of great trial, first as a simple and very humble serviceman, and then after a few months in his capacity as priest.

It was signed: Don Angelo, military chaplain.

He meant to write a short biographical account but it turned into a volume containing nearly five hundred pages. It is certainly not the definitive biography of Radini. The interval of time was too short, but what prevented it more than anything else from being complete was Don Angelo's natural reluctance to criticize things and people, combined with the care he took not to hurt people's feelings. A veil of extreme reserve covered those events which involved popes, priests, and laymen holding responsible positions. But those pages might serve as a basis to anyone wishing to compile a more complete history of Radini's episcopacy. Even when he was back among his soldiers he did not interrupt his spiritual contact with the bishop. He spoke of him to everybody. Besides, it was one way of engaging in those simple conversations which he so much enjoyed and in which he could conceal the depth of his culture and his intellect. Several of his brothers had also gone off to the war. On the feast of St John in 1917, their father's birthday, five of the six children were missing from the family reunion. At last the armistice came. The soldier-priest could now, rather than enjoy a well deserved rest, satisfy his desire to return to his former activities. Families were reunited and the young ordinands who had left for the front were coming back to the seminary. Don Angelo was not slow to resume his former employment.

At the seminary the new post that was allotted him was that of spiritual director. Was there anyone better equipped than he to give a sympathetic hearing to the outpourings of these young men coming back to the seminary, their souls tormented, distracted, or just irritated? In tending the wounds, no less deep than those that he must have seen in the hospitals, he discovered within himself a depth of spiritual and paternal feeling that quite surprised him. To build up a priest's soul again, to set it on the right path, to restore his confidence, and to imbue him with enthusiasm for new ambitions, was indeed an absorbing work and all the more worthwhile in that it did not interfere with his inner silence and his meditation.

He spoke to the ordinands about God, the Church, and their vocation with a warmth which derived from the remembrance of his own trials. He guided their minds towards peace, towards a maturity of spirit largely made up of surrender to God but also of restraint of spontaneity. When he commented on the psalms in the morning periods of meditation, it was easy for him to dwell on those in which the tumult of the mind grows calm through an expression of confidence in God. In the history of the Church and in the writings of the early Fathers he found an infinite variety of material that brought strength and encouragement.

Yet his interest was not confined to the seminary. Radini had directed his footsteps towards certain spheres in which he certainly intended to continue his previous apostolate. Before the war, in the rooms of the *Casa del Popolo*, the headquarters of all Catholic activity which had been set up during the early years of his priesthood, he had given lessons to the religious school for women and young girls. It was there that one day in 1909 a member of his audience had entrusted him with a letter for the bishop. In it the first Roman secretary of the Union of Catholic Women gave encouragement to any form of initiative that might be taken at Bergamo in favour of the new movement. If the matter was not to everyone's taste, for many felt convinced that women should not emerge from behind the four walls of the home, it nevertheless roused Radini's sympathies. He did not hesitate, therefore, to appoint his secretary as ecclesiastical adviser to the movement. This led to criticism after the war. The movement developed all kinds of activities in favour of education and assistance for young women of every category: employees, saleswomen, nurses, refugees, tram conductresses and telephonists. In the upper town the whisper was heard: 'This good man Don Angelo wanted to organize even the telephonists. Couldn't he have been satisfied with the sacristans?'

It was not only the sacristans whom he organized. Another field of work had also been close to his heart before the war, that of the young men. In this sphere also he had begun with conferences at the *Casa del Popolo*. So successful had been his series of lectures to the Circle of Youth on religious history that the public university—one of the most public-spirited steps ever taken by Bergamo—begged him to give the same series to its members. The last course, organized in the first months of 1914, had been given on the theme, so dear to the heart of his bishop: 'Church and School.' It consisted of ten lectures, the subject titles of which are not without interest:

1. The Church, learning and the school. General principles.
2. Christianity and Greco-Roman learning.
3. Schools throughout the pagan world before the time of Charlemagne.
4. The universities and scholasticism.
5. Astrology and alchemy, and the intellectual aberrations of the Middle Ages.
6. The Church and the Renaissance.
7. The Church and modern scientific thought.
8. The great Christian educators.
9. The true origins of the State school of today.
10. Modern struggles for freedom of teaching.

In this way he had introduced himself into the world of young men and of schools. In the upper town there was no lack of scholastic establishments, and from every corner of the province students came, transported to the little square in groups by a new funicular railway. This journey, besides wasting precious studying time, also exposed them to moral temptations in gatherings where laxity tends to follow long hours of restraint.

Don Angelo believed that a hostel which would make them welcome, without imposing the strict discipline of a college, and allow them to work off their natural exuberance ought to win the support of those who were most sympathetic. He found what he wanted within the walls of the ancient palace at Marenzi, just halfway between the bishop's palace and the seminary, and he opened it in November 1918, at the beginning of the first scholastic year after the war. The students turned up in force, and Don Angelo undertook an experiment in that hostel which, for one year, was entirely his responsibility, even financially. He was certainly one of the first in Italy to take such a step. It turned out very well and although sometimes he heard himself described as naïve he had no desire that *carabinieri* methods, which were the denial of justice and freedom, should be applied to his students. He did not conceal the fact that they sometimes abused their freedom. On more than one occasion their turbulence and high spirits went too far, but he had a horror of ruthless methods. He preferred a reasonable degree of discipline. He wanted a relationship in which there was, on both sides, a certain cordiality.

The fate of the hostel, after he left, made him rather sad. His successor came in for criticism on the grounds that Christian standards in the hostel were inferior to those of an ordinary Christian family and that the young people were allowed too much freedom. When this successor in his turn gave up the management he observed in a report to the bishop that the religious programme had been that of his predecessor, but he made it clear that, in his opinion that programme was in perfect accordance with the aims of the institution and the ideas of its founder, Don Angelo, with whom he was in complete agreement.

The list of daily, weekly, and monthly religious exercises carried out at the hostel is quite substantial. It mentioned, for example, daily Mass with prayers and a short commentary on the Gospel. Naturally there were not the same number of exercises as there were in seminaries and novitiates, but experience has now shown that that number is too high for young laymen and does more harm than good. When the new management took over it soon became apparent that they considered their primary job to be the winding up of the students' hostel. Other reasons also influenced this decision; among them a reduction, arising from the transfer of some schools to the lower town, in the number of those pupils who still found it inconvenient to return to their *pensione*. But the way in which this matter was handled caused one of those vexations which occurred at intervals in those years for Don Angelo and, indeed, throughout his entire life.

Nevertheless the work he had begun was carried on by the enterprise of others who had been encouraged and inspired by him. All the institutions established in this troubled period after the war to help education and young students owe at least part of their existence to him. In order to co-ordinate the various educational activities, the bishop, Mgr Marelli, had asked him to elaborate plans for a society, the *Opera di Sant'Alessandro*. As with so many tasks that he undertook, he ended up by shouldering the full burden of it almost alone. The accounts that have survived of the meetings of this association, all carefully drawn up by Don Angelo, show that he was the main force behind it: the setting up of other hostels in the lower town to take in students, the formation of a single administration for the various Catholic educational colleges, an approach to the Roman authorities, and so on.

Once again he was following the teachings of 'his' bishop,

carrying out in full, after many deviations, what might be called the provisions of his personal will and testament. He was looking to the future; he realized that he was not only guiding souls at the present time, whether in Church services or outside, but that he was preparing men to give courageous Christian witness in the heart of the society of tomorrow. He had a liking for the work. His mind was at peace, the field of work clearly marked. All he had to do was to stimulate and to develop. It was a happy experience and one that was well worth while. But at this point his life was to take an unexpected turn.

In early June 1921, he received a note from Cardinal van Rossum—known as the 'red Pope'—who was head of the Congregation for Propaganda, inviting him to Rome, at the personal instigation of Pope Benedict XV, to direct the Association for the Propagation of the Faith. At Bergamo this was known as the 'Association of the Pennies', for the contribution required to extend the work of the missions throughout the world was equivalent to a penny a week. Was Don Angelo to give up the rewarding work he was doing for a post in Rome, the purpose of which was to collect funds? Certainly from the papal point of view it was an act of kindness and trust, for the Pope had himself been a great friend of Radini's, but are popes necessarily the best judges of the importance of a post which tends to get lost among the ramifications of the Roman congregations?

He wrote seeking the advice of the Metropolitan of Milan, Cardinal Ferrari. The cardinal, stricken by a serious disease of the throat and almost dying, could no longer speak, but he replied at once in light-hearted vein: 'Dear professor, you know how fond I am of you. The will of the red Pope is the will of the white Pope, and therefore the will of God. Drop everything and go; a great blessing will go with you.' He obeyed and on January 18, 1921, climbed for the first time the steps of the Palace of Propa-

ganda in the Piazza di Spagna. He was received by Mgr
Laurenti, the future cardinal, who spoke encouragingly to
him. The work that was being entrusted to him was still in
its early stages; they had not even thought of providing
him with an office. Only with difficulty was a corner found
for him to work in.

On the steps of the palace he had met Mgr Bugarini,
who had been his superior in the Roman seminary, and
who now offered to take him in until a suitable lodging
could be found. Having thus made first contact, Don
Angelo returned to Bergamo to finish the school year, but
he got acquainted with his new job by going to Rome
whenever the opportunity arose, and each time he felt very
unhappy about it. To overcome this mood he used to go
into the church of St Ignazi to pray.

At Rome in April he learned of his nomination as a
prelate in the papal household. He was being given consolation, he told himself, before he had even begun work,
but he took the honour very seriously. And so it was
that at length he took leave of his friends in Bergamo, and
in particular of his young people, dressed in a violet cloak.
He left for the capital in the full heat of summer. On St
John's Day he had made a brief appearance in his home
village. The country women, seeing him at the altar in his
violet cloak, had asked his mother: 'But what is your son
doing, dressed like a bishop?' 'Bah! These are matters
which the priests arrange among themselves', she had
replied. From that day on she was only to catch glimpses
of her son.

The new work of the young prelate consisted of reorganizing the Association for the Propagation of the Faith in
Rome along national and international lines. It was—and
still is—one of those organizations by means of which
Catholicism maintains its missionary effort throughout the
world. It originated a hundred years ago in France, at
Lyons, and was one of that country's greatest glories. Other

countries had followed her example, and in Italy, particularly in the northern regions, the movement had made great strides after the recommendations put forward by the Roman pontiffs to the faithful of all countries.

It had as sister organizations the Association of the Holy Childhood and the Association of St Peter the Apostle for the native clergy. The idea was that the Propagation of the Faith, the most important of these associations, should serve as the principal instrument for the centralization of the funds necessary for all the missions. In Italy it had been organized on the basis of regional committees which meant dispersion of energy and loss of efficiency. Mgr Roncalli began, therefore, by visiting the Italian dioceses and talking to the bishops and diocesan directors of the association with a view to creating the psychological atmosphere favourable to the setting up of a unified control. Being blessed with a conciliatory nature himself, he was well fitted for this mission. His action was supported by Cardinal van Rossum who sent instructions to the bishops themselves. On a higher level still, the Pope in person gave vigorous encouragement in writing to the whole missionary movement.

Benedict XV, who died in February 1922, was succeeded by Cardinal Ratti who took the name of Pius XI. One day, just before the conclave, Roncalli, who knew him well from the days of Radini, met him at the Ambrosian library in Milan and expressed his good wishes. The cardinal had replied by saying that the greatest achievement that could be expected of the new Pope was the spreading of the Gospel and of the spirit of peace throughout the world. No sooner had the Pope been elected than Roncalli presented himself at the Vatican. He arrived at the very moment when the new pontiff was going into the Sistine Chapel to receive the third homage. Cardinal van Rossum who had caught sight of him approached him at once with the joyful news: 'Listen, monsignor, while I was presenting my vows to the Pope, immediately after his election, he said to me: "Cardinal, I would very much like the work in connection with the Association for the Propagation of the Faith to be completed as soon as possible." ' Some weeks later there appeared the *Motu Proprio 'Romanorum Pontificum'* by virtue of which the work of the association, and of its two sister bodies, was raised to papal level, thereby concentrating all its activities in Rome. This *motu proprio* had been prepared with the collaboration of Roncalli. It meant more travel, and this time abroad to make contact with the various national councils. France, Belgium, Holland, Germany, and Austria, each saw in turn the full force of his missionary fervour.

At the heart of the central council a privileged place was kept for France to whom was given the credit for having launched and established this far-reaching work. Roncalli was a member of the council, not only as the Italian representative but also by reason of his experience on the national level and his relations with various outside bodies. He was made responsible for co-ordinating the work of the association with that of the other bodies sharing the task of helping in the missionary movement. The wise and prudent measures taken at that time are certainly one of the causes of the notable advance that was given to the whole work of co-ordinating Catholic missions. Roncalli watched the work growing under his eyes. The small weekly offerings of a penny, which the association preferred to larger but less frequent gifts, continued to accumulate year after year as the various contributions were directed into the one fund. The Pope found in it ever growing resources for the needs of the missions. But it was even more satisfying to watch from his central observation point the harmony created by an increasing missionary zeal, by enterprise, prayer, and ceaseless activity. The vision of this rhythm animating the whole body of the Church eventually gave Roncalli the conviction that he had found the sphere of his vocation. This participation in a work which extended his horizons beyond the limits of a diocese and which gave him a keen sense of universality—the most characteristic note of Catholicism—brought him profound satisfaction.

The Holy Year 1925 thus found him on the crest of a wave of steady religious fervour. Travelling for the propagation of missions, sharing in the work of congresses, talking to students and seminarists—it was from these sources that his joy flowed. That same year the Pope wished to mark the two-way movement, from Rome out to individual souls and from them back to Rome, by some event. To this end he thought not only of distributing artistic pamphlets, as a permanent memorial to the glorious event, but also of organizing a missionary exhibition, a symbol of the different aspirations and of the unifying mission of the Church. He called once again on Roncalli to prepare and direct this exhibition. For him it was the last burden and the last achievement connected with a work to which he had devoted himself for four years. In a pamphlet written at the beginning of the year he invited the Italian clergy to place that time of grace in the light of the missionary ideal: 'Holy Year, missionary year'. Little did he know that within a few months he would be called to realize this ideal in a very concrete manner.*

* See *La propagazione della fede*. Scritti di Angelo Giuseppe Roncalli, Roma, 1958 (published under the auspices of the *Union missionaire pontificale du Clergé*).

1. Sotto il Monte: The ruins of St. John's, the former parish church of the district and a favourite retreat of Don Angelo.

2. Rome, March 19[...]
Mrs John Kennedy vi[...]
Pope John.

3. November 1902:
gelo Roncalli recalled
military service.

4. Rome, 5 May 1961:
Queen Elizabeth II
visits Pope John.

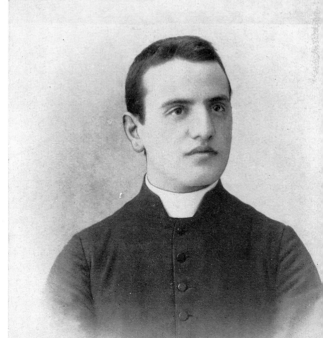

5. Rome, 10 August
1904: Don Angelo on
the day of his first
mass.

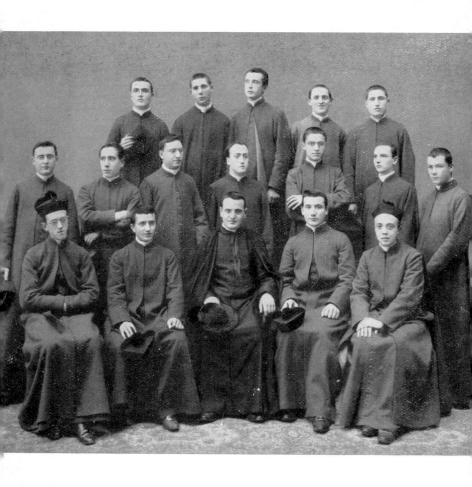

6. Rome, 3 March 1905: Don Angelo and fellow students on his departure from the seminary of Rome to become secretary to his bishop Mgr Radini.

7. Bergamo, 1921: Mgr Roncalli, recently appointed a papal domestic prelate, with members of the university students' association at the moment of his departure for Rome.

8. Rome, November 1960: With the British Prime
Minister Macmillan.

Bergamo, 1915:
rgeant in the
my medical serv-

10. Rome, March 1925: Part of the deputation from
the province of Bergamo for the consecration of
Mgr Roncalli as bishop. Behind him are his father
and mother with four of his brothers and three of
his sisters.

11. Plovdiv, August 1925: At a retreat with Bulgarian priests.

12. Istanbul, 1935: As Papal Delegate with some of his clergy after the investiture.

13. Istanbul: As Papal Delegate, with his secretary Mgr Giacomo Testa, on a path by the Golden Horn.

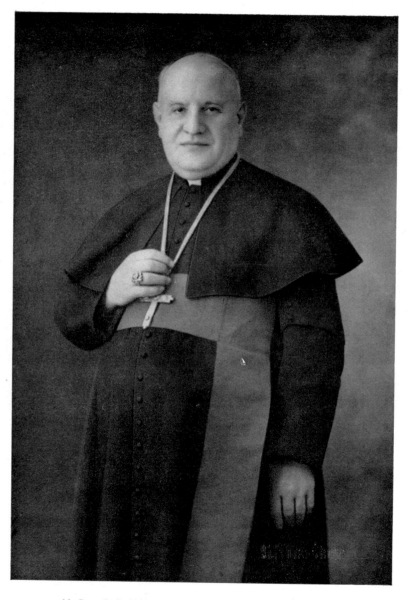

14. Istanbul, 1941: On the back of this photograph he himself wrote: 'This is Mgr Roncalli at sixty. This is the best age: good health, improved judgment, more easily disposed to view things dispassionately, but with gentleness and a confident optimism.'

15. Paris, at the Nunciature, February 1949: In conversation with Cardinal Suhard, Archbishop of Paris.

16. Paris, at the Elysée Palace, 15 January 1953: The
new Cardinal receives the biretta from President Auriol.

17. Paris, February 1953: At a farewell dinner; Herriot seated beside the departing Nuncio, and, left to right, a guest, Pinay, Gouin, Monnerville, René Mayer, Bidault, Pléven.

18. Venice, 15 March 1953: The new Patriarch makes his official entry in procession along the Grand Canal.

19. Venice, Epiphany: Visiting children with poliomyelitis.

20. Venice: The Patriarch with two of his principal
collaborators in handling the relations between the
dioceses placed under his care: the Apostolic Delegate
in Turkey, Mgr Giacomo Testa (left), and the Internuncio from Cairo, Mgr Pietro Oddi

20. Venice: The Patriarch with two of his principal collaborators in handling the relations between the dioceses placed under his care: the Apostolic Delegate in Turkey, Mgr Giacomo Testa (left), and the Internuncio from Cairo, Mgr Pietro Oddi.

21. Rome, 28 October 1958: The homage of the Cardinals in the Sistine Chapel after the election of the Supreme Pontiff John the Twenty-third.

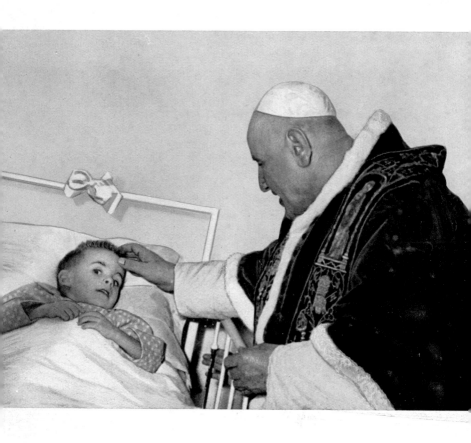

22. November 1958: Pope John visits the hospitals of Rome.

23. His Holiness John the Twenty-third at work at his desk.

24. 15 December 1958: The late Archbishop William
Godfrey of Westminster receives the cardinal's biretta.

25. December 1958: Visiting the prisoners at the Regina Coeli gaol in Rome.

26. February 1961: With Archbishop John C. Heenan of Liverpool.

THE BULGARIA OF BORIS III

O N October 23, 1923, the Balteuxin Agency issued the following information: 'On the occasion of his visit to Rome, M. Kalkov, the Bulgarian diplomat, was able in the course of conversations with the Holy Father and Cardinal Gasparri to establish the basis of a reciprocal agreement on religious matters of interest to the Holy See and to Bulgaria. That agreement might take the form of a concordat.'

During the whole of the following year, however, nothing was heard of any moves by the Holy See towards the formation of a diplomatic plan of action. Actually Pius XI was carefully watching Bulgarian political resurgence and in particular he was trying to find the right man for this delicate mission. In 1924 he dispatched to Bulgaria Mgr Tisserant, later to become a cardinal, and Father Cyril Korolewsky to acquire books needed by the Vatican Library. He also instructed them to study religious conditions in that country and to bring back further information about the inclinations towards union with Catholicism which had been attributed to the Orthodox Metropolitan, Stephen. On their return they both recommended sending a permanent representative who could watch the situation closely. The Pope at once got into touch with Papadopoulos, the liaison officer of the Eastern Congregation, and without going through the usual bureaucratic channels, he singled out Roncalli. The Holy Year was hardly two months old. On March 3 the national director of the

Association for the Propagation of the Faith received his nomination as titular archbishop of Areopolis (the former bishopric of Palestine). The choice surprised him but left him perfectly calm. Later he was to write: 'Actually, to be nominated a bishop or to remain a simple priest has some importance for the eyes but does not mean very much to the mind of one who seeks the glory of the Lord and not the brief splendour of earthly rewards.' But, unknown to him, there was about to begin a journey which would advance him much farther. He decided to meditate in a kind of retreat before the episcopal consecration. In a letter written on March 15 to some friends in the priesthood he expresses in these words the simple, humble and pious thoughts that were his at that time:

I am here, in an ancient Roman villa, alone and apart in order to prepare my soul for the episcopal consecration on Thursday, the feast of St Joseph. From here my thoughts go out to you who, better than anyone else, can understand and help me. I thank you for the kind words you sent me on the occasion of my nomination. I am happy that this honour should redound to our congregation. Otherwise I feel only confusion. Nevertheless my mind is calm and my heart at peace. I give proof of my obedience by overcoming my reluctance to give up certain things in order to explore others, and I remain untroubled. Yes, *obedientia et pax*, that is my episcopal motto. May it always remain so.

But you, my dear colleagues, have the duty to help me at this time by your prayers, especially on the feast of St Joseph. Joseph, by the way, is my second name; I am happy to take it, but I would be happier still to take the virtues that are characteristic of that saint, for they form the fundamental qualities of a good representative of the Holy See. I am delighted by the assurances which Don C. gives me of the continued progress of the Propagation of the Faith, specially at a time when my heart is grieved by the thought of leaving an association which has been the inspiration of my life these past four years. Thank you also for that consolation.

It had taken him a long time to decide on his episcopal motto. All his life it was to remain the truest expression of

his activities. He had come across it in studying the life of
Baronius and had referred to it, while still a young priest,
in an article devoted to that great historian of the Church
at the time of the third centenary of his death. Towards the
end of that article, he confessed that he had been unable
to leave the powerful figure he had been outlining without
recalling an episode which had impressed him at an early
age.

> For many years there was to be seen in Rome about vesper
> time a poor priest crossing the Saint-Angelo bridge each day
> making his way, deep in thought, towards the Vatican Basilica.
> The children who used to stand at the gates of the temple
> begging were pleased when they saw him coming—according to
> Arrighi—and said to each other: 'Here comes the priest with the
> big slippers!' referring to the large shoes he wore. The priest
> came up to these young boys who knelt down round him. To
> each one he gave a penny; then entering the Basilica to pray he
> approached the bronze statue of St Peter, and after kissing the
> Apostle's feet, he always repeated the words: *Obedientia et pax.*
> That man was Baronius.

In this short simple formula, regularly repeated, the young
priest had found his one rule of conduct and, he added, the
true secret of his success.

Roncalli was consecrated on March 19 in the church of
SS Ambrogio e Carlo, at the hands of Cardinal Tacci. On
April 25, in the company of a Belgian Benedictine, Dom
Constantine Bosschaerts, he made his entry into the Bul-
garian capital and took up residence at No. 3, Linlina
Street, in a small but pleasant lodging, next door to the
church of the *Sveta Bogoriditsa*.

They lived in an atmosphere of war. Nine days before,
on April 16, a bomb had exploded in the Orthodox
cathedral in Sofia during the funeral of a political figure.
The cupola had collapsed, killing or wounding hundreds
of people. Miraculously King Boris had escaped, but the
government's reaction had been terrible: curfew, search
warrants, mass arrests. A short time before this the king had

succeeded in ridding himself of the Communist dictator, Stambuliski. After the Treaty of Neuilly (April 27, 1919) which established the defeat of Bulgaria, compelling her to hand over part of her territory to Greece and part to Yugoslavia, Stambuliski had governed Bulgaria and endeavoured to show favour to Russian interests. Russia, after the setback of the German revolution and the failure of Bela Kun's *coup d'état* in Hungary, had begun her attempts to bolshevize the Balkans and aimed at making Bulgaria the centre of the Union of Slav Agrarian States. It was a foreshadowing of the peoples' republics of today.

The life of King Boris had been dramatic. His religion was Orthodox although that of his brother, Cyril, and of his two sisters, Nadeyda and Eudoxie, was Catholic. The tangled situation was the result of the religious politics practised by his father, the Czar Ferdinand, an ambitious sovereign who had led Bulgaria to defeat in the Balkan war and in the first World War. In order to curry favour with the powerful Czar of Russia, Ferdinand had not hesitated to sacrifice the faith of his son by making him adhere to the Orthodox religion. On two occasions he had sent deputations to Leo XIII, first an Orthodox bishop, and then Manini, Catholic Bishop of Sofia. The Pope merely replied to the latter: 'I am surprised that a Catholic bishop should know so little about religion.' Nothing could shake the purpose of the Pope. Then Ferdinand himself tried one last approach and dared to present himself at the Vatican, surrounded by high court dignitaries. But hardly had he got on to the subject of the reasons for his visit before the Pope rose indignantly from his throne and with an imperious gesture showed him the door saying: 'Leave!' 'He chased me out like a dog', the Czar announced to his followers. Back in Sofia he made known his notorious proclamation: 'After consulting the highest religious authorities I find myself obliged to sacrifice that which I hold most dear: my son.' Boris had therefore embraced the

Orthodox religion and bowed to his father's orders. On succeeding to the throne after the defeat of 1918, he had declared in his first proclamation to the people: 'I, the faithful son of the Orthodox Church . . .' It was his profession of faith and the official indication of his adherence to the national Church of Bulgaria. His action marked the triumph of Orthodoxy.

Nevertheless Bulgaria remained wide open to intellectual currents and to western culture, thanks to the numerous Latin religious communities, both of men and women, which laboured with admirable generosity and self-denial. In addition to the Assumptionist Fathers and the Brothers of the Christian Schools, with their colleges at Plovdiv and Sofia, we need to remember a whole series of schools run by nuns at Sofia, Plovdiv, Varna, and Rutschuk. Several lay schools, run by Italians, Germans and Americans, also exercised a good influence there.

One hundred years ago there were virtually no Catholics of the Eastern Rite in Bulgaria. On the other hand there was in existence a community of the Latin Rite, called the community of the Pavlicanes, originating in the conversions made as far back as the seventeenth century by the Franciscan Fathers among the old Manichean heretics established in the north round Rutschuk on the Danube and near Plovdiv in Thrace. Altogether they formed a group of 50,000 faithful, under the jurisdiction of two Latin bishops: Peev, a Franciscan, for Sofia and Plovdiv, and Theelen, a member of the Passionist congregation, for Rutschuk.

But in 1840 new factors had arisen even for the Catholics of the Slav Rite. In the movement which in the nineteenth century had led the Bulgarians to demand their independence of the Phanar of Constantinople (the see of the highest patriarch of the Orthodox Christians), an influential minority had begun to look towards Rome with a view to joining the Catholic Church. At Constantinople delegates

representing 2,000 Bulgarians had embraced Catholicism.
On January 21, 1861, Pius IX had consecrated as bishop
of the Bulgarian Catholics of the Slav Rite, Sikolski, an
elderly archimandrite officially recognized by the Turkish
Government. This marked the beginning of fresh conversions, and at the end of several weeks there were 60,000 of
them. One modern historian is not afraid to describe it as
'the greatest movement of union with Rome for centuries.'
Unfortunately Russia was watching events. On June 18,
1861, Sokolski suddenly disappeared on board a Russian
boat. He was taken to Odessa and later interned in a
monastery at Kiev. This blow led to a severe crisis among
the converted Bulgarians and in no time their numbers
were reduced to a few thousand. Towards the end of the
century Catholic missionaries, Assumptionists and Lazar-
ists, undertook the revival of this community, especially
among the Bulgarians living in Macedonia and Thrace.
After the first World War there remained a core of about
seven thousand faithful who, having escaped massacre and
deportation, had taken refuge on the soil of the new Bulgarian kingdom.

By the time Roncalli arrived they were in a wretched
state. Some had been able to establish themselves in Latin
religious centres, others had taken refuge in Orthodox
villages where, from lack of a spiritual leader capable of
organizing them and keeping them together, they ran the
danger of being absorbed by their separated brothers;
others again, even less fortunate, lived a life of isolation in
localities bereft of any religious support. Pius IX had
received some intimation of these difficulties, and it was
this that had decided him to send to Bulgaria an Apostolic
Visitor, with the task of studying the situation and proposing suitable remedies. Roncalli was to provide the Catholics
of the Eastern Rite with a hierarchy and a clergy; he was
to regroup the faithful scattered in too many localities, and
to concern himself with the fate of the 400,000 other

refugees from Macedonia and Thrace, whatever their religion, who were in material or spiritual need. A vast field of action of a purely missionary nature was opening before him. From now on diplomacy was to take second place. It was the first time for a thousand years that Rome had entered into direct relations with Bulgaria.

The day after his arrival he received the delegates of the Uniate* refugees who were captivated by his gentleness. They simply could not believe that they were talking to the envoy of the Pope who wished to make them feel the love with which the Pope had looked upon this Church, so small yet so loyal and so sorely tried. On April 30 at six in the evening King Boris gave him an official audience and expressed his sincere gratitude for the papal benevolence shown towards one section of his subjects. The conversation turned on a variety of points: the apostolic visitation, the Orthodox Christians and the Metropolitan Stephen, religious orders, and Catholicism. The Visitor was much astonished at the culture, good sense, and gentleness of the king. The king could find something to say on any subject and sometimes spoke at length with surprising competence, showing an interest even in the smallest things. Some of the advice which he saw fit to give, the Visitor found very much to the point, even later on. Above all he expressed his pleasure that the Pope should have sent an archbishop to look after the interests of the Bulgarian Catholics. Ecclesiastical titles counted for a good deal in the East.

No mention was made in this conversation of the religious position of the king. But in emphasizing how pleased he was that the Visitor should be concerning himself with the Orthodox Christians, he seemed to imply a desire to see himself also delivered from the chains that bound him, through a return of his people to the Church. When the Visitor left the palace it was half-past nine.

* The name given to the Christians of the Eastern Rite united to Rome. As used by Orthodox Christians, however, the term is derogatory.

The following Sunday he celebrated Solemn Mass in the Latin parish church. In his sermon he made known the aims of his mission and also expressed his regret at having to speak in Italian. He added, however, that soon he would be able to deliver it in French, and even in Bulgarian, and thereby draw closer to those people to whom he had been sent. This design had to remain no more than a wish. With so many duties and with so much on his mind that he could not possibly have foreseen, he never succeeded in attaining a sufficient knowledge of Bulgarian for him to make himself understood. The next twenty days were spent making contact with people, things, and surroundings. The little house in which he lived was new and clean, although it was not finished. It was so small that the worthy Don Stephen Kurtev, who lived there before him, had to go to bed in the kitchen. The Catholic groups in Sofia, composed of two ethnic elements, Thrace and Macedonia, were divided. On the whole they were intelligent and active people, but as hot-blooded and as prone to intrigue in love as they were in hatred, and always excited and noisy. It required all the Visitor's patience and great tolerance to restrain these people in which, nevertheless, there was so much goodwill.

The first apostolic journey began on May 19. Various reviews published by the Congregation of Assumptionists and also its domestic bulletins enable us to follow quite closely the Visitor at the principal points of his journeyings. From Sofia he went to Burgas, second seaport of the kingdom, and from there to Yamboli. From that town he struck out into the villages of Gadzilovo, Topuzlari, Doruchi and Sliven, an important commercial centre. Then he went on to Stara Zagora, a growing and highly promising city, in which the Resurrectionist Fathers worked in poor conditions. As for the more important groups of Catholics of the Eastern Rite, they were scattered about the villages which lie on the frontier of Greece and Turkey, in the area on

both sides of the River Maritza which had Svilengrad as
its centre. Nevertheless, before leaving on a new and more
difficult journey, he took the opportunity, as though by
chance, to meet the Metropolitan Stephen. The intellectual
vigour of the man, who was accepted as the main representative of the Orthodox Bulgarian world, did not dazzle
him. His desire for union with Rome, of which he spoke so
much, was not accompanied by a sufficient knowledge of
Catholicism in its highest and truest manifestations. He had
no proper idea of the depth of the internal life of the
Church, and the few glimpses of it which he was given by
the Visitor quite astonished him. But still the ice was
broken, and Roncalli felt sufficiently encouraged to hold
other interviews.

Then he left on a second journey. Seeing the proximity
of Svilengrad to the town of Andrinopolis which is on
Turkish soil and which had been the most important centre
of the Unionist movement in 1860, he wished to pay a
visit to these places, which were rich in memories. This
excursion of June 9 was more useful to him in getting to
know the Bulgarian Church than the reading of a thick
volume of history. The region was now abandoned by the
population which had emigrated, and everywhere was
desolation. The religious institutions which had formerly
flourished, the churches, the icons, the fittings, everything
was in a state of neglect. The prophecy of the old monk
Pantaleimon was being fulfilled. A visit to the splendid
mosque of Sultan-Selim at the time of vesperal prayers only
deepened the sadness of his soul. He returned to Svilengrad
whence he set out again for Pokrovan with the intention of
making a long car journey through a mountainous
countryside which was extremely beautiful but deserted
and dangerous. Waiting for him at the halfway stage was
the police patrol which had been provided to protect him
from mishaps. After a drive of thirty miles he arrived on the
banks of the Arda, a little tributary of the Maritza; there

he paused for a short time to take refreshment, then crossed the river in an old boat and found on the far side horses ready to convey him to Pokrovan, their wooden saddles covered with goatskin. The village was entirely Catholic. The church was pretty but the presbytery was no more than a small Turkish barn: four walls roughly made of stone, with no lime either inside or outside. The light from a few cracks barely relieved the darkness. In the corner stood two beds which the priests gave up to the Visitor and to his companion, Father Privat Belard, an Assumptionist. Once again the travellers were to hear from the faithful the story of the massacres committed by the Turks in 1913 before leaving the country. Still on horseback he made his way to Ateren, then in heavy rain he passed through a wood and reached Armuth: in these two villages the Catholics lived in wretched huts near a little church, itself not much better than a hovel, where there was not even a tabernacle. The torrential rain continued until his arrival at Pokrovan on the banks of the Arda where a car was supposed to be waiting. But the chauffeur, fearful of brigands, was not at the meeting-point. There was nothing for it but to remount and to go back up the far slope. There he was met by soldiers guarding the frontier who took him to their officer's room. He spent the night there on a hard bed while his companions, stretched out on the ground, made do with blankets. An *araba*, a simple cart drawn by oxen, was summoned by telephone and arrived two days later to fetch him.

On his departure the officer, of the Orthodox faith but very friendly, advised him to conceal his pectoral cross, his ring and the acorns on his hat in order not to attract the attention of robbers. In those thickly wooded mountains they did not encounter a living soul, apart from a long caravan train of refugees making its slow way up from Svilengrad. The day before brigands had attacked the mail coach and left the driver lying injured on the road. But the Lord watched over Roncalli's journey. At Svilengrad, after a change of carriage, they headed for the fields of Thrace, for the places hallowed by their association with the old monk Pantaleimon. At Mostratli two priests were still living who remembered the exploits of that ascetic, who had built a convent now occupied by the Assumptionists. His body lies at Soudzac, one of the most beautiful villages in Bulgaria, some twelve miles farther on. Roncalli's visit to Armutluk, another village about ten miles away, was unforgettable. Old women and strong young men came running to meet him, leaving fields covered with ripe corn, and his departure seemed to cause them much sorrow. After stopping at Derviska Moghila, where a priest who must have originally been farmer, joiner, and mason rolled into one, had a great influence among the Orthodox, they made the journey back to Svilengrad. A visit to Plovdiv, the most important town in Bulgaria after the capital and a well-known centre for Catholics of the Latin Rite, brought his journey to an end.

There remained Malko Ternovo to be visited. At the outset, on account of the distance of the place and the dangers of the journey, the Visitor had been advised against going as far as this remote enclave of Bulgaria which lay beyond the former Turkish frontier near the Black Sea. But Malko Ternovo was the citadel of Catholicism in those parts—a sort of Bulgarian Vendée—and so Roncalli gladly accepted the pressing invitations addressed to him from that quarter. His travelling companion was Don Stephen Kurtev who came more and more to identify his life with Roncalli's. Relations between Catholics and Orthodox were somewhat strained in that area, and when Roncalli delivered his sermon in the church, he felt himself watched and even spied on. He went out of his way to show himself milder than usual, and the following day the vice-prefect himself, a scoundrel who had seriously wounded a Catholic the year before, came with the mayor to pay his respects. The Visitor spoke to him about peace and sent him away satisfied with his visit.

He was glad to get back to Sofia. It had not been a pleasure trip for him, but although he had never had a special vocation for missions, he had felt himself to be not only a bishop but a true missionary. He smiled at the remembrance of the simple ceremonial of those visits. First came the entry into the church with its adoration and prostrations and the kissing of the icons which always made such a good impression on the faithful. Then followed the installation on the simple episcopal throne which was placed in front of the rows of pews. The congregation sang an anthem or hymn in their own language. The sermon was delivered in a strange fashion: the Visitor uttered three brief thoughts and these were then translated by a Bulgarian Father; then three more thoughts and a fresh translation, and so he continued for half an hour surrounded by an attentive audience. The affection that was felt for him showed itself in the warm and spontaneous reception he was given. At the first sight of him the bells would ring out. The faithful of both rites formed a lane as he walked; the youngest members threw flowers. The Visitor celebrated Mass for them. He gave communion and confirmation. He liked to be present at the Slav liturgical rites. With utter simplicity he allowed himself to be photographed in the middle of groups which the entire population tried to join. By the evening he was extremely tired. Throughout the day he used to feel compassion, but above all sorrow caused by the continual spectacle of misery and neglect. Like a father surrounded by his children he allowed people to gather round him. He listened to them, encouraged them through his interpreter, and held out his pectoral cross and his ring to be kissed. It was the good shepherd among his flock and he believed that he had returned to the charming simplicity of the early days of Christianity.

His journey did not go unobserved in the rest of the

country. On his return to Sofia he was surprised to find himself being interviewed by journalists. One of these interviews, which was published by *La Bulgaria*, a daily newspaper in Sofia, on August 7, 1925, has come to light.

The Apostolic Visitor, His Excellency Mgr Roncalli, did us the honour of receiving us recently. We went into the courtyard of the Uniate church of Sofia where stands the monsignor's little white house. A Bulgarian priest showed us into a simple and pleasing room. The door of the monsignor's office was soon opened and we saw His Excellency get up, leaving his work table covered with books. On a shelf were standing the works of the Fathers of the Church and the great Italian writers, Dante, Petrarch, and Manzoni. The monsignor is still quite young; there is in his face a striking energy, simplicity and gentleness. His welcome was friendly and without fuss. He explained to us, with a vivacity common to his countrymen, the objects of his journey to Bulgaria and his first impressions of the country. 'I came here,' he said, 'to transmit to the Bulgarian Catholics the blessing of the Pope who has always had a profound respect and an ardent love for the noble Bulgarian people. My mission is to organize the religious life of the Bulgarian Catholics who, although in a minority, have become quite numerous since the arrival of a flood of refugees from Macedonia and Thrace. I shall certainly have many questions to study and decide, for example the organization of Catholic schools and churches, and mixed marriages between Catholics and Orthodox. It seems to me that by religious discipline and instruction it should be possible to help the Bulgarian Catholics, and at the same time respect their institutions, customs, rites and language. My impression is that generally speaking the Bulgarian people possess great Christian qualities. Certainly they are basically good. Nevertheless it is necessary to develop their love of religious things, of the Eucharist and of the cult of the Holy Mother, the great shield of the Christian world. I have already been able to watch the Bulgarian people closely; I wish to learn their language and I am at the moment studying their history. I have already visited a large part of your country, among other places the celebrated valley of the roses, Kazanlik, Sliven, Yamboli, Plovdiv, Tirnova Seimen, Svilengrad, and many others. My impressions are excellent. Your soil is wonderfully well cultivated; everywhere one can see the handiwork of the pains-

taking Bulgarian people who have transformed their country
into a magnificent garden. I have also enjoyed the beauty of
your countryside which might be compared to that of Lombardy
and Calabria. I have been delighted by the simplicity and the
kindness of the population who received us everywhere with the
utmost sympathy and with a touching hospitality. It has also
been interesting for me to observe the Turks who in the celebration of their religious rites, prostrate themselves before God.
I should also add that I have witnessed the complete tolerance
of the Bulgarian people with regard to racial and religious
minorities.' The face of Mgr Roncalli (the article continued)
lights up with real joy when he is speaking of our country and
its simple, gentle peasants. He told us that he believed firmly in
the future of Bulgaria and paid a compliment to the shrewdness
of His Majesty the King. Monsignor believes that Boris III has
all the qualities of a monarch who is devoted to his people and
he admires his high culture. Then he spoke to us of the problem
of diplomatic relations between the Holy See and Bulgaria: 'It
would be a good thing and an immense advantage for your
country to be represented at the court of the Holy See, but it is
still too early to establish such relations.'

We assured Mgr Roncalli that Bulgarian opinion was well
disposed towards him and that the self-denial and sincerity with
which he was accomplishing his noble and heavy task had
aroused admiration.

The opinion of the journalist was not a mere formal compliment. Roncalli had given pleasure especially in the
trouble he had taken not to harm in any way the susceptibilities of local authorities, both civil and religious. The
latter had kept a particularly close watch on him. The fact
that he provoked no clash might be set down as a rare
diplomatic success. In a speech to the Sobranie (National
Assembly) the Minister of Foreign Affairs and Culture,
M. Bourov, made a discreet but clear allusion to the
presence of the apostolic Visitor in Bulgaria, praising the
perfect tact with which he was accomplishing his task. The
government had, incidentally, a special motive in being
considerate to the Pope's representative. Thanks to the
liberality of Pius XI the Minister had been able to return

to Mutana Liaptchev, wife of the President of the Council, a considerable sum of money on behalf of all the refugees who had had to leave their homes in Macedonia and Thrace.

Before the end of 1925 Roncalli was able to return to Rome taking with him some indication of the revival of Catholicism in Bulgaria. The Holy Year was an occasion for organizing two Bulgarian pilgrimages to the throne of St Peter. The second, about one hundred strong, was presented to the Holy Father by the apostolic Visitor on October 16. Pius XI openly expressed the joy he felt at knowing how much his respresentative was esteemed and loved by the Bulgarian Christians. In a private audience the Visitor presented his report. He had only fulfilled the first part of his task. He now had to proceed to the second part which received the full approval and blessing of the Holy Father.

In the course of these visitations the Visitor had taken a large number of notes on the real religious conditions of the faithful and of the eastern clergy. These latter, in particular, although filled with zeal, lived an isolated existence in the midst of hardship which slowly sapped their energy. Moreover, the religious training received at the seminary could not be described as satisfactory. Roncalli realized that what the clergy needed above all was to be given a feeling of solidarity in order to reawaken and stimulate in them a sense of their responsibilities and in order to lighten the burden of solitude which in the long run stifled all enterprise, so he began by introducing an annual retreat over which he presided whenever he could. The first was held in the Saint Augustine College of the Assumptionist Fathers at Plovdiv. Twenty-five priests of the Eastern rite came, in spite of the inconveniences and the heat of August, to take part in it. The presence of the papal representative was a great comfort to them. Roncalli realized that they were regaining confidence. Rome was not abandoning them to their fate, and these workmen in a vast organization which was the admiration of the world entered with more feeling into the main stream of Catholic life. Moreover, that was the feeling which had to be infused into all the Uniate Catholics. He himself presided over their first congress, held at Yamboli in the seminary of the Assumption, and took note of the easing of tension and the contented atmosphere which spread among the faithful after years of sad dispersion and neglect. But the most important problem still remained: that of the training of the clergy and the establishment of the hierarchy. Having been without a leader since 1920 the clergy and the congregation had no longer any sense of the stability of the Church. They needed someone to guide and sustain their activities. With this in mind Roncalli had had his eye on a young priest, thirty-five years old, modest and unassuming, who was fulfilling the function of Administrator and who had shown unmistakeable signs of zeal and especially of wisdom. His name was Don Stephen Kurtev. Born outside the Roman faith, of Bulgarian Orthodox parents, as a child he had been taken in by, and had pursued his studies at, the little seminary at Karagatch-Andrinopoli which was run by the Assumptionist Fathers. In the course of his studies he had embraced Catholicism and from Karagatch he had gone, on the completion of his secondary studies, to the big seminary at Kadikog (the former Chalcedon) a suburb on the Asiatic side of Constantinople, where he had finished his preparations for the priesthood. Thereafter he had devoted himself to pastoral work in Bulgaria.

In proposing him for this high function Roncalli had shown how much confidence he felt in the qualities of a humble worker. Before taking him to Rome for the episcopal consecration he kept him by him for a long time in the hope that he would absorb something of the spirit of Italy and of Rome. He took him with him on his holidays, so that he might get to know Catholic life as well as possible;

he even took him to Bergamo and introduced him as his *protégé*. Eventually he arranged for his consecration at Rome by Cardinal Tacci on December 5, 1926, in the church of S Clemente so dear to the heart of Orientals who come to venerate the tomb of Saint Cyril, like his brother an apostle of the Slav people.

This consecration was also, no doubt, a token of esteem and sympathy on the part of the apostolic Visitor for the congregation of the Assumptionist Fathers. It was, so to speak, the crowning of the work to which the congregation had devoted itself for many long years in its eastern mission, that of training native priests and preparing for union with Rome. After the ceremony and before returning to Bulgaria Mgr Cyril Kurtev attended a Unionist festival on January 28, 1927, organized in his honour at Kadikog by his old seminary. A few days later his enthronement took place in Sofia. Roncalli felt that in presenting him to the Bulgarian Church he was making a gesture which would open new horizons. In his speech, delivered in French, he declared that he felt he had accomplished the first task set him by the Holy Father and he humbly expressed his satisfaction over it. The presentation of the new bishop was later made to all the parishes in Bulgaria. Shortly afterwards, on February 25, he wrote, among others, to Father Saturnin Aube, provincial vicar of the Assumptionists in Constantinople:

Mgr Kurtev conducted himself with humility and dignity during the various manifestations of respect that were organized in his honour. The time is not yet ripe to think in terms of a more or less striking success. I apply to Mgr Cyril constantly the Biblical saying: *Ecce puer meus, servus meus . . . non clamabit nec accipiet personam nec auditur vox ejus foris . . . nec erit tristis, nec turbulentur, donec ponat in terra judicium . . .* He is possessed of the Spirit of the Lord and at the same time of a perfectly Catholic and Roman spirit . . . He will make his way and with the help of the prayers of those who were mother and father to him in his youth he will go far . . .

The future was to confirm what he had foreseen. When the Communist storm which was later to descend on Bulgaria started to blow, Kurtev proved that beneath his modesty he concealed the strength of the apostles and martyrs. As the apostolic leader of the Bulgarians of the Byzantine-Slav rite, he paid in long periods of suffering and imprisonment for the courage of having stayed at his post and having resisted the pressure of those who wanted him to break with Rome. He is at the present time the only Bulgarian bishop still alive: Ivan Romanov who had been proposed by Roncalli as apostolic vicar of Sofia and Plovdiv, and Eugene Bossilkov, elected Bishop of Nicopolis in 1947 for the Bulgarians of the Latin rite, have both disappeared and must have died in prison as the result of bad treatment.

The future of a Church and its clergy is bound up not only with a stable hierarchy but also with the possibility of a sound ecclesiastical training at the seminary. The idea of a Bulgarian seminary which could provide a clergy well equipped for a difficult ministry in which prudence— prudence in doing good—was so necessary but at the same time was liable to sap all apostolic initiative, came to Roncalli at an early stage of his sojourn in Bulgaria and grew stronger as his mission was unexpectedly prolonged. While getting ready for Mass in the Uniate church the morning after his arrival in Sofia he had seen from his window the branch of a peach tree in bloom and had told himself that by next spring he would be far away. But since then two years had already elapsed. It was true that the immediate aim of his mission had been accomplished, but the complete plan which he had thought out after long and careful observation had still to be put into operation. For all the area it covered Sofia was certainly not a very large town and the Catholics in it represented a minority com- pared with other Catholics scattered throughout the kingdom. But as the capital this town was very important. It might be compared in importance to little Bulgaria in relation to the rest of the Slav world. The arrangements which the Holy See was to make on behalf of the little group of eastern Catholics in Bulgaria were to give to the wider movement of the union of the churches its first and most effective impetus. Numerous symptoms suggested to Roncalli that they might be on the threshold of a great spiritual movement which would have its beginnings in Bulgaria. That country was therefore the ideal ground on which to carry out a bold experiment. Sweeping changes were needed, for the requirements were enormous. At Kavaklj sixty families of Catholic refugees had been successfully grouped together. The Russian Orthodox priest celebrated religious rites in an unsalubrious hall which in this urban centre exposed the entire community to the scorn of the Orthodox. Those of the priests who had shown signs of spirit and goodwill were beginning to get discouraged. They feared that in spite of the original promises they would be once again deserted.

Roncalli trembled at the thought that for lack of means this time of opportunity for the Church might be allowed to pass. The time was ripe for the undertaking of something on a large scale, a noble and worthy affirmation of the vitality of Catholicism. His original plan had been to introduce into Bulgaria a group of new men, distinguished for their doctrine and their holiness, alien to politics and nationalism, respectful observers of the eastern rite, men who would become Bulgarian with the Bulgarians, who would organize works of social assistance and spread historic, artistic and religious culture. Such a plan certainly needed considerable organization. The first requirement was that he should himself remain in Bulgaria until such time as the spiritual field was completely prepared and sown. All those round him urged him to prolong his stay. Rome was quickly convinced of the need, the more so since the Visitor had clearly made up his mind: 'I hope that the Lord will help me not to let slip even once from my mouth, nor from my heart, the desire for a change.'

Yet Rome had to consider carefully the programme put forward by Roncalli. Such an experiment was new in the recent history of the East. First of all the men called on to bring it to reality had to be trained. The Congregation of the Eastern Churches which had taken on this field of work some years before from the Congregation of Propaganda, found itself unable to provide them. The Visitor soon saw clearly that he must give up his dream. The sorrow he felt at doing so went deep and took a long time to wear off. His motto 'Obedience in peace' was put to the test in a small way.

An illness, short-lived but unpleasant, hindered him for some time from devoting himself wholeheartedly to work. Mgr d'Herbigny, passing through Sofia in the course of a long journey ordered by the Holy Father, found him ill and in bed. But his suffering was primarily of the spirit. The virtue of patience had never seemed so useful to him before. He sought serenity through a task well done. He wrote:

> Quiet but busy days. When there are no letters to be written and no visitors to receive, I study languages a little. I take an interest in the world at large by reading the papers, either of this country or from abroad. I can give myself up calmly and regularly to worship and this brings me great comfort and helps me to endure the little pricks from the straw on which I lie like the Holy Child.
>
> The wonderful chance to study the East in the East is given to very few. I am in the state which Saint Francis de Sales calls perfection, that is to say I ask for nothing and I refuse nothing. The Lord knows that I am there. That is enough for me.

Yet the real solution, the spiritual one, he found in Rome during one of his annual visits. By accepting that it was impossible for the Holy See to support his plans he understood that it all depended on the will of God and at the same time he felt a supreme joy. Some time later, recalling this state of mind, he wrote to a friend who was going through a serious ordeal:

We too, my dear Don P., sometimes need to be brought to a standstill by God's grace; under its influence the mind finds peace again. Do you remember what I said to you last year on the subject of my anxiety concerning the ministry with which I was entrusted in Bulgaria? Well, on my arrival in Rome I received a precisely similar shock which restored perfect peace to me. It is not that the reasons for my troubled mind last year have ceased to exist; no, they are all still there, almost as powerful as before. But I found a reason for life and a reason for suffering; and so I live and suffer willingly. I am happy with my lot, from which I believe the Lord will draw numerous advantages for myself, for those souls and for the Church, whose humble servant I am in this country. From the outset of my episcopacy I have recited each day one of the prayers of the *Exercises* of Saint Ignatius, and I still say it.* Well, one morning when I was suffering more than usual, I became aware that my state indicated precisely that my prayer had been granted.

His complaints became milder and milder: 'I am constantly at work here, although my really important plans for the future encounter a thousand obstacles. I see clearly that in this soil I shall always be a humble sower without ever being able to be a builder. Patience. We must not seek our own glory.' And, his mind now quite content, he observes: 'We often wait with impatience for great and resounding successes. We want, so to speak, to see them and to touch them every day. If the results of our efforts do not stand out we think we are going backwards instead of forwards. We are mistaken.'

While he was in Rome in 1929 one plan seemed to be coming to fruition, and that was the one for the seminary.

* He is no doubt referring to the prayer: 'Receive, O Lord, my whole liberty, receive my memory, my intelligence and all my will. All that I have and possess was given to me by you; I give it back to you entirely. Do with it as you will. Give me only thy love with thy grace and I am rich enough and ask for nothing more.'

The training of the Bulgarian clergy had previously been entrusted to various Latin religious congregations, in particular the Assumptionist Fathers and the Resurrectionists. While recognizing their great value he thought that the problem ought to be tackled on a larger scale, 'with the support of new men and conforming to a single ecclesiastical pattern.' The seminary ought to constitute a centre of attraction and at the same time of radiation for the whole of Catholic Bulgaria, it ought to be the symbol of a refound youth and the heart of a powerful renewal.

To this end a piece of land not far from Sofia had been purchased at the end of 1929 and it was thought that things would begin to happen, but that was as far as it went. As a result of unforeseen difficulties and the lack of funds the building plans had to be abandoned. Once again the Visitor was very upset, but he faithfully left the matter in God's hands. Furthermore, in order that his obedience should be inward as well, he tried to make himself believe that a reduction in the number of Catholic Bulgarians made it possible to leave things to follow their own course in spite of the inconveniences they presented. He bowed his head, absolutely resigned, and he realized that Bulgaria was going to be a great problem, but that he must not stop hoping. He recalled the story of the Forty Martyrs of Sebaste, which he had read in a work by Father Cesari during his years in the seminary. The number forty seemed to him to have a symbolic significance, showing him the need for watchful perseverance to the end, that is to say until the limit fixed by God. This thought sustained his courage. He also consoled himself by reading over and over again a chapter from the *Introduction to the Devout Life* by Saint Francis de Sales on the subject of patience. Never had it seemed as precious as it did then.

The year 1929 was the year of reconciliation. Radini's former secretary thought he must be dreaming when he heard the announcement. It was a great lesson to him and a great encouragement. He declared simply: 'One protests as far as the rules allow; one waits; one suffers. Then the Lord intervenes; deliverance follows, and safety.' From a distance he had been able to appreciate even better the feeling of satisfaction and relief that had spread throughout the Catholic world as a result of the settlement of the painful conflict between the Church and the Italian State. He felt more than ever inclined to benevolence. To a friend who was thinking of consecrating a book to the memory of Radini, 'the avenging, unvanquished champion of the rights of the Church, of the liberty and sovereignty of the Sovereign Pontiff', he suggested that it was no longer timely, at a moment when a new spirit was abroad, to 'relight the fire and stir the ashes of past battles.'

The solution of the Roman Question was, however, going to have repercussions in Bulgaria. It was known that King Boris was seeking the hand of Princess Giovanna, the daughter of the King of Italy, Victor Emmanuel III. As King Boris was of the Orthodox religion there would have to be dispensations on the part of the Holy See. In such a delicate situation the Catholic Church required absolute guarantees concerning the religious rite which was to consecrate the union and the Catholic education of the children in the future. If recent rumour was to be believed, and it had penetrated as far as Bulgaria, the following light-hearted conversation took place after the signature of the Lateran Agreements between Mussolini and Cardinal Gasparri:

> Mussolini: After this agreement has been signed it will be easy to settle the little matter of Bulgaria.
> The cardinal: Nothing easier: just one signature.
> Mussolini: Nothing but paper-work! Cannot the matter be settled among friends?

Clearly, such questions could not be settled without solid guarantees, but the mistrust of the Holy See was on the point of vanishing. The conditions to be submitted to King Boris were agreed and Roncalli found himself engaged day after day in a very complicated matter.

The king had no intention of submitting to the conditions laid down by the Vatican. He knew with how much suspicion the Orthodox Church was following the matter. They could not understand a royal marriage taking place outside the national Church. There was no lack of newspaper articles and strongly worded campaigns. His submission, his readiness to accept Catholic requirements, it was said, were really in direct opposition to his profession of fidelity to Orthodoxy. The whole story of his life and of the gesture made by his father was suddenly confronted with a manifest denial. From the way events subsequently turned out, many believed that the king had from the start intended to act a part. On this point the doubt has not altogether been removed. During the months that preceded the marriage, Roncalli was frequently invited to the palace to discuss the difficulties of the affair. His friendliness had without any doubt won the Czar's confidence. Showing much patience he sought to persuade him to accept the conditions of the Holy See, taking care at the same time not to offend the susceptibilities of Orthodox circles.

He certainly did all he could to make sure of the king's sincerity. At the same time he took stock of the extent to which religious interests were involved and of the diplomatic repercussions that could be expected if the negotiations were brought to a successful conclusion.

At length he thought he had sufficient proof of the king's sincerity to be able to reassure the Holy See. The king and the Italian princess had signed all the undertakings entrusting themselves explicitly to the canons of the Catholic Church and in terms which inspired absolute confidence; a confidence that was strengthened, moreover, by the important signatures that the documents bore. A letter, written on October 24, the eve of the royal wedding, shows us, nevertheless, that the king was feeling some hesitation at the thought of the consequences of his act.

As to your own affairs we will speak of them another time. Let me first get out of this period which is one of no small anxiety, considering the mass of very awkward circumstances. You will readily understand that a success such as the Holy See has achieved with its royal wedding deserves the closest study if the fruits that are to be expected from it are to be really *in aedificationem*, and if the slightest want of tact is not to arise which might compromise everything, even after the wedding was over. Here, things are going pretty well; but it is natural that the devil should get up to all his tricks, *quaerens quem devoret* . . .

Tomorrow the marriage will take place at Assisi. Here the Orthodox, poor people, are embittered—I am speaking of the religious leaders—and do not know to which saint to turn. It is certain that difficulties will arise. I have done my best to forestall them and my soul is at peace, come what may. Who knows? Who knows? May Saint Teresa of the Child Jesus arrange matters perfectly!

What he feared, however, fell far short of what was going to happen. The marriage was celebrated on October 25 but hardly had he returned to Bulgaria before Boris had the marriage repeated according to the Orthodox rite in the cathedral of Saint Alexander Newsky. In order to excuse this indefensible action and the grave lack of fidelity to the agreement he had signed, the claim was made that there was nothing more to it than a nuptial blessing, but there was every appearance of its being a repetition of the sacrament. At least the solemn ceremonies had been meticulously prepared to produce in the eyes of the public the impression of a repetition of the marriage, or at least of an addition to it. This disloyalty surprised even some Orthodox circles and Siniev, the Bishop of Varna, raised his voice in public disapproval of the king's conduct. Roncalli was profoundly disturbed by it. At first he tried to believe that the king had agreed to the ceremony simply in order to guard against the inevitable religious counter-offensive. He felt that everything that had happened was not only the work of men but of the darkest spiritual powers. In any case something had to be done, however painful it might be: 'Here my days are spent surrounded by storms. The business of the nuptial ceremony in the Orthodox church has caused me much trouble. I console myself with the hope that a greater good may come out of the evil, and I am content to have kept calm, even at the moment of the gravest steps which my conscience bade me take.'

What these steps were it is easy to imagine. Naturally Rome had to be informed. One question which had to be raised with the utmost delicacy concerned the responsibility of Queen Giovanna in the affair. Had she been capable, in the extremely difficult situation in which she found herself, of seeing clearly the significance of the action she had been made to take? Had not her eyes been closed to the true nature of the ceremony by all that had been suggested to her as to the purely ritualistic value of the ceremony? And even supposing she had been fully aware of the events, what moral possibility was there for her to oppose them? The Delegate could not, for the moment, give a sure answer to those questions. The impression made on the Vatican was, naturally enough, considerable, the more so since thousands of false rumours of imaginary negotiations and absurd transactions had been circulated, based on the guarantees that had been required and given. There had been no question of any transactions in a matter on which the Church has always been particularly strict, even when grave interests are at stake.

The matter was judged to be so serious that Pius XI in his address to the cardinals at Christmas 1930, when he offered to the world as his Christmas present the en-cyclical on Christian marriage, said that a royal marriage had made it more opportune and more necessary than ever. Recalling the gravity of the obligations undertaken by the contracting parties, he denounced the attempts that had been made to deceive public opinion. That speech was not designed to make the papal representative's task in Bulgaria any easier. Reaction at Court, in the government and in the religious camps was naturally very lively. People went so far as to give credence to the rumour that the Visitor would be asked to leave Bulgaria. One member of the diplomatic corps confided in Roncalli that this departure would perhaps take place the day after Christmas.

In spite of this, he showed a great deal of serenity. He knew that the Holy Father had been satisfied with what he had done and it mattered little to him that others should accuse him of naïvety. As for Bulgaria, he was certain that he 'had been able to tell the whole truth to everybody without compromising himself in the eyes of the government or of King Boris.' No action was taken. For many long months a serious tension existed which called for a great deal of calmness and patience on his part. A rupture would have seriously displeased him especially at that time when Rome was thinking of setting up a proper apostolic delegation in Sofia.

The delegation was not yet of course a nunciature, nor was it recognized by the government. But it meant that Rome was represented in the Bulgarian Church. It was a sign of the importance which Rome attached to the problems and to the future of this corner of Christianity. To obtain the Bulgarian Government's official recognition of the person of the apostolic delegate appeared to him to be so important that it certainly deserved, now that his duty had been done, a little indulgence.

Everything went well, and the establishment of the delegation took place on September 26, 1931. Shortly afterwards he wrote: 'Everything went off well and in perfect order. So far there has not been the slightest discordant note. No need to tell you how happy I am about it. But you know how much patience has been needed to reach this point.' And lest he should feel any inclination to boast, he added: 'Now I return to Master Kempis.' *The Imitation of Christ* was indeed his favourite book from which he was constantly drawing examples of sacrifice, detachment, and humility.

On this occasion the residence of the delegate had been transferred to a more spacious building decorated with the help of Italian friends. In the little chapel to which special attention had been paid there hung the copy—ordered from Rome—of one of the three tapestries representing the Trinity which had formerly been displayed above the Sistine altar: there could be nothing more significant in those countries where the *Sveta Troitza* was more highly venerated than in the West. In the red reception-room there stood out, in a large golden frame, a gentle figure of the Saviour Christ, brought from the presbytery at Entratico, a small town in the province of Bergamo. His solitude had also come to an end. The Holy See had attached to him a private secretary: Don Giacomo Testa, a very young priest who was to become his most faithful colleague, his most intimate confidant, and his spiritual son.

Up to that point he had kept in his house an elderly Bulgarian father, Father Methodius Ustichkoff, a great cigar-smoker, a conscientious member of the Orthodox Synod, translator of *The Imitation of Christ*, a volatile man, but one who did not forfeit one's respect even when he was weeping like a child or full of exuberance. But at that time his poor state of health was causing grave concern, as was the number of people of every description coming and going round him and taking advantage of his kindness.

In this way the so-called diplomatic life began. On the occasion of the tenth anniversary of the election of Pius XI, diplomats and ministers made their first appearance in the house of the delegation and during the ceremony of February 14, 1932, the delegate read his speech in French and Bulgarian. On January 31, King Boris had received him in a friendly audience which lasted an hour and a half and in the course of which he bestowed special honours on him. Yet an even harder trial than the previous one awaited him. On January 13, 1933, there was born a daughter, first fruit of the royal marriage, and King Boris hastened to have her baptized with great ceremony by the Orthodox Archbishop Stephen. There was no longer any doubt about the loyalty of the king and Roncalli was completely dismayed. Doubts had begun to be confirmed before the birth of the child, and he had immediately warned the Holy See of it. With great consideration they sent him a few days before the event a personal benediction to comfort him in the difficult situation in which he might find himself.

On January 15 the Havas Agency put out the following announcement: 'M. Musrov has received the apostolic nuncio* who protested against the Orthodox baptism of the baby princess, the responsibility for which action rests on the Bulgarian Government. Mgr Roncalli has informed the Pope of it.' The delegate had also presented himself at the royal palace but had not been received. This refusal roused him to vigorous protest. In fact, from what he learned in the course of the next few days, the king was not alone responsible. Interference by the Orthodox religious authorities weighed heavily upon the government. In the contacts he had succeeded in making with the queen he was able, nevertheless, to convince himself of her innocence. The queen had looked on powerless at what had happened without ever giving formal or tacit consent. While she was still confined to bed the king had come to take the baby into his room and had had her baptized in the palace chapel in the presence of dignitaries who had been assembled without knowing the reason for it. The Queen Mother of Italy had arrived at Nice thinking that she would be the Catholic godmother of her grand-daughter.

* An agency mistake. As we have stated, Roncalli was the apostolic delegate.

The conduct of the delegate was entirely dignified.
Except for what was required of him officially, he refrained
from all recrimination. To a friend who visited him shortly
after these events he said simply as though replying to his
inquiring glance: 'He deceived me!' His voice betrayed
deep sorrow and his gesture let it be understood that he
would rather talk of other things. And then he thought
that all that had only been allowed by God for the greater
good of the Church. He even began to diminish the
responsibility of Boris, saying that this state of affairs was
only 'the outcome of the original mistake, that of old
Ferdinand.'

In the midst of exultant Orthodox and of Catholics who,
according to reports at the time, showed considerable
annoyance, he insisted on a serene dignity. No move on
the part of the Catholics was to lay them open to the charge
of disrespect. It was for the Pope to protest publicly. While
waiting for the secret consistory of March 13, 1933, in
which he knew that the Sovereign Pontiff would speak of
the incident, he advised Queen Giovanna to make her
devotions in the chapel of the delegation, instead of going,
as had been her custom, to the church of Saint Joseph
where she was in danger of rousing protests from Catholics
who knew only half the facts.

Those were in any case months of unpleasantness. When
the consistory met, the tone of Pius XI's speech to the
cardinals was, as might have been expected, very vigorous.
He made known 'his very pained surprise', recalled 'the
formal and explicit promises made in full awareness of the
facts, written and signed by the royal hands'; said that he
knew from irrefutable documents 'how the responsibility
was divided and that consequently he neither ought nor
was able to inflict canonical penalties on, nor even to with-
hold his benediction from, a mother who is already
distressed and who protested her innocence in all that had
happened.'

Naturally, rumours of the transfer of the delegate were again put about. Neither from the Vatican's point of view nor from that of the Bulgarians did it seem possible that anyone could survive in such a critical position. Even before the date of the consistory, March 1, 1933, the *Popolo d'Italia* released the news of his nomination to the nunciature of Rumania in place of Dolci who was marked out as one of the new cardinals. Even in government circles in Bucharest the nomination was given out as certain. It was taken as a sure sign of the confidence of the Holy Father in him, but the Pope, even if he had the idea of doing it, did not give effect to it. Mgr Valerio Valeri, his friend and old school companion, was sent to Bucharest. Some years later they were to meet in Paris in circumstances that were equally delicate, but this time for Valeri. Even the delegate thought a change was probable:

> Whether I change posts or remain here a long time; whether I become a nuncio or am nominated a bishop in Italy; whether I have a post in Rome or finish up as a canon—these are all matters of indifference to me. Nor do I worry what the world may say, for the world judges by appearances and is nearly always wrong. It is enough for me that I have the support of a clear conscience and to know that the Holy Father is satisfied with my humble activities. I have had the proof of all that in recent months. Why should I worry about anything else?

In fact, both in Rome and in Bulgaria, it was reckoned that he had the new situation well in hand. On March 19 the Queen insisted on being present at the solemn Mass which he celebrated in the great church of Saint Joseph. In the glare of public limelight, he presented his vows to her and offered her a beautifully bound missal. Thus he was anxious to show that on his side, and not only on the side of the Queen, the incident was closed without any mental reservations.

Indeed, some months later he reopened the doors of the delegation to the Bulgarians and the worthy Father

Leopold, a Franciscan, returned to the palace as the queen's almoner. Roncalli was already occupied with the future. 'The days pass quickly', he said, 'we must live and above all seek peace.' Once again he found himself in high spirits. He would not have exchanged his post with anyone, not even with a cardinal. And yet about Christmas time in 1933 the rumour went round that the queen was expecting another child. The rumour was quickly scotched. The queen herself took part in the mission preached by the delegate in the Latin church, and on Christmas Eve she made her communion *coram populo*. Then came his first visit to Court, on March 28, 1934. Well received and surrounded with little courtesies, Roncalli wrote: 'Apart from the affair of the baptism, etc., he is a good man. But what a mystery the human heart is! We must pray for him.'

It was now ten years since he had arrived in Bulgaria. The grandeur and poverty of the East lay spread out before him. Eastern Christendom in particular had revealed to him its charm as well as its decadence. Dissension between the Christian confessions had been the daily spectacle of his life. Had not he himself been the first victim of it? Mutual prejudices made brotherly love impossible. The downfall of Christianity was inevitable if a fresh wave of charity did not succeed in regenerating the minds of men and in overthrowing absurd secular barriers which were the outcome of a profound lack of understanding.

What a great need there was, on one side as much as on the other, for knowledge, meekness, and penitence! What a lot of suffering would be needed! Roncalli liked to recall the grief of an elderly Armenian bishop who had spent himself in apostleship in various Eastern countries. During one of the early years of his apostolic visitation the venerable prelate had knelt before him in tears and as he kissed his hands said: 'Your Excellency, we read in the Gospel that our Lord forgives all sinners but that one sin will never be forgiven, neither on earth nor in heaven. Which sin is that, Excellency? Would it not be the sin of the division of the Church?' The great sorrow of the Armenian bishop had become to a certain extent his own. He had at once grasped that his mission in Bulgaria was to present Catholicism in all its broadness of mind and of heart. He was happy when some aspect of Catholic life made a good impression on the Orthodox; whether it was the public assistance distributed by the Holy Father or his own solicitude for the victims of the earthquake of April 1928 ('There are certain circumstances', he wrote at the time, 'in which a small thing done in time is worth more than long wars or a task lasting several years'), or the beauty of the liturgical ceremonies, or even the scholarship revealed in Catholic books.

In December 1927, on the occasion of the death of Petit, a former archbishop of Athens and a great Orientalist, he wrote his first letter in French to the head of the Catholic college in Plovdiv:

> I should like to have presided at the funeral service of the much lamented Mgr Petit. I should have liked to have expressed something that has not been mentioned in the various eulogies addressed to the immortal scholar who has left us: the meaning and the value of his learned apostolate. May God raise up other generous souls to carry on the furrow ploughed by Mgr Petit, and thereby to be able to show with what breadth of scholarly understanding the Catholic Church treats questions of Orthodoxy. This way of serving the Church by means of erudition is one of those which impresses the minds of our separated brothers most.

He liked to attend in person demonstrations held by the Catholic Unionist movement. In September 1928, when the XV Social Week was being held by Italian Catholics in Milan, Roncalli took an informal part in the meditation and discussion over, and arguments in defence of, the celebrated Encyclical *Mortalium animos* of Pius XI on the steps to be taken to realize true Christian unity. Then in

September 1934 he presided at the successful Congress of Byzantine Studies held at Sofia.

In spite of everything, the best way for him to reach the dissident brothers was the establishment of friendly relations. In order to understand each other and to love each other it is first of all necessary to know each other. So long as people remain apart, they may go so far as to be mutually suspicious, and this will lead to mistrust, if they do not actually regard each other as beyond the pale. And so the delegate was happy, on visitations, at receptions and on every kind of occasion, to open his heart to all. He did not fail to attend the banquet given by the Hungarian Minister, which took place shortly after the unfortunate incident of January 1933, although the Metropolitan Stephen, the man who had baptized the baby princess, was also present. He made a point of going privately, during Holy Week, to the Orthodox cathedral where he took pleasure in admiring the splendid religious ceremonies.

These were small gestures, but well-meaning ones, and were not without importance with regard to the vast problem of Church unity. When he left Bulgaria, a priest summed up his impression in these words:

> By his personal behaviour, by his affability and his understanding of the situation, he made an effective contribution to the *rapprochement* of minds by banishing certain prejudices which persisted in some quarters. His term of office in Bulgaria will certainly mark the beginning of a new development in the outlook of our separated brothers, an evolution which will continue slowly but surely.

In the meanwhile providence was about to prepare him for another field of experience in the East before providing him with the opportunity for developing his full powers. On November 24, 1934, he received his nomination as apostolic delegate to Turkey and Greece.

If Catholic circles saw him depart with profound regret, feeling among all classes of society was no less strong. The national press was unanimous in praising the noble figure who was leaving. The articles which appeared showed that his work had been well understood by everybody. As representative of the Holy See, although not officially accredited to the Bulgarian State, he had managed, during his stay, to make himself liked by successive governments and to maintain friendly relations with them. It was emphasized that although he had been obliged to proclaim the rights of the Catholic Church in painful circumstances, he had nevertheless acted with such tact and courtesy that he had preserved the goodwill of the sovereign. His influence had rapidly extended beyond the limits of his jurisdiction but without harming anyone; he had even been approached for help. The very fact that he did not wear official dress had enabled him to act with more freedom. He had represented the Church solely in her religious interests without pursuing other objectives. The delegate, for his part, was sad at the prospect of leaving. Suffering had developed his love for the people. Some days before he left he wrote to Cardinal Tacci, of the Eastern Congregation: 'After ten years this country has become dear to me.'

He freely expressed his affection in the farewell sermon which he gave on Christmas Day in the church of Saint Joseph before a crowded congregation. This sermon, which was broadcast and published in *Istina*, the Catholic newspaper in Sofia, ended with these words:

To you also, my brothers, I give my blessing. Do not forget the man who will remain always, come wind or weather, the fervent friend of Bulgaria. In accordance with an old tradition of Catholic Ireland all the houses put a lighted candle in the window on Christmas Eve, as an indication to Saint Joseph and the Virgin Mary, in search of a refuge on that holy night, that inside the house round the fire and the well-stocked table, a family is waiting for them. Wherever I may be, even though it be at the ends of the earth, if a Bulgarian away from his country comes past my house, he will find in my window the lighted candle. He has only to knock on my door; it will be opened to him, whether he be Catholic or Orthodox: friend of Bulgaria, that title will be enough. He can come in and I shall extend to him a very warm welcome.

He left Bulgaria on January 4, 1934. Ten years before, on his arrival, he had found at the station only M. Peef and a few good people who had come to meet him. Now the entire diplomatic corps was there. King Boris had sent two of his representatives and Stephen one delegate. At Plovdiv, in spite of the lateness of the hour, clergy and congregation organized a demonstration of goodwill as the train passed. A Catholic, who was also a lawyer and a former deputy, took advantage of a few minutes' halt to tell him that the Bulgarians would never forget him and would love him always. As the train left loud applause broke out and voices shouted a farewell greeting. Roncalli had to move away from the doorway to conceal his emotion and his tears.

Once in the course of his early apostolic wanderings he met by chance an old Orthodox monk, who had bowed very low in the eastern manner on learning that he was the Catholic bishop. Then as he kissed his hand, the monk said: 'Monsignor, I wish you the gentleness of David and the wisdom of Solomon.' He was not, at that time, always certain of having shown the wisdom of Solomon, but about the gentleness of David he felt no doubts.

Chapter Six

THE TURKEY OF ATATURK

I N these words Roncalli wrote to Bernareggi, Bishop of
Bergamo, on December 30, 1934:

> Thank you for your kind thoughts and good wishes. I am
> nearing the end of my mission in Bulgaria, a mission for which
> I can now see that I must give thanks to the Lord. On Friday I
> leave for Istanbul and on the feast of the Epiphany my new
> ministry begins. As it is pouring with rain in that country, I
> shall have to keep to the walls and get along as best I can.
> Who knows, I may end up by making a long journey in spite of
> the vicissitudes and difficulties which I am told await me there.
> It will be something to be allowed entry to the country, as I
> hope to be.
> Excellency, each of us has his cross to bear and each cross takes
> its own particular form. Mine is fashioned entirely in the style of
> this century. Your prayers will help me to bear it honourably
> and with a joy which is not altogether displeasing to our Lord.

The allusions in the letter to the delicate political and
religious situation in Turkey are clear enough. The Turkey
to which Roncalli was going was the Turkey created by
Mustapha Kemal—later known as Ataturk—the new
nation which had escaped from the disaster of the first
World War after fighting alongside the central empires
against the Allies. Neither the support of Germany nor the
proclaiming of a holy war had prevented the dislocation
of the vast Ottoman Empire. Its capital, Istanbul, had
become an international Babylon. The old sultan, Mahomet XI, sheltering behind the ramparts of the Yildiz, with
a harem of three legitimate wives (the third was a girl of

fifteen and the daughter of one of his gardeners), thirty concubines and numerous slaves, was completely sub-servient to the will of the conquerors. The national territory was invaded by the Greeks who, after landing in Smyrna on May 15, 1919, tried to extend their domination. All Turkish sovereignty over Arabia, Iraq, Syria, Palestine and Egypt was reckoned to have ceased.

Mustapha Kemal, after turning against the sultan and reorganizing an army and a parliament at Ankara, left the city and managed to create the Turkish republic out of chaos. The republic, after a protracted war of liberation against the Greeks, got rid of the sultan and when its representatives arrived at the Lausanne Conference to-wards the end of 1922 its prestige was so high that they were able to negotiate very advantageous peace terms with the great powers. Then the transformation of the old State began under the direction of Mustapha Kemal. Nothing of the old Turkey of the sultans was to be allowed to survive. Istanbul was relinquished as the capital in favour of Ankara which lies at the centre of a territory that is essentially Turkish. A new constitutional law proclaimed the absolute secularization of the State, the substitution of Sunday, the day of rest, for Friday, the day of Moslem prayer, the adoption of the Gregorian calendar, of European customs and the alphabet, of a new civil code based on the Swiss model (by virtue of which polygamy was abolished) and of a new penal code based on the Italian model.

At the time of Roncalli's arrival not all these reforms were in force. It is difficult for a western mind to appreciate the size of the revolution which they entailed. It is enough to consider what the emancipation of Turkish women meant in a Moslem country. Even the suppression of the *ciarciaf* with which they veiled themselves, called for a ruthlessness on the part of Ataturk that amounted at times to cruelty. If one still comes across a veiled woman in the back streets of old Istanbul or behind the walls of the citadel at Ankara, one can be sure that she is over 60. The old world of Pierre Loti's *Désenchantées* has completely disappeared.

A large number of reforms went against the laws of the Koran and united every religious and traditionalist group against the courageous head of the government. Nowadays the other Moslem countries look upon Turkey as no longer enjoying religious orthodoxy. The Lausanne Conference had important consequences, even for the western and Christian communities who had been established in Turkey for centuries and who represented a sort of varied mosaic of intelligent and active people. Century-old questions had been settled at Lausanne, among them that of 'capitulations', agreements concluded by former treaties, in accordance with which the old Ottoman Empire could only exercise over foreign elements a jurisdiction limited by privileges and innumerable exemptions. The new State had done away with all those restrictions. The Christian communities, delivered on the one hand from disapproval by a Moslem State, were obliged on the other hand to come to terms with the nation solely on the basis of Turkish law. A state of affairs that had been quite convenient and advantageous was disintegrating and giving way to a period of uncertainty. Catholicism itself, which had been sustained up to that point by the European powers, now found itself without any protection and was exposed to blows that were inescapable because they were aimed indiscriminately against every religion, including the Moslem.

In the archives of the cathedral of the Holy Ghost in Istanbul, a chronicle is kept containing accounts of the most important events in the life of the Church. The entry for January 6, 1935, written in French, reads:

January 6, 1935, will always be remembered in the annals of the apostolic vicariate of Istanbul: if the sun did not shine, it was largely compensated for by the face of the hero of this family feast day which was radiant with kindness. Arriving incognito in Sofia on Saturday morning . . . Mgr Roncalli was welcomed by the clergy, the religious, and the faithful in the basilica-cathedral on the morning of the Epiphany . . . Everyone was much uplifted by the reverence with which the prelate kissed the great cross when it was presented to him, in accordance with custom, by the arch-deacon of the cathedral, Mgr Collaro. The cross symbolized the one which he was taking up. The effect was the same when Mgr Roncalli sprinkled the crowd through which he later passed with such dignity, bestowing paternal benedictions with a serene smile. Words cannot adequately describe the scene of the swearing of the oath of fidelity which followed the reading of the papal bulls establishing him in his duties. In the course of this act of canonical respect, Monsignor was not content to present his pastoral ring to each one in turn; in his paternal way he gave them a kiss of peace accompanied by an appropriate word or two which no one will ever forget.

Such an account will hardly surprise those who were present in St Peter's at the coronation ceremony of John XXIII, or who saw it through the medium of television.

It was in this way that Roncalli began his new life in Turkey. It was not his first visit to that country. The last time he left it he had written, in reply to a letter from Guillois expressing the hope that he would soon return to Istanbul, that having already visited Turkey seven times, he had no desire to exceed that biblical number which was the symbol of perfection. And yet at the beginning of 1930, when the post fell vacant in Constantinople, his name had already been repeatedly mentioned. In the end it was Margotti who was nominated, an intelligent bishop, speaking twelve languages, extremely zealous, who got through a lot of work in a short time: March 1931 to June 1932, pastoral visitation; a synod in March 1933, and as early as the beginning of 1934 the announcement of another pastoral visitation in order to consolidate the results of the first. But his overpowering zeal, which paid scant attention to what he considered unreasonable objections, and his modern methods of apostleship, which were customary in the dioceses of northern Italy, were not understood and were interpreted as an attack on rights and privileges established by tradition, although in fact they were nothing more than abuses. As a result friction was sometimes unavoidable, and rumours began to circulate in Istanbul and Rome. In Greece, too, similar difficulties began to arise, and the Holy See, although fully conscious of the merits of its delegate, decided to show moderation by withdrawing him. He had become involved in a controversy from which it would have been difficult to dissociate himself on his own. Diplomatic life is, alas, only too familiar with such episodes.

Roncalli, who had been in a position to appreciate his predecessor, little knew that he was referring to himself when he wrote in June 1933 to a friend: 'In Constantinople Mgr Margotti is hard at work. This year he summoned the synod, the first of its kind; and in my opinion this will be of the greatest service to his successors.' He was himself to inherit just that awkward problem. It was known that a slight rupture had taken place over the past few years between the delegation and the clergy of Istanbul. It was necessary to re-establish an atmosphere of confidence, which is the basis of all collaboration, but it was also necessary to safeguard the work of his predecessor, and to avoid giving the impression of demolishing what had been built up. Margotti's principal colleague was the young secretary of the delegation, Dell'Acqua, who had devoted to this apostolate all the enthusiasm of his early years of priesthood. The new delegate kept him by him for six months. 'His metal is of good, reliable alloy.' Thus he described in a letter the man who was one day to be among the most intimate colleagues of his pontificate. That appointment meant continuity with the preceding administration and recognition of principles that were still valid. Not that he was in favour of strong-arm methods. He saw men in a different light and had different ideas about improving them. His invincible optimism led him to place implicit trust in everyone and to respect scrupulously, in pastoral oversight, other people's forms of privilege and autonomy so long as they were acceptable. When it came to obtaining those results his stock of patience was inexhaustible; instead of giving orders he preferred to persuade, invite, wait until circumstances were favourable for the solution he had in mind.

Among the secular clergy of Istanbul was one who was particularly venerated, Collaro, who had been vicar-general and who was now a curate of the cathedral. The holiness of this priest did not recommend him for administration or outside activities, but he spent long hours in the confessional giving guidance to laymen and priests. His good nature prevented him, in his position of responsibility, from showing that vigilance and courage without which the intuitive gifts of the heart cannot be put to use. Roncalli was well aware of all that but at the same time he appreciated the priest's thorough and intimate understanding of local conditions as they affected the Church and his long experience of the religious feelings of the country. Consequently he turned to him whenever he was called on to give judgement.

When, later, in July Dell'Acqua was recalled to Rome, the duties of vicar-general were in fact resumed by Collaro, but it was not until two years later that his official nomination came through. Acting with the greatest delicacy the delegate had listened to the voice, not only of his own inclinations, but of reason and prudence. At the same time, good relations between the delegation and the clergy were ensured at an early date.

I enjoy my work (he was able to write as early as February 3, 1935). I ought in any case to find it more to my taste because there is less of it. I try to perform my duty with charity and gentleness, endeavouring to keep calm, which is one of the great secrets of success. I find myself surrounded here by people of the highest quality, all of them anxious to help me in any way they can, even to the point of being willing to swallow the pills ordered by Mgr Margotti to make them better and which in his time they could not take without making faces. What more could a man ask?

For the first time Roncalli felt himself to be truly a bishop and a shepherd. Up to that point he had never had a diocese. At the time the function of apostolic delegate in Turkey included that of administrator of the apostolic vicariate (a department reserved for the missionary territories), and the Catholics of the Latin Rite were under his immediate jurisdiction for any matter connected with the religious life of a diocese. He had his cathedral and he had his flock. It was certainly a small diocese, but complete in its components, so that it needed the same care and attention as a vast one. Moreover, there were at that time a considerable number of faithful Catholics in Turkey. The Catholics of the Latin Rite in Istanbul had a glorious history stretching back several centuries, in the course of which they had known tragic moments owing to the constantly changing pattern of Ottoman political life. At that time there were reckoned to be some fifty to sixty thousand faithful in the whole of Turkey, including the Greek, Armenian, Syrian and Chaldean communities. But this number was still on the decline. The reforms brought in by Ataturk made life increasingly difficult for westerners and naturally led to a reduction in the number of Catholics. The activities of the Church, which was ignored if not positively opposed by the government, gradually lost their importance and intensity; the position taken up by the Church itself became a purely defensive one directed against the gradual erosion of its foundations. The whole framework—welfare, education, cultural life—was visibly threatened. The intention was to make everything appear, superficially at least, first and foremost Turkish and openly secular.

When he left for Turkey Roncalli was quite well aware that he was taking on work which was considered very humble in certain religious circles. Certainly, his nomination as nuncio in Bucharest, which had been rumoured some years before, would have meant much more. He wrote:

> What can I tell you about myself? Well, I am very happy. Many people in Europe and Asia pity me and call me unfortunate. I do not know why. I am doing as I am told, nothing more. Certainly I am saddened by the spectacle of the gradual and fatal decay of many things which formed the backbone of Catholicism and nationalism in days gone by. Unpleasant times and painful situations may be in store for me, but I direct my gaze steadily upwards and onwards.

Seeing his field of activity so much restricted may have saddened him but it also stimulated him. Being unable to embark on large-scale programmes, he decided to devote himself to less ambitious work, to his bee's work or ant's work, as he liked to describe it. He would pursue a double object: to sustain and revive the Catholic life of the faithful, and at the same time to demonstrate to the Turkish rulers the purely spiritual nature of the Church's activity and her capacity to survive even without the political protection of the western powers.

His work as a bishop, therefore, had its priorities. Sermons, religious ceremonies, spiritual aid, exhortations to be calm and peaceful, and general encouragement. Above all he desired that his priests and his flock should see in him not a reformer but a guide able to make use of the will and the energies of others. The Catholic parish churches in Istanbul looked to him to breathe life into their religious practices. He did not centralize the expressions of Catholic life round his cathedral, but preferred to allow each church to arrange its ceremonies in its own way. The fact that he had to seek far and wide for his flock did not make him afraid that he would get out of touch with them and be less loved for it. He would rather pay a visit than call a meeting. Even his visits bore the mark of consideration. He would arrive 'on tiptoe'. He came to the conclusion that the more trouble he took to issue his orders gently, the more immediate and wholehearted was the response of his colleagues. His first pastoral visitation on February 2, 1938, was announced in these words: 'I shall make a point of behaving paternally in any matter covered by the ✓ primary object of the visitation; and all the more so because the zeal which burns in the breasts of my priests of the regular and secular clergy never ceases to rejoice the heart of the shepherd.' Each one of the religious groups working in the different sectors of Catholic life in Istanbul felt itself the special object of his love. Moreover, it was impossible to involve the delegate in petty jealousies and red tape. An atmosphere of mutual esteem was maintained by praise equitably bestowed in public, while the inevitable short-comings were enveloped in respectful silence. He never missed an opportunity to express his gratitude to those who were helping him in his ministry. If a member of one of the religious communities died, the delegate would not fail to be present at the funeral service and often gave the address. We have seen the addresses given by him in French on the occasion of the deaths of the Superior General of the Brothers of the Christian Schools, Father Junien-Victor (October 30, 1940), of Father Bruno of Paris, of the Capuchin Friars Minor (August 14, 1943), of Father Jean of Capistrano, vice-rector of the seminary of Saint Louis (September 2, 1942).

In 1939 the first centenary of the founding of the Little Sisters of the Poor took place. Roncalli wished the celebrations to be public, as public as the good they did. Of all the Catholic institutions in Turkey, this one was perhaps held in the highest esteem by the other Christian bodies and by the Turks themselves. In the hostel in Bomonti any poor person, whatever his nationality, religion, or creed, found willing help in old age or distress. More than two hundred hospital cases were cared for there, maintained by charity.

The participation of the pastor in the sufferings and the joys of the Christian family was thus complete and sincere. The poor, especially, had the power to move his heart. In February, 1937, the old sacristan of the cathedral died in the Jeremiah Hospital. Roncalli took part in the modest funeral service 'in order to show', as the cathedral magazine said, 'that the Church, like the Lord whom it represents, takes note of the merits of the humble as much as those of the powerful.'

There were also the more ceremonial occasions when bishop and faithful filling the cathedral felt they understood each other, felt that they were met together in perfect communion of thought or of religious and human feelings. The great liturgical ceremonies provided the shepherd with the opportunity to reveal some new aspect of his soul. The words he uttered were never impersonal or pedantic. Even in the sermons he gave explaining the great mysteries of Christmas, Easter or Whitsun, involving a greater degree of dogma, it was possible to detect the beating of a heart which sought to make itself understood with as much delicacy as it did clarity. To read those sermons written in French is to be left in no doubt as to the theological and biblical depth to which they attain without ever becoming abstract or losing their persuasive power. The very style is an effortless combination of intensity and lucidity, suggesting an intimate knowledge of great orators like Bossuet.

The death of Pius XI was a memorable date in the history of the religious life of Istanbul. The disappearance of the great Pope who had shown him so much friendship moved Roncalli to his depths. He fixed February 19, 1939, as the day for the celebration of the funeral service and himself arranged the details and took an interest in the decoration of the church. In the middle of the central nave he had erected a large catafalque surrounded by candles while from the vault of the cathedral were draped huge black bands which covered the catafalque. Above the high altar was suspended a white cross on a black background and the banners which hung from the stalls were also in black. The pillars were covered with red cloth and from the tops of them hung violet drapes. In contrast with all these outward signs of mourning the lavishness of the ceremony itself was designed to proclaim to the world that though the Pope dies the Church lives on, and that in spite of its grief and tears it rejoices at the never-failing promise which its divine head has given to be always at its side. Everything possible had been done to give this ceremony the character of a world-wide homage to a great figure who was disappearing from the scene. Members of the international diplomatic corps and representatives of other Christian bodies were gathered side by side. The patriarch of the schismatic Greeks, was represented by his first secretary; the Armenian patriarch of Kum Kapu had sent two bishops; the Great Rabbi was present in person accompanied by a civic dignitary. The ecumenical character of this assembly was again emphasized at the end of the prayers for the Pope. On such occasions it is laid down that five absolutions shall be given round the catafalque. By a happy inspiration the bishop arranged for the other four officiants to be of the Eastern Rite, in order to give living proof, in the variety of ritual and tongue, of the unity of the Church round its head. And so in succession there went forward the Melchite patriarchal vicar, Mgr Scismu, the Bulgarian officiating priest and the Greek and Armenian bishops, each one giving the absolution in his own language, Arabic, Bulgarian, and so on, and according to his own particular rite. The final absolution was given in Latin by the celebrant. The effect on the congregation was tremendous. Roncalli was unaware as he took this service that his mother was being stricken by the last crisis of an illness from which she would not recover.

The next day the papers of Istanbul published a long account of the ceremony with extracts from the address given by the bishop. This panegyric which was deliberately kept free of all those rhetorical flourishes which Orientals so much enjoy, had impressed those present with the purity of its message. Often the speaker's own conception of the papacy would shine through what he said; he had also included a number of his own reminiscences.

From my many meetings with him I carried away the impression of a simple and robust faith. Looking always to the future and to heaven, Pius XI never entertained a doubt; his faith was a reflection of the assurance of divine promises, it was the *scio cui credidi* of St Paul. The last time he received me, in September, he said among other things: 'I have no fears for the future of the Church, I have no fears. God keeps his promises.' The same stout faith upheld him in 1918 when he was nuncio in Poland. It was a time when, at the height of the retreat, the occupation of the capital by the bolshevik army was expected at any moment: 'I am staying in Warsaw,' he announced. 'This morning I said holy Mass and offered my life to the Lord. That is all I need for peace of mind.'

In the same way, after his election to the supreme pontificate, there immediately arose the question: Should he bless the crowd from the great outside balcony of St Peter's or follow the example of his predecessors? He paused a moment, then said firmly: 'I am called Pius, which means peace, the forerunner of peace; I shall give the benediction from the balcony to the city, to Italy, to the whole world.' That gesture in itself reveals the kind of man he was. His whole pontificate is summed up in that first benediction.

A few days later the bishop announced in a circular to clergy and faithful the election of the new Pope.

His Holiness Pius XII, remarkable for his piety, his gentleness and his wisdom, is going to occupy the chair of St Peter. His ministry is one of reconciliation and peace. The Pope is both father and pastor for all Christian nations, irrespective of constitution or politics, and of the millions of faithful who live in them. And even beyond the Christian flock which is his more especial care, he sees only the children of God, worthy of respect, understanding and love.

Might it not have been the future John XXIII speaking?

Thus, the little Catholic community in Istanbul felt that it was not living on a desert island, or lost in the middle of hostile territory. The unfortunate effects of the social and political isolation in which they lived were alleviated by the thought of the invisible bonds which secured them to the world of the faithful.

When Roncalli arrived in Turkey, there was a certain amount of reluctance on the part of the press to refer to him by his title of Apostolic Delegate. This was a sign of the prevailing attitude. It was accepted that he should carry out the functions of delegate to the faithful, but there was to be no official acknowledgement of his position. Margotti, finding himself denied the status of representative to the government, had done what he could to establish official relations with the diplomatic corps outside government circles, but the Turkish Government authorities had frowned upon his efforts. Shortly after taking up his duties, the new delegate was asked to sign the letters, addressed to members of the diplomatic corps, announcing his arrival. 'These are quite unnecessary', said Roncalli, after a hasty glance through them. 'But, your Excellency, it is the official notification of your arrival.' 'Quite unnecessary', he repeated. 'Let it be clearly understood, here and now, that in this country the apostolic delegate is a representative with no diplomatic standing.'

This gesture did not mean, of course, that the delegate had given up all hope of making contacts in circles most likely to keep him informed of the government's attitude. He was content at first to approach accredited diplomats as the opportunity offered simply in order to discuss religious matters coming within their province. At Easter, he decided to send each of the Christian diplomats a short letter of greeting, containing a delicate allusion to his position and to his need to show special consideration towards the authorities of the country. This letter produced the desired effect. At the delegation and in the embassies, cordial meetings were held in an atmosphere of friendliness and confidence. The delegate's position was becoming more clearly defined.

Such information concerning the attitude of the Turkish rulers as could be obtained from those nearest to them was hardly encouraging. Roncalli had a good idea of the reasons for this. Foreign diplomats were now realizing that the Turks were no longer an element to be exploited for the benefit of the countries concerned, and that they could no longer, as in the old days, be influenced by threats. They were afraid, and the Turks, seeing this, became bolder and more self-assured.

Did the Church have any grounds to fear a lack of protection? He soon realized how artificial the rise of nationalist feeling had been which, for fifty years, had predominated on the banks of the Bosphorus. The atmosphere of luxury in which various foreign institutions carried on their work was sometimes simply a cloak for privileges which were not enjoyed by the Turks themselves, who were too often considered incapable of being civilized. Thanks to the measures of a charitable and cultural nature that had been taken by some nations, Catholicism had been able to survive in the East, but very few attempts had been made to graft it, so to speak, on to the main body of Turkey. In spite of the exhortations of the Holy See—which had lately become more pressing—to obtain Turkish converts, to study the language and to get as close as possible to the mentality of the people, almost nothing had, in fact, been accomplished. Everything had been kept just as it was under the watchful eyes of the foreign powers. But once the leaders of the country developed a national conscience, the whole position was upset. The last straw

came when those very same foreign authorities to whom
the Church had hitherto so easily given way, not only
refused any assistance at all on occasions, but were seized
with panic and advised unconditional surrender.

The delegate, therefore, did not regret that the Church
had remained isolated but independent. He wondered
whether it was really so impossible to come to an agreement
with the Turks. Information which reached him concerning
the atheistic and irreligious spirit of that time gave the
impression that nothing could be done. The wives of
ministers and high-ranking Turkish officials did not hesitate to ridicule the religious practices of the European
wives, for in the clubs and social circles of Ankara it was
fashionable to proclaim oneself an atheist. All this, Roncalli
was able to see for himself. At the time of the earthquake
which rocked the islands of the Sea of Marmora—at the
beginning of his stay in Istanbul—he saw, too, that it
would be dangerous even to offer help. The organs of the
Catholic press were obliged, one by one, to cease publication. Soon there remained only the *Vita Cattolica*, a little
paper not much more important than a parish magazine,
and even this was finally suppressed. The publications
issued by other religious sects met with the same fate. The
Turkish Government refused to tolerate religious propaganda of any description.

Catholic schools became, in their turn, subject to
restrictive measures. With education now being handled by
the State, Catholic institutions languished through lack of
pupils and funds. Before the end of the 1934–35 school year
it had become necessary to consider a serious reduction in
the number of schools. The Christian Brothers closed four
out of their eight schools in Istanbul and in Smyrna; the
nuns of the Order of Our Lady of Sion closed two out of
their three schools but were proposing to expand the
remaining one, the School of the Holy Spirit, situated near
the cathedral. The Oblates of the Assumption were re-

called to Paris; as for their schools, in Istanbul and in
Haidar Pasa de Fanaraki, these also would have to be
closed if no assistance were forthcoming. Other institutions
were in a similar position. The delegate was very upset,
for he knew that the Holy Father had expressed the wish
that the schools should at all cost remain open. Several
departures were put off in accordance with his wishes; the
Sisters of Charity of St Vincent de Paul, the Ivrea nuns,
the Franciscan Sisters of Gemone, by dint of many self-
imposed sacrifices managed to stay on.

Wherever the Catholics withdrew, the Turks hastened
to install themselves. The delegate was particularly worried
about the School of the Holy Spirit which belonged to the
delegation and which was situated near the residency. It
contained only Catholic pupils and was indeed a sort of
training-ground, from which a number of recruits might
be expected to emerge. If it were transformed into a
Turkish school, there would be no Catholics with the
qualifications required by the government for the post of
head teacher. By taking over this school, the Turks would
be occupying the most important Catholic post in Istanbul.
Another problem was also arising: the question of religious
dress, the church vestments and the cassock worn by priests
and the habit worn by monks, nuns and brothers. Ataturk
would not tolerate in public any outward sign of religion
or any special form of dress. It was difficult to protest since
the whole nation had abandoned the fez and adopted
western headgear. Even the Moslem imams themselves had
to submit to the new regulation which came into force on
June 13, 1935. From that date priests, brothers and nuns
might wear only ordinary dress in public. This was a
serious cause of trouble between the delegate and the
Turks, and yet the former persisted in his feeling of sympathy towards the nation; even Ataturk's revolution had,
in his opinion, positive and encouraging aspects. He felt
one could not but see signs of a *rapprochement* with Christian

civilization in this movement which had overthrown the old Turkey, proclaimed freedom of individual conscience, abolished polygamy, substituted Sunday for Friday as the weekly day of rest and endeavoured to bring the Turkish nation up to the level of European civilization, a civilization impregnated with Christianity. After all, Ataturk's subjects were unbelievers, groping their way towards the most sacred principles of human law—principles which the Gospel, far from suppressing, had illuminated; they were not apostates, denying nineteen centuries of Christian civilization, as were the Russian bolsheviks, the Spanish communists, the barbarians of Mexico and the Nazis of Germany. There were possible points of contact with them, from a practical if not an ideological standpoint. Roncalli was rather inclined to agree with what the Minister of the Interior, Chukru Kaya Bey, had said to the Italian ambassador, shortly before the delegate's arrival: 'The Catholics ought to be grateful to us for the service we are doing them by finally getting rid of the Moslem religion and leaving the way open for the advance of Christianity— at some far distant date.' The minister himself, whose daughter was a pupil of the Sion nuns, although her father was supposed to be a Freemason, replied to the Ankara priest who asked him if Turkey was not following in the footsteps of Mexico: 'We are not the least bit interested in what is happening in Mexico; our policy is exclusively Turkish. We have contact with the Russian Soviets, but we are going our own way'; and as a sign of friendship he promised to make the priest a present of his first civilian suit.

It was in any case obvious to the delegate that the mere abolition of Friday as the Moslem day of prayer and the substitution of Sunday as the day of rest—although it might seem an insignificant change to western eyes—rendered a greater service to Catholics than the law forbidding religious vestments caused them harm. Anyone who had lived in the East for any length of time realized how serious a blow had been dealt to the Moslems by this single act, which was already detaching the Turks from the main body of the disciples of Mahomet. Not surprisingly, they were protesting that Ataturk wanted to make Christians of them. Many Christians in Turkey, however, failed to grasp these simple facts. For his part, the delegate, in his very brief Lenten instructions (he had not dared to prepare a pastoral letter) informed the faithful that they were also to pray 'for this strong and vigorous nation which is seeking the path of its noble ascent to the summit'—and he maintained his phrase in spite of the protest of a Turkish woman, a former pupil of Sion and the only one to become a lawyer in Istanbul. 'The Turks today', she declared, 'are already too sure that they have reached the summit of progress; they even imagine they can now give lessons to others.' His occasional contacts with Turks and with foreigners, all more or less involved in politics, showed him clearly that the Catholic Church could afford to take a calm and benevolent view of the new constitution. He suggested to Turkish public figures that they, in their turn, should consider the Catholic Church in the light of her present attitude, instead of looking back to the time of the Crusades when 'force of circumstances' had obliged her to follow a policy of warlike confederations and military campaigns in order to save Europe. By another historical comparison, drawn from his great store of learning, it was easy for him to illustrate that the new Turkey, although she had every-thing to fear from the armaments and the politics of certain nations, had no reason at all to fear a peaceful, purely spiritual power. Of course, it was natural that the Church should protest against the secular bias of the Turkish movement and she could not but suffer with those of her sons who were being sorely tried, but she still retained confidence in a noble cause, while frowning upon some of the methods employed.

By looking at things in this way, the delegate managed to create in those around him an attitude of complete calm. It was useless, after all, to waste time regretting a past which, in relation to the spirit of the Gospel and from the point of view of the Turkish people, had not always been an entirely honourable one, and had too often, in fact, had only the outward appearance of the Catholic faith. The present trials were to be borne in silence, protecting one's interests, of course, as far as possible, but always with the utmost correctness, thereby making it clear that the religious life of Catholics, even at its strongest, was not an element of disorder but rather of peace and social progress. Meanwhile, the time should be spent in preparing for the rebirth of a purely Catholic apostolate, freed once and for all from clannishness, from disputes between different nationalities and rivalry between monastic communities.

The question of the religious habit was, of course, a delicate one, particularly in the East, but the delegate's view was that too much could be made of this. The French ambassador, whom certain religious orders had asked to protest, received the prompt and rather tart reply: 'Please bear in mind, *Monsieur l'ambassadeur*, that capitulations have been out of fashion for some time, and that we are now the masters in Turkey. This is a question of internal administration. France may, if she wishes, send her fleet to uphold the privileges of her monks—but it will not be the same as in 1914. This time, we shall be ready for her.' There remained the possibility of trying to obtain permission to wear religious dress at any time in private life; this was readily granted. Like every other religious leader, Roncalli had applied for the personal right to wear ecclesiastical dress. He considered, however, that the matter was not really important and decided, should he be granted exemption, to take advantage of it with moderation. He did not agree with the Orthodox patriarch who, it was said, had made up his mind, if permission were refused, to

remain cloistered for ever in the Phanar. He entirely disapproved of those religious communities who invoked their
reluctance to give up wearing the habit as an excuse for
leaving the country, thus abandoning scholastic and other
work which could never be resumed.

In spite of the pessimism of many Cassandras, there was
nothing oppressive about the way the measure was enforced. Police officers visited convents in an attempt to
persuade the nuns, and priests were invited to go to the
Kaimakan to submit their explanations in person, but the
authorities were inflexible. Even the request for personal
exemption submitted by the delegate was refused. The
privilege was only granted to heads of Turkish religious
communities. It was of course a severe blow, but, once
again, there was nothing to be done except obey. The act
of obedience was in fact carried out with a certain amount
of ceremony. The bishop forbade the wearing of ordinary
dress before the new law actually came into force, in order
to make clear, by the very act of submission, how repugnant
such measures directed against religious liberty were. He
therefore decided that on June 13, the feast of St Anthony,
all the Catholic clergy should assemble in the church of
St Anthony, in the very centre of Pera, so that the giving
up of the religious habit should become, in a way, a
sacrifice offered to God. After the ceremony, a procession
of priests in ordinary clothes, somewhat embarrassed by
the curiosity of the Turks and by the sadness in the eyes
of the Christians, made its way slowly out of the church.

Among the older priests, for whom it was indeed hard
to have to appear in public wearing an ordinary suit after
so many years of wearing the cassock, came the bishop
himself, smiling, even more genial than usual—one would
have said almost amused by the proceedings, a living
example of the saying that *l'habit ne fait pas le moine*. He had
not insisted on any uniformity of dress, or any particular
colour, his only stipulation was that it should be suitably

dark. For church ceremonies and at home, as allowed by the law, ecclesiastical dress was to be put on again; this meant frequent and often inconvenient changes but—as he pointed out—they would benefit from such gymnastics which were known to be excellent for the health. In due course it became clear that the law even had certain advantages. At a time when youth was losing all sense of religion and when xenophobia sometimes led to crude and vulgar behaviour, priests were thus preserved from the antics of scoffers and practical jokers. Moslem fanatics themselves, in certain central regions of Turkey, were also deprived of a pretext for the unpleasant demonstrations which had formerly been quite frequent. Today, the law is still in force but there is a certain amount of toleration. Catholic bishops and a few of the older priests now wear the Roman collar instead of a tie. No religious leader, however, wears monastic habit in the street, in spite of the privileges granted.

Roncalli's chief concern, however, was to find some point of contact by means of which he could start to bring Church and nation closer together. He could scarcely believe that among the Catholic priests and even among the faithful themselves it was so difficult to find anyone who spoke Turkish properly. Of course it was a difficult language, as he had himself discovered after a few lessons, but on the part of people who had been in the country for years, even generations, this ignorance of the language was a sign of negligence, of lack of interest and even of contempt for the nation which was giving them hospitality. In foreign surroundings and among a people that needed to be won, the Church had undoubtedly neglected a unique opportunity to demonstrate one of its most attractive assets: its universality.

He felt instinctively that the Turks would greatly appreciate any mark of respect that could be shown and he therefore started to introduce the use of the Turkish language in official documents. Profiting from his experience in Bulgaria he would, before preaching a sermon in the cathedral or in one of the churches, have an extract from the Gospel read to the people in Turkish. He recommended that at the end of eucharistic ceremonies (such as the Benediction) the congregation should recite the *Laudes divinae* in Turkish, instead of Italian or French. Translation of the prayers was found to be extremely difficult. How was 'God' to be translated into Turkish? By 'Allah'? But could 'Mary, mother of God' be expressed as 'Mary, mother of Allah'? The translations sounded very peculiar, to the Christians as well as to the Turks, and from a theological point of view they were far from perfect. The word 'Tamre' (God) was finally adopted, but this did not solve all the difficulties. It showed that Christianity was having to make certain efforts from within in order to adapt itself to the situation. The recommendation soon became an order as far as the cathedral was concerned, not without some grumbling and protests from the more narrow-minded among the Catholics who criticized the consideration being shown to the Turks at a time when the latter were most unaccommodating. But people were obliged to pick up the leaflets distributed to every pew and to try and read out the unfamiliar words. In this way, the custom spread. February 26, 1936, was the final day of important celebrations in the church of St Anthony. The church was packed, mostly with men, many of whom were of the Orthodox religion, and Turks (the Turks venerate St Anthony even more than some Christians). The fathers of the order, to please their bishop, had the prayers recited in Turkish. It was a lesson for everyone, Catholics included. The bishop did not worry too much that the majority of the faithful did not understand the words. It would encourage them to emerge from their selfish and unfortunate isolation and, in any event, it constituted a mark of respect to the nation which was giving them hospitality.

On a recent visit to Istanbul we were again able to hear these prayers chanted in the cathedral, to a simple but suggestive tune composed by Fr. Montico. In those surroundings and in that atmosphere the singing seemed to have a deep meaning.

Meanwhile, in Ankara, every action of the apostolic delegate had been carefully noted. Two ambassadors, representing France and Italy, said that the tact and friendliness shown by him in a situation of singular delicacy had aroused sincere admiration at the Ministry of Foreign Affairs. The fact that his influence had inspired a dignified attitude on the part of the entire Catholic clergy was also greatly appreciated. The Turkish imams and the members of the Greek Orthodox Church had shown themselves much more stubborn; the latter, in particular, seemed determined to make it difficult for the Greek Government by their continual recriminations and they never ceased harping on the days of the Great Byzantium. Eventually the situation began to improve. Early in 1937 the delegate visited Ankara on the invitation of the Austrian ambassador; the Catholics, some thousand strong, who belonged to the diplomatic corps certainly deserved a visit. Ankara was far from being the wild and inhospitable place it had often been painted. In fact it struck the delegate as being a splendid modern city in a magnificent position. Embassies were building villas, the lavishness of which was in proportion to the importance of their respective governments. The city was the centre of an intense activity. In its midst the mind of the nation could be seen strong, healthy and freed from all artificiality. The delegate could not resist making an approach to the government. He left his card at the President's house and at the Ministry of Foreign Affairs, where, he had been told, the under-secretary, M. Numan Rifat Menemencoglu, was the proper and most important person to contact. Through Monsieur Guillois, who had accompanied him to the capital, he inquired whether his visit would be welcome; 'Most welcome', was the reply. Thus for the space of half an hour two diplomats met face to face, conversing in a friendly manner, weighing their words carefully but at the same time concerned to make their respective positions absolutely clear:

—As I am in Ankara on work connected with my ministry, I am very happy to have the opportunity of presenting my respects to a representative of Turkey.

—And I am very happy to meet you personally and to tell you that the Turkish Government has the deepest respect, both for you and for the great and illustrious traditions which you represent.

—I thank you. I hope that the Turkish authorities have, for their part, noted the way in which Catholics have respected the laws of the country, even when these are sometimes far from acceptable. The suit which I am wearing is one example.

—Of course, but we would like to point out, with great respect, that we are allowing you complete freedom to conduct your ministry, so long as it is not contradictory to our laws— even though we do not care for titles which give the impression that we have relations with a religious power, a very respectable one, certainly, but one that is alien to our way of life.

—I understand. That does not prevent the power in question from rejoicing in Turkey's progress, nor from detecting in the new constitution several of the fundamental principles of Christianity . . . even though the religious spirit in which they are applied naturally does not receive its approval.

—A non-denominational State is our fundamental principle. It is, for us, the guarantee of freedom.

—The Church will take good care not to dispute it. But I am optimistic by nature. I always prefer to dwell on the things which make for unity, rather than on those which tend to separate. Since we are in agreement on fundamental principles, we should be able to go at least part of the way together. As to the remainder, we must have confidence. Meanwhile, on our side, a few steps have been made in the right direction. The Turkish language has been brought into the Church.

A smile was the only reply, indicating that the discussion was drawing to an end.

On his return to Istanbul the delegate could not make

up his mind whether or not he had reason to be pleased. It could certainly not be said that there had been absence of frankness on either side. He decided to maintain fairly distant relations, while awaiting a further opportunity.

In 1939 Ataturk died. Roncalli was in Athens, where he had gone to settle the serious problems which had arisen between the Greek Church and the government, but he did not fail to give instructions to the delegation and to the apostolic vicariate in Istanbul to join in the nation's mourning. Of course it was necessary not to overstep the bounds and to avoid any public manifestation of a religious and liturgical nature. A month before, the Orthodox patriarch had ordered public prayers to be said by his faithful, who were Turkish subjects; but the government had formally opposed it, and this served as a warning to the Catholics.

Ismet Inônu was elected President of the republic; a gallant leader on the Sangaria battlefields during the war of independence, he had later shown himself to be a shrewd negotiator of the Lausanne Peace Treaty and an active collaborator of Ataturk. Although it was Ataturk who had had the courage to demolish the past and lay the foundations of a new Turkey, it was the dogged Ismet who had worked this transformation, who had placed his intelligence and his conscience at the disposal of Ataturk. By choosing him as successor Turkey had given a further proof of its wisdom. All traces of division and disagreement between leaders had in fact vanished in the face of the country's needs. Roncalli hastened to send a telegram of congratulations in the name of the Holy See. It was difficult to know in advance what might be feared, or hoped for, from the new President. As a man, Ismet had always shown himself to be a model of integrity and dignity. As a political figure, he was, however, rather different from Ataturk; convinced that it was imperative for the nation to preserve the non-denominational character of the State, he yet remained, in private life, very much attached to Moslem traditions and practices. It seemed likely that this dual personality, faithful disciple of Mahomet and resolute supporter of a strictly secular State might add to the difficulties of Catholic life in Turkey. Those close to the delegate were convinced that it would be so, but he preferred once again to wait and to hope. The period of waiting proved to be a long one, in spite of a number of important opportunities which occurred. On the death of Pope Pius XI memorial services were held in the cathedral and an invitation to attend was sent to the Turkish Government, but they did not reply. Then came the letter from the three leading cardinals of the Church giving the official announcement of mourning to the governments concerned. Still no reply, on the pretext, rumour had it, that Roncalli's position in Turkey was merely that of a distinguished guest.

When the papal letter arrived from Rome informing the government of the election of Pope Pius XII the delegate wondered whether, at some time previously, he had committed some grave error of form. By making yet another approach did he not lay himself open to a flat refusal and, worse still, might he not be exposing the Pope to an affront? He realized that no matter to which address the document in question was sent, it would finally reach Numan Menemencoglu, now Minister of Foreign Affairs. He therefore decided to forward it to him as the most reliable and most authentic interpreter of the opinions and attitude of the government. Courtesy combined with open tactics seemed to him the best possible means of obtaining for it the reception it deserved. We have been fortunate enough to see extracts from the letter—dated the end of April—which accompanied the papal document.

> Your Excellency, I still recall with pleasure the courteous reception which you were kind enough to give me when I personally presented my respects to you, at the Ministry of Foreign Affairs, on the evening of January 4, 1937. You were

good enough to tell me on that occasion that by receiving me in this way it was your intention to signify the respect in which the Turkish Government held the functions of my spiritual ministry.

It is now in the name of that same spiritual ministry that, in all simplicity and without any ulterior motives, I take the liberty of entrusting to the kindness of your Excellency the missive forwarded to me by . . . (the new Pope).

It contains the autograph letter in which the new head of the Catholic Church announces his election.

By this traditional act of sovereign courtesy towards the heads of State of all the nations of the world, without any distinction of political regime or religious persuasion, the new Pope, Pius XII, is making a primary gesture in favour of that universal peace . . .

This is a natural, and at the same time, a spontaneous and cordial gesture on the part of the new Pope towards the most illustrious new President of the strong and noble Turkish republic which is called upon to play an increasingly important rôle among the oldest-established and most vigorous nations of the modern world.

If, in carrying out the task which has been entrusted to me, I have deemed it preferable to take advantage of the kindness of your Excellency, avoiding any other channels, please attribute my action to the sense of discretion, understanding and respect with which I have always tried—modestly but with all my heart —to inspire my personal conduct as head of this Catholic community.

The letter was simply sent off by post.

The document was accepted and Roncalli felt sure that it would receive consideration. That in itself meant a great deal to him. After receiving Menemencoglu's reply, also sent through the post, he sought the opinion of someone very well acquainted with the customs of Ankara, and was advised that the letter was polite but not encouraging. Menemencoglu recalled that during the pleasant conversation between them he had taken the liberty of stressing the essentially non-denominational character of the Turkish Government which did not permit any official relations with religious organizations. There was, however, one sentence which seemed to the delegate to mitigate somewhat the rigidity of the position. The writer said that the attitude of the Turkish Government must not be taken to imply any unfriendly feeling towards the Holy See. Contrary to the opinion of his advisers, he held the view that the reply might have been 'much more disagreeable'. Deep down the leaders remained essentially Moslem in their sentiments, even while seeking to rid themselves of their former beliefs. It was certainly kind of them not to have treated him more harshly. Indeed, the consideration given to him personally, over a period of five years, had never varied; the press was now allowed to refer to him by his title of Apostolic Delegate. The Church, he felt, had therefore not been obliged to retreat but had even taken a step forward. He had in any case always been careful not to give the impression that he was intent on gaining official recognition of his position. He was in Turkey simply to perform the tasks of his spiritual and pastoral ministry. So long as he was free to do this the question of official recognition was of secondary importance. Such opportunities gave him, however, a chance to make his presence known and to express his esteem and his gratitude.

The apostolic library of the Vatican had recently reproduced the famous map of the Danube countries and bordering regions, by Giacomo Castaldi, of which it had, up to then, possessed the only copy. The Holy Father had decided to offer a reproduction of this map to each of the interested governments. This time, the delegate was sure that such a token of esteem, of a purely cultural nature, would be well received by the Turks, since it concealed no ulterior motive. The intermediary was to be the Polish ambassador, Michel Sokoviev; it was after the German and Russian invasions of Poland and the delegate had offered help for his country's refugees. The delegate mentioned it to Menemencoglu, who appeared to appreciate the courteous gesture very much and undertook to obtain for the ambassador an audience with the President of the Council, Dr Refik Saydam. The ambassador presented himself as the official representative of a friendly power, but he was also, of course, a representative of one of the greatest Catholic nations of the world. A letter from the bishop accompanied the Holy Father's gift, expressing the conviction that Turkey, open now to all forms of culture and progress yet still mindful of its own history, would be interested to discover in this beautiful map traces of its own military prowess which had won the admiration of the entire world. The gesture was perfectly appreciated. The President of the Council wrote later to the Polish ambassador that he had been very much moved by the Holy Father's attention and that he was the more appreciative of the gift because of the manner in which it had been offered. The library of Istanbul University was chosen to receive the gift from the Pope. There it is still cherished.

Those who are acquainted with the world of diplomacy may smile at these trivial episodes; but in this connexion Roncalli applied two principles which were very dear to him. The first is one of the basic rules of human wisdom for those who can appreciate small things and who have learned to bide their time: *Gutta cavat lapidem*—the drop of water wears away the stone. The second is a rule which is also a Christian virtue, practised by those who put their own person and pride second to the task they have to accomplish and are willing to sacrifice themselves for it. It is reflected in the words of the prophet as he offered himself to his persecutors: *Dabo frontem meam percutientibus*—I will turn my forehead to those who strike me. A letter written at that time said: 'Of the apostolic delegate—and I am speaking here of his title—there can be no question at the present time. But you will see, in the end, that the *Dabo frontem meam* and its sequel will prevail with the help of God.'

A delicate question arose between the Turkish Govern-

ment and the delegation; it concerned property owned by
the latter in Pangalti, the residential quarter of Istanbul;
it was here that the delegate's house, the cathedral and
the School of the Holy Spirit were situated. The title to the
property was in the name of 'the apostolic vicar, son of
St John Chrysostom, French subject'—a relic of the time
when France, under the 'Capitular Acts', conferred its high
protection on the Church in Turkey. The new regulations
relating to patrimonial titles called for an amendment of
the inscription itself, but the time limit for such an amendment had expired without it having been possible to find a
legally valid title. Legal action by the government therefore
threatened to deprive the delegation of its patrimonial
property. The war, on the one hand, and the extreme
delicacy of the matter, on the other, caused the proceedings
to drag on for a number of years. Roncalli was still dealing
with it during his period as papal nuncio in France. In
Paris, at that time, the Turkish ambassador was none other
than Numan Rifat Menemencoglu. The lawsuit ended late
in 1947 and the delegation lost. But by then—far away
from Turkey—relations between the former delegate and
Menemencoglu had become more relaxed as a result of
the more cordial atmosphere, and the nuncio realized then
that he had not worked in vain. Negotiations were opened
with the Turkish Government, with a view to coming to
some arrangement which would be more satisfactory than
a fiercely contested legal victory. It came, however, as a
great surprise to hear from the diplomat that Turkey
would like to have official relations with the Holy See and
that he himself would willingly co-operate to that end. It
seemed to Roncalli that the spirit of goodwill was probably
moving faster than the times, but he was delighted with
such a hopeful prospect, remote though it was. Many
years later, as Patriarch of Venice, he wrote to an influential friend in Turkey: 'I should like to have news of Menemencoglu who, I am told, has returned to his own people

after a long period of service in Paris. He was always so friendly towards us that I feel sure that he will welcome my greetings.'

The war which broke out in 1939 spared Turkey; but the chances of the nation remaining neutral appeared slight. From the beginning, in spite of all that had been whispered about their sympathies with Russia, the Turks accepted from England and from France a considerable number of favours: the cession of the Hatay territory and large sums of money and military supplies. The Minister of Foreign Affairs had paid a lengthy visit to Moscow, but without giving in to the Russians, much to Molotov's disgust. Everything seemed to point to a Franco–British attack through the Black Sea. The largest hotel in Istanbul—the Pera Palace—which had closed down through lack of tourists, now reopened in order to house the many British pilot officers, sleeping four to a room, who had arrived in the country as instructors. At night dozens of ships crossed the Bosphorus, bringing arms and men. During the day they sheltered in one of the many bays of the Sea of Marmora, resuming their voyage at nightfall. But the Turkish leaders were not at all interested in entering the war. Although parliament had approved the arrangements made with the British, neither the President, Ismet Inönu, nor the chief of staff, Fetzi Cakmak, had any intention of yielding to pressure. Without fuss, and helped by the turn military events had taken, the German ambassador, von Papen, knowing very well that he would not be able to bring Turkey into the war on the side of Germany as in 1914–18, was doing his utmost, by a combination of flattery and threats, to persuade her to remain neutral. A commercial treaty, the culminating achievement of this shrewd ambassador, showed better than anything else the atmosphere in Ankara at that time; and so it was that when, towards the end of June 1940, the diplomats from Paris and London renewed their efforts to get Turkey to enter the fray, recalling, among other things, the enormous sums paid out to her, they received from Ismet Inönu, the following reply: 'As regards the money—you have only to name the date on which you require reimbursement.'

Keeping a close watch on the military situation, veering sometimes to one side and sometimes to the other, Turkey arrived at the year 1945 without having been drawn into the turmoil, ready to declare war on Germany along with the others as soon as the latter should collapse, in order to be one of those nations that held the fate of the world in their hands. Neutrality made Turkey, and especially Istanbul (as it did Switzerland and Lisbon) a centre for espionage and international dealings. One million Jews for 10,000 motor-cars; many such Nazi bargains were clinched in Istanbul. Roncalli had become one of the Vatican's most important sources of information. Requests for information and messages calling for the greatest vigilance came frequently from Rome. He thought that his reports contained little more than what was published in the press; but at the Vatican details sent by him personally were considered invaluable. Actually, his facts did not come from the newspapers alone. High-ranking diplomats were now only too ready to approach him, fully conscious of the influence exerted by a neutral power in a neutral city. The intense spiritual efforts in favour of peace made at that time by Pope Pius XII, to which even the warring nations paid the closest attention, the possibility that the Vatican might assume the rôle of mediator, or at least make known its views when the time came to reach a settlement round the table or before the international courts, such considerations led the majority of diplomats to maintain good relations with the apostolic delegate. The latter was quick to realize the delicate nature of his new position. His secretary had recently been taken from him and transferred to the government secretariat, where certain people were trying to take advantage of the youth and inexperience of the newcomer in their midst. It was more than ever necessary to proceed warily and be discreet. The delegate decided, first and foremost, to remain aloof from every quarrel.

One of the main difficulties was the fact that he was Italian. Fear of Italy coming into the war, then her definite entry on the side of Germany, naturally threatened his reputation for impartiality. Only his extreme discretion enabled him to retain the confidence of every diplomat and of all the faithful—and it was the latter, above all, who were his chief concern. The large French colony was bitterly upset after the fall of France in 1940. Its sense of patriotism was deeply hurt and there was much bad feeling towards the Italians who, it was said, came into the war in order to deal the death blow to France. The only thing to be done was to console the faithful and remind them of eternal things, in order to fuse nationalist feeling with that of universal love. This was the spirit which moved the delegate to compose the following addition to the prayers offered in the church of St Anthony that Istanbul might be preserved from the horrors of war: 'What we are asking for ourselves, we ask also, with the same sincere desire, for all those with whom we live, being all of us brothers, despite the differences of religion, nationality, historical tradition and social position.'

At the services those who were distressed by events and who felt tempted to give way to hidden feelings of hostility, constantly heard a passionate appeal for peace and understanding. They were reminded that true Christianity requires a love which destroys all feeling of national resentment and they were urged to widen the field of vision of their judgement until it extended far beyond their personal experience, which was inevitably limited. Italians, French, Germans, Maltese, Greeks, etc., should consider

themselves part of one great community. While naturally
sharing in the suffering of their respective countries,
officially at war with one another, they must acknowledge
their own wrong-doing and the sorrow caused to others.
In his Easter address in 1941, the delegate told them:

> Each one of us tends to judge events from the narrow view-
> point on which he stands—that is to say, from the national point
> of view of his country. This is a great illusion. We must rise
> above events and courageously look upon the situation as a
> whole; we must lift up our minds until we lose sight of the
> barriers which separate the combatants one from another. Love
> of one's country is one of the noblest and most delicate of all
> human feelings and comes within the scope of charity and the
> teachings of the Gospel; it can and should lead each one of us
> to make the maximum personal effort, with passion, even with
> heroism. But it will not provide us with a perfect philosophy of
> war and peace, either now or in the future.
>
> By continually seeking to name those responsible for the
> present catastrophe, by endeavouring to apportion to each his
> share of the blame, we would be assuming an impossible task
> and at the same time we would cause disputes and arouse
> bitter protests on either side. For no one will ever admit that he
> is in the wrong. Actually, every one of us is at fault; there comes
> a time when every individual is involved in what happens to all
> the rest.

Reflecting the state of their mother country, members of
the French colony were the most anxious. In Istanbul, the
followers of Pétain and the Gaullists formed two distinct
groups hostile to one another. Even the religious communities were not immune from this psychological conflict.
A young Lazarist missionary had already left the St
Benedict monastery and gone off to Cairo where, it was
said, other French priests had gathered under the leadership of a Carmelite Father, well-known as a teacher of
asceticism, to participate in the liberation movement.
Three other young priests, of the Order of the Assumption,
who had arrived in Istanbul from Plovdiv when the
German army entered, were waiting at Kadikoy for an

opportunity to follow their example. In addition, pressure was being exerted on the delegate to take authoritative action in favour of one side or the other. It needed all his wisdom, and sometimes his delicate and paternal sense of irony, to remain aloof from the disputes. A French priest, after preaching the Lenten sermon in the cathedral of the Holy Spirit, left for Beirut immediately after Easter to support the Gaullist movement. He later returned to Istanbul and called to see the delegate, pleading with him to speak to the French community in favour of the followers of de Gaulle. The delegate let him have his say, then, seemingly lost in meditation, he said, with obvious regret: 'I read in the bible that the patriarch Jacob also had sons who disagreed among themselves. But he, the father, *rem tacitus considerabat*—considered the matter in silence.' The delegate maintained this same attitude of reserve even in diplomatic circles.

Gradually, the formally correct attitude adopted by those acting from political motives yielded to his inflexible integrity and he began to be entrusted with genuine confidences which had hitherto been concealed from him, and in which disgust at the lies of both sides mingled with hopes of a peace based not on crumbling treaties and false alliances but on the principles of the Church and the dictates of men's conscience. The time came when he had received so many proofs of confidence and witnessed such unanimous approval of the spiritual values proclaimed by Pope Pius XII in his Christmas message in 1940 and 1941 that he took the liberty, in September 1942—being fully aware of the slaughter that a prolongation of the war would cause—of suggesting to the Holy See that it might perhaps be the moment to issue a call to peace. In Istanbul, people felt the need to gather as closely as possible round the delegation, not only Catholics, but also Greeks, Armenians and Jews. Here, in the midst of the general distress, they were able to find never-failing understanding.

Some Greeks who had listened to one of his sermons fully appreciated his admission that

> between Christmas and Easter I considered it a duty of my sacred ministry to return to the country which is suffering most of all, that is to say, to our brothers in Greece. You will understand, then, when I say that my heart is still full of sadness at the unforgettable sight of so much physical and moral suffering in that beloved and noble country, a suffering which can only be relieved by the spirit of charity . . .

He also, one Christmas night during the war, appealed with great feeling from the pulpit for alms on behalf of the starving children of Greece. He did not really expect much response from his small, poverty-stricken congregation, but he hoped in this way to encourage feelings of peace, to put an end to prejudice, to break down barriers and bring men together.

The Jews, for their part, knew very well that the delegation was always being pressed by the Palestine Agency in Istanbul, or by the Chief Rabbi of Jerusalem, Dr. Herzog, to forward to the Holy Father or to the nuncio in Budapest requests in favour of persecuted Jews. His good offices often had the desired effect and many unfortunate people were relieved of their sufferings or received material assistance in this way; but because of the serious difficulties attaching to such intervention, he was eventually obliged to stop. One of the diplomats who was closest to Roncalli was von Papen. This acquaintance went back to the days when the latter was going through a difficult time in his relations with his own government. Von Papen was thinking more about post-war Germany than the Germany of that time, and some people strongly disapproved of one of his speeches in which he seemed to give the impression of holding himself in readiness for a mission on behalf of his country with which providence would not fail to entrust to him. It was impossible, however, to have absolute confidence in his political convictions and Roncalli received

warnings against becoming too familiar with the great
diplomat, but he was able to maintain relations with him
on a purely religious basis.

Roncalli's time in Turkey was coming to an end. He
was, however, to make one more approach to the Turkish
Government in spite of the precautions taken by that body
to avoid any such contact. He asked Sukru Saracoglu, the
head of the Cabinet, for permission to help those interned
in the concentration camps of Yozgat, Kirshir and Corum
—most of whom were Austrians, though holding German
passports. He wrote then to this head of a secular government, stating that his sole aim in making the request was
a desire to help those poor people by bringing to them the
comfort which they had a right to expect from his religious
ministry. Had he been able to assist them materially, he
would willingly have done so. He offered as a guarantee
that he would carry out his task with the greatest delicacy,
and spoke of

> the memories of ten happy and peaceful years in Turkey, in
> which country, having refrained from any bias in political or
> other controversial matters, mindful solely of my spiritual
> ministry, and being animated by a deep feeling of understanding,
> respect and real friendship for the Turkish people, I can claim
> never to have given the civil authorities the slightest cause for
> suspicion, either in my personal relationship or in the execution
> of my modest duties.

The favourable reply which he received on this occasion
was an admission of the truth of his remarks.

At the beginning of the war, Roncalli had celebrated
his sixtieth birthday. He noted the passing of the years
with a certain nostalgia tempered, of course, to a considerable degree by that detachment from life which he had
continually practised and by his total acceptance of the
will of God. Two feelings, in fact, now contradicted one

another in his mind: the conviction that he had passed his best and, on the other hand, the persistence within him of a feeling of youth which prevented him from noticing the weight of the years. More and more often he would recall memories of his beloved bishop and master. In July 1936, he had already written the following lines: 'When I think that at my age, Mgr Radini was on the point of dying, I am tempted to think of myself as an old man. It is necessary to fight against such feelings; despite outward appearances, youth of mind and spirit must be preserved. For this is pleasing to God, a good example, and helpful to one whose duty it is to communicate joy and optimism to others.' On his sixtieth birthday, sending his photograph to a friend, he wrote on the back: 'Here is Mgr Roncalli, aged 60. This is the best age: sound health, a more mature judgement, a disposition to see things more clearly, to judge with gentleness and optimism.' But he had felt himself to be at the final cross-roads in his life:

> With the idea of sanctifying the first few days after my sixtieth birthday, I spent a week in Terapia as chaplain to the poor nuns who have come from Roumania. I followed the spiritual exercises and meditated on the *Miserere*—four verses each day—in the strictest solitude and silence. This was how I wanted to enter into the final period of my life, old age. A peaceful setting of the sun. May our Lord make what remains of my poor life as profitable and as edifying as possible.

The impression of being near the end of his life was further strengthened by the rapid disappearance of so many of the figures dear to his youth. Each one as it faded away left him with a feeling of regret. He did not rebel against the idea of the solitude to which this would lead, but accepted it with feelings which, although not entirely devoid of sadness, left him with the comfort of pleasant memories, and the hope of an early reunion.

> From far off the sad news reaches me of the death first of Mgr C. and then of Mgr R. These two prelates, differing in

appearance and in merit, have been very much a part of my poor life. The first, as a fellow seminarist in the early days, that is to say when I was in the third grade, and the other as director during my time at the seminary. How I admired and liked him! His disappearance leaves a gap in my memories of a youthful apprenticeship which I like to recall. But, thank God, I prefer to look forward rather than back. Even my most cherished memories of persons and of things linger as if to remind me of the reunion which we can expect. Life is rather like a long sea voyage. We say goodbye with tears when leaving those we love —but lo and behold, when we reach our destination they are waiting for us on the quayside.

He was therefore not really tempted to dwell on the past, and was pleased with the continual changes taking place all around him. He was ready to welcome any new assistants: they seemed to be coming to him younger and younger, but he loved them for their youth and for the fresh energy which they brought to the service of the Church. He liked to cross swords with them and to show them that if he lagged behind in the race, it was not by very much. He knew that young people were quick to take the lead but, thereafter, were equally quick to fall behind. And being used to trials and difficulties, he undertook the task of comforting them and urging them forward. 'Being sixty years old', he wrote to a friend, 'does not in any way affect the elasticity of my mind, which does not care to dwell on the past. The other day a Carmelite wrote to me that your illness had depressed you somewhat. But I refused to believe that Don G. is letting himself go. Your spirit is too strong not to hold out and not to discern with joy, in every happening, the divine will of Our Lord.' What pleased him most was to find himself without ambition. 'I am not yet', he would say, 'thanks be to God, obsessed with the idea of obtaining a cardinal's hat.'

He enjoyed to the full the inner peace and freedom which resulted from his contentment with what each day brought. He never complained or showed any trace of selfishness or anxiety. Moreover, he combined complete detachment from financial preoccupations with a spirit of generosity which enabled him to receive his guests in the grand manner. The emoluments of a diplomat of the Holy See were not at that time—nor are they now—unduly lavish. Even so, he found a way to be generous as if he were a really rich man. He even decided that the Holy See should benefit from his love of giving. For some time he had been longing to brighten up the delegation's premises situated in a rather dull corner of the Olcek Sokak, although only a short distance from the magnificent Avenue de Pangalti. After the chapel had been redecorated, it was the vestibule's turn and Luigi, an artist and general factotum from Bergamo who had followed him around since his days in Sofia, transformed it into a magnificent entrance hall. The delegate wrote to inform his superiors as soon as the work was completed, adding that everything was already paid for.

The Holy See felt it could not be outdone in generosity by a poor bishop in a far-off land. No one doubted that the benefactor (who would have been immensely happy to see his gift accepted without any fuss) had gone well beyond his means; the Holy Father therefore invited him in a fatherly way to submit his account. He resigned himself to it, but not without feeling rather hurt, although everything had been done with the utmost consideration for his pride. The fact remained that he was mortified. For the first time in his life it seemed to him that, after receiving so much from the Holy Father and from the Holy See, he had been able to make a concrete gesture of devotion and gratitude. He had done so simply, acting like a good son, like a *humilis episcopus ecclesiae Dei*, without any notion of furthering his own ends, and now the Holy Father's own generosity took away all the inner meaning and all the joy which had inspired his gesture. Naturally, this money which had reached him through the channels of charity would be paid out again in full for a similar charitable cause.

He looked round and soon found a way to dispose of the money. At Bergamo the bishop, wishing to modernize the seminary, was building an additional wing for the teaching staff, and a new library. Roncalli's gift took the form of the complete works of the Latin and Greek Fathers in Migne's edition—350 precious volumes which he had obtained from an Armenian convent with the aid of the Catholic patriarch, Mgr Agagianian. He paid about two million lire for them, sharing the expense by accepting half the amount from the generosity of another Bergamo prelate, Mgr Gustavo Testa, the apostolic delegate in Egypt, an old and intimate friend of his.

Breaking the news to the Bishop of Bergamo, he wrote: 'Please do not worry that I may have deprived myself on your account. If I am granted a few more years to live, I shall easily manage to straighten things out. St Louis was admirable in the way he combined innocence with penitence. For my part, I would like to become perfect in the handling of wealth and the practice of poverty combined.'

Chapter Seven

THE GREECE OF METAXAS

DURING the time he was fulfilling the function of apostolic delegate at Istanbul, Roncalli assumed the same responsibility for Greece. It was an entirely different world. Turkey was a nation in full vigour, being born again. Greece, continuously threatened by revolution, was struggling for her life. In the former the Moslem and decidedly oriental influences were beginning, as a result of agitation that showed signs of violence, to accept western civilization. In the latter an over-refined culture was stagnating, even showing a tendency to decadence, owing to a spirit of grudging conservatism. The two countries had been divided against each other for centuries. A peaceful state of affairs had been brought about quite recently by Ataturk and the Greek premier, Venizelos. The treaty of friendship, signed at Ankara in 1930, the first in the history of the two countries, provided official if not popular recognition of the end of secular hostilities. But, in fact, it merely recognized the defeat of the Greeks; their assault on the Turkish world must be considered as repulsed. A few years before, on every river bank and in every port of Asia Minor, particularly Istanbul and Smyrna, Greeks swarmed, nurturing in the depths of their hearts a political ideal—that of the Byzantine Empire—which was still very much alive centuries after the empire had disappeared. The withdrawal of population which had been, a short time before, laid down by the Treaty of Lausanne had condemned them to a dreadful exodus: two million Greeks, saying goodbye to the places of their birth, their homes, and their fields, had returned to their national soil, a real invasion of discontented, anxious people with nothing to call their own.

In Greece, too, the Catholic religion was in a minority. There the shadow of the old Schism which tore the East away from Rome, was darker than ever. Greece has always been the country in which Orthodoxy assumes the rôle of inspiration and spiritual guidance. Istanbul has, it is true, as former capital of the Byzantine Empire, an official pre-eminence over Athens and shelters, in the Phanar, a patriarch who is considered in the Orthodox hierarchy as *primus inter pares*, but the real life and centre of Orthodoxy is to be found in Greece. On this soil Catholicism resisted with a strength born of despair, alongside an Orthodox Church that was solidly organized and supported by the government. The Catholic hierarchy had remained, in its form, the same as in the Middle Ages. Owing to the fact that the mainland had gradually gone over to the Ortho-dox, the episcopal sees had survived only in the islands of the Ionian and the Aegean Sea, together with isolated dioceses, reduced sometimes to a few thousand faithful. The Bishops of Chios, Santorin and Crete each had only a very small flock in one single parish. The Greek Govern-ment had ever since the far off days of national independ-ence (1830) exercised the function of principal guardian and controller of the Orthodox Church and had more or less ignored the Catholic Church. Moreover it was impos-sible to create new episcopal sees, for the sole claim to their recognition by the government was their existence under the old Turkish regime before the creation of the Greek State. For the same reason the presence of the Latin archbishop in Athens was not legally admitted. After Greece's military disaster in Turkey, large groups of Greek Catholics of the Byzantine Rite together with Armenians, led by their bishops invested with exarchal authority, had

crossed into Greek territory, creating fresh problems of
organization for the Church and raising difficulties for the
government which inclined to the view that this shift of
population gave the Catholics a chance to proselytize. It
was an impossible situation, especially in Athens, where no
fewer than three Catholic bishops of the Latin, Byzantine
and Armenian rites caused a certain amount of confusion.

Until 1932 there had not really been an apostolic delegation in Athens. Actually, the Bishop of the island of Sira
already possessed the title of apostolic delegate but his rôle
was limited to a delegation of powers for the mainland of
Greece. Suddenly in 1932 came the announcement of the
nomination of Mgr Margotti as apostolic delegate in
Istanbul. The Holy See had a foreboding of the precarious
state of Catholicism and of the extreme danger that existed
of a state of tension building up between it and the government which it would be impossible to dispel. Unfortunately,
as often happens in Greece, the rejoicing had been carried
too far. The delegate's mission had been exaggerated until
it was made to look as though he had been charged with
the duty of entering into diplomatic negotiations. That
gave rise to misunderstanding and bad will on the part of
the government. The Minister of Foreign Affairs, A.
Micalacopulos, took it as an insult, believing that the Holy
See had tried to accredit a Catholic prelate without the
customary bilateral agreements. In spite of all the reassur-
ances as to the strictly religious nature of his mission,
Margotti had not succeeded in convincing the Minister.
It was not long before difficulties began to arise, and the
government even went so far as to refuse him a visa. To
counter all this petty obstruction and to reach Greek
territory he had to resort to a number of expedients.

From Sofia, Roncalli had been able to follow these
changes of fortune, and from the moment he arrived in
Istanbul the thought of his visit to Greece caused him much
anxiety. Rome, questioned as to the possibility of an

improvement in relations, let it be known that Greece had not shown the slightest intention of recognizing the apostolic delegate or of allowing any increase in the number of bishops. It looked like being difficult, therefore, even to obtain a visa for entering Greece. When the delegate called on the Greek consul in Istanbul to ask for one, he made a point of not insisting. He merely laid before him the difficulties of his apostolic mission. Shortly afterwards he was informed that the government had allowed the visa on condition that the journey should not last more than eight days and should be carried out *en touriste*. This restriction did not affect him much.

Roncalli's arrival in Athens in the early days of May 1945 took place without any sort of ceremony. In order to avoid rumours, he had written to the bishops asking them not to make any special arrangements. But the Archbishop of Corfu, in his eighty-ninth year, and the Bishop of Santorin had insisted on going to meet him at Brindisi. It at once became apparent that a meeting of the episcopate would be of the first importance. Three or four days later, after hasty notification by letter, all the bishops assembled in the presence of the delegate. The meeting did much good and at one stroke changed relations with Rome for the better; Roncalli's genial and fatherly spirit inspired confidence. Many distressing situations were given an airing and the delegate did not fail to show his compassion for the sometimes tragic conditions in which Catholicism was struggling. All at once questions of the utmost gravity were brought forward—the lack of agreement with the government, the unsatisfactory administration of the Latin seminary, the danger of mixed marriages. Fortunately considerable agreement was reached between the bishops, even between those of different rites. The common danger united them. The question of mixed marriages raised acute problems for the bishops and clergy. The faithful who streamed in ever-growing numbers from the islands to the towns succumbed at once to temptation. Caught between the requirements of the Catholic religion and the government regulations protecting the Orthodox code, they tried everything they could, often to the extent of lying, to obtain Catholic marriage from the priest, only to go on from there with an easy conscience to the Orthodox Rite. In this way the gradual defection of half the Greek Catholics was inevitable. It was possible to be strict with the faithful by enforcing the regulations, both old and new, of the Holy See; but the evil went deeper and arose from the conditions imposed by the Greek nation on a Catholicism whose requirements it misunderstood. The delegate perceived at once that hearts were embittered and he understood that his mission was to pour oil on their wounds. For his part he did not fail to send indirectly to the Greek authorities an expression of his respect. In his eyes courtesy came first. Indirectly also there came to him an echo of the government's appreciation of the fact that he had been discreet and self-effacing. He had, moreover, scrupulously avoided all contact with members of the diplomatic corps in Athens. He noticed that until the moment of his return to Istanbul he was being followed; but he did not take offence at the thought that perhaps he had roused suspicion. He desired nothing so much as that his purely spiritual mission should be properly understood.

The following year things went a little differently and he was able to present himself in person to King George II, bringing with him a personal note in which Pius XI congratulated the monarch on his recent election to the throne. His reception was cordial and the delegate spoke openly and with confidence of the problems which occupied his mind. He also explained how desirable it was that the papal representative should get a rather better hearing. He found that the difficulties did not arise from the royal family. King George observed that in the traditions of his house there was goodwill towards Catholicism and a certain familiarity with the Vatican. Likewise at the Ministry of Foreign Affairs deference was not lacking. The attitude towards the delegate was full of respect, and the matter of his passport was soon settled. At Istanbul he had been granted only the customary eight days; now he could stay as long as he liked and obtain the diplomatic visa. They even showed themselves quite disposed to forget the past and to conclude agreements with the Holy See on specific points which, although secondary, were not without importance. For the rest, the Catholics had only to make their desires known for them to be sympathetically examined. Roncalli began to feel more hopeful. He did not conceal from himself that agreement over fundamental problems was for the moment impossible, but he did not approve of those round him who spread pessimism. He told himself that the most influential person in the Ministry of Foreign Affairs and Culture was the Orthodox Metropolitan. There was no doubt that even if an agreement were reached everything would have to pass through his hands. Nevertheless, Roncalli, ever confident, wrote in a letter:

I should be so happy to have you here with me in Greece. The season is just right for making journeys. If, on my return, you are in the mood for it, I shall tell you about the various visits I have been able to make. But perhaps what will interest you the most is to know that here too the drop of water ends up by wearing away the stone: *gutta cavat lapidem*. The new king received me well. I was also able to go to the Ministry of Foreign Affairs and engage in useful conversation with the Director of Ecclesiastical Affairs. Who knows? I am not thinking of a *concordat* but of a *modus vivendi* of which there is great need, if only to ensure for this country, that is to say the Catholics in it, the continuity of regular relations among the bishops themselves and between them and the Holy See. May the Lord help me in this.

These faint hopes sustained him on his return to Istanbul and in his retreat on the island of Buyuk-Ada, in the Sea of

Marmora, where he was able to work more peacefully in the summer months.

In September he returned to Athens. He had been charged with the task of acquiring a large iconostasis for the Byzantine rooms of the Pinacotheca in the Vatican. He took advantage of the opportunity to present his respects to the government. This time it was the President of the Council in person, M. Metaxas, who received him. Metaxas was a dictator and at the present time Greek opinion of him is inclined to be critical. But the delegate had set all his hopes on this meeting and the dictator appeared almost to encourage them by asking him to draw up the main points of an eventual agreement. The proposal was sent off by him during a lull which marked his return to Istanbul. Some months elapsed before a reply was received, and unfortunately in the interval the atmosphere had grown a little more heated. A Catholic newspaper, which appeared in Italy, had seen fit to criticize the Olympic run organized between Athens and Berlin, and this caused a certain irritation. A little later the outspoken attitude of a French ecclesiastic towards a well-known anti-Catholic, a director of religious affairs in the Ministry of Culture, provoked a lawsuit. These events greatly upset the delegate. So much effort, all wasted by lack of tact! It seemed to him that charity must inspire men to greater efforts to endure many things in silence. However, not all the mistakes were on the Catholic side. More disturbing was the news which circulated concerning the preparation of a new civil code in which the laws regulating marriage would be determined according to the requirements of the State.

The Church was in serious danger. Up to that time, although the balance-sheet of marriages showed a loss, the rite celebrated before the Catholic minister was tacitly recognized as valid. Everything was confined within the framework of canon law; from there the marriage passed

to the civil domain. If the Catholics found that the new
provisions were unacceptable to them, they would be
forced to put themselves outside the law and to act against
the State. A lively discussion was known to be taking place
in the governmental committee responsible for drawing up
the code. Those partisans of civil marriage who were at
least prepared to safeguard the freedom of conscience of
the non-Orthodox party, seemed to be in a minority. More
numerous were those who, convinced of the religious
character of matrimonial union, demanded that it should
be contracted in the presence of the Orthodox minister in
his capacity as an officer of State. This latter solution
would impose the Orthodox Rite on all Catholics, if they
were to obtain a valid marriage. At the beginning of May
1938, Mgr Roncalli was once again in Greece. He could
now come and go as he pleased, but he used the privilege
very sparingly. At the assembly of bishops that was
immediately convened this grave question was on the order
sheet. A committee was set up, composed of Mgr Calavassy,
Bishop of the Greek Catholics in Athens, and Mgr Vuccino,
Bishop of Sira. It prepared a report to be presented to the
government expressing the lively concern of Catholics whose
liberty of conscience was threatened, and appealing to the
State to recognize also the competence of the Catholic
ministry. The report was handed, some weeks later, to the
Minister of Justice and to the President of the Council
himself. As a precaution a second supplication was addressed to the Holy Father. In it a request was made that
it should remain possible, while firmly recognizing the
necessity for the celebration of marriage according to the
Catholic Rite, to appear before the Orthodox minister,
considered purely as a State function, without incurring
censure. In the early days of September the bishops were
once again assembled at Timos on the occasion of the
national Eucharistic Congress organized by the Jesuit
Fathers. There the news came that the official journal had

just published a royal decree concerning the dreaded measures.

The apostolic delegate who was present in the midst of the general turmoil recommended calmness. Any hasty step must be avoided and above all they must not give way to theatrical gestures. The new code had not yet appeared and amendments might be obtained which would render the decree less offensive, but he did not intend to intervene in that way. The tactics he had adopted were to make himself as unobtrusive as possible. In Athens he had stopped presiding at the annual festivals in the cathedral and had even removed the delegation's residence from an area which he considered too exposed to the precincts of the cathedral under the disapproving glances of those who would have liked to control his movements. He believed that if there were some advantage to be gained, the best method of obtaining it would be to get the Greek Catholic hierarchy to act through the mediation of one of its members who was on good terms with members of the government. This restraint at least made it possible to continue the exercise of his pastoral ministry to the limited extent still allowed him. He knew that in Greece also he had come primarily as a pastor of souls. Vuccino was charged with the task of making contact with the government. He found himself given every help by the delegate who did his best to smooth out difficulties. It was going to be a long and arduous business. In Catholic circles pessimism spread. Fundamental relations between the Church and the government of Metaxas showed no signs of improving and repeated incidents only increased the feeling of irritation: difficulties over episcopal nominations, for example, laws against Catholic proselytism, the humiliating treatment of foreign ecclesiastics passing through Greece, even when for no other purpose than study, and obstacles put in the way of building a Latin seminary. The goodwill of certain ministers clearly came up against the obstinacy of others. The point was reached when it was forbidden to celebrate Mass for those Catholics who came to Kefissia, a summer resort not far from Athens.

Roncalli was upset, not so much by the facts themselves, as by the lack of understanding they revealed between the two parties. Nevertheless, the reactions aroused in Athens by his approach to the Ecumenical Patriarch of the Phanar in Istanbul had been symptomatic. On the death of Pius XI the patriarch had, on the invitation of the delegate, been represented at the pontifical Mass celebrated in the cathedral of the Holy Spirit. Another representative of the Orthodox Church, who had been given the place of honour, took part in the *Te Deum* in the thanksgiving service for the election of Pius XII. Roncalli had thereupon seized the opportunity to act, and on May 27, 1939, he had made a personal visit to the Phanar. Received with every courtesy by the Patriarch Benjamin, who was accompanied by the metropolitans of Heliopolis and Laodicea, he had thanked him in the name of His Holiness for his participation in the mourning and later in the rejoicing of the Catholic Church. This meeting was probably the first that had taken place between them for centuries. For anyone who understood the traditional tension between the two Churches the event had an extraordinary significance in spite of the attempts of the press to belittle it. 'It was simply a courtesy visit between the two Churches', commented the Greek Orthodox newspaper in Istanbul. But the delegate was convinced that the road to union was being constructed by means of these contacts and marks of courtesy. He thought he had good reason to believe that the most formidable barriers could be overthrown by the heart. In Athens these events had roused attention and the most reactionary elements could not resist accusing the Ecumenical Patriarch of having deviated from the line of conduct which the Orthodox Church deemed it right to adopt in regard to Catholicism.

As for the law relating to mixed marriages, no progress had been made. Roncalli was living quietly in Istanbul when a message came from Rome requiring him to make a journey to Greece. As matters in that country always caused trouble he decided to prepare himself for it with the greatest care and patience. As things stood he no longer expected anything to be gained. The evil went too deep and men were victims of mistakes for which they were not entirely responsible. The latest report sent to Metaxas by the assembly of bishops, dated January 16, 1940, virtually came to nothing. A decision concerning the crucial point had already been taken. The only civil officer for mixed marriages would in future be the Orthodox minister. The code was expected to come into force in July 1941. An exception was made for marriages contracted before the publication of the code. Never had Roncalli felt more mortified and offended; but these disillusions taught him the importance of loving the world and the Church. It was grievous for him to note that the seamless garment of the Church was rent by the brothers of Christ Himself. Statistics drawn up by Mgr Calavassy show that if the Catholics had been left to enjoy their freedom in the matter of marriages, there would have been from the end of the last century 200,000 more of them, simply by a calculation of births. Today, there are estimated to be only 50,000 Catholics in Greece in spite of immigrations in the past decade. It has been a slow but inexorable struggle.

That was not the only disillusion Roncalli experienced in Greece. There, too, he had been considering the training of the clergy. The seminary which had been run until 1916 by the priests of the archdiocese of Athens, had later come under the direction of the Assumptionist Fathers who had been obliged to close it from lack of support and recruits. The Jesuits had reopened it in 1931, then handed it over two years later to the Marian Brothers. Excellent teachers though these lay brothers were, they were not suited to the work of theological training. There was nothing to be done except to put up with the situation and to wait until it was possible to supply the remedy. In the course of the episcopal assembly of 1938, the delegate announced that the Sacred Congregation of Propaganda was studying a proposal to reorganize the work on a new basis. But it meant a long wait. At that time the Congregation of Propaganda abandoned its jurisdiction over the Eastern Latins and handed it over to the Eastern Congregation, which had good intentions but was restricted in means. In the meantime the questions of finding staff and a site on which to build had to be solved. The problem was further complicated by the fact that permission had to be obtained from the Greek Government which reserved to itself the right to approve first of any school intended for ecclesiastical training. The difficulties did not frighten the delegate. Although he did not enjoy full freedom of action he did everything he could to bring the project to reality. Friction seemed probable between Jesuits and Assumptionists. The latter were supported by one of their colleagues, Vuccino, Bishop of Sira, but the other bishops showed themselves favourable to the Jesuits, and it was to them that the delegate turned. His efforts seemed to be on the way to succeeding, when suddenly the Jesuit Superior in Athens informed him that he must for serious reasons give up the direction of the seminary. Without bitterness the Assumptionists came back into the picture, and the delegate proposed their candidature to the bishops at their meeting in January 1940. Then the 'serious reasons' having ceased to exist, the Society of Jesus offered itself once more for the direction of the seminary. The bishops agreed. The removal of suspicion between the two religious bodies must have been rather difficult; but the fathers, like Vuccino, gave evidence of good faith and everything worked out well in the end.

The bishops had agreed on the island of Naxos as the seat of the seminary, where an old monastery was at their disposal. Local resources were also there in abundance and the place was quiet, more favourable to the training of seminarists than the distracting noise of the capital. But the monastery had been expropriated by the government which had taken advantage of a dispute between the old occupants and the Church over the right to the property, to take possession of it. It was therefore necessary to obtain the handing back of the building and to seek at the same time approval for the project. Roncalli, without hoping for immediate success, persisted in the belief that he would not be met by a blank refusal, but the two bishops responsible for negotiating the matter were met only with fine promises. It was soon realized that any form of insistence would be useless. It is only quite recently that the Holy See has been able to build a Latin seminary in Athens.

In spite of everything, Roncalli loved Greece and the Greeks very much. Thanks to his classical and Christian upbringing, he admired the country of Homer, Plato, and Phidias, he was deeply interested in her heroic history, and in the land itself which had been the cradle of some of the most ancient and flourishing cities in the early days of Christianity. On his arrival in that country his constant preoccupation was, it is true, of a pastoral kind. The delegation alone remained the pivot of his activities. He insisted on getting to know personally all the dioceses, even the very smallest, and learning about the real conditions in which Christians lived. With the utmost charm he visited each institution and centre of religious activity. His long experience enabled him to form in time definite opinions. In Greece, even more than at Istanbul where his duties as resident bishop confined him to the town, the passion of the travelling missionary was aroused in him.

He was seldom far from it; besides, there were few Catholics living outside the Bosphorus. Cianakkale (formerly Troy), Smyrna, Ephesus, and Tarsus had naturally attracted him. But Turkey, apart from Istanbul, is not rich in ancient Christian monuments. The long period of Moslem domination had removed the traces of a very flourishing primitive faith. Greece on the other hand is still full of the remains of Byzantine Christianity. Priceless treasures are scattered over the whole country: churches, monasteries, pictures, mosaics, materials, manuscripts, illuminations and a thousand other objects, especially liturgical ones. Resembling a kind of rampart facing Asia Minor, the eastern strip of Greece offers a unique spectacle. It is a veritable confederation or republic of monasteries going back almost a thousand years and continuing the traditions of a way of life that was austere and contemplative, rightly called 'angelic'. That the monks are of the Orthodox faith does not alter the fact that there is to be found there the remains of one of the most venerable and suggestive forms of Christian spirituality. Roncalli contemplated with delight this distant and unusual world and was sorry that it no longer possessed the flourishing vitality of earlier days. The monks of Mount Athos received with astonishment a visit from the representative of the Bishop of old Rome. He, for his part, stopped in wonder before this array of convents, hermitages, capitular rooms and refectories. Even more curious to him were the famous 'meteors', built like so many eyries on the jagged basalt rocks, rich in simple works of art deriving from the genius of the monks themselves and from the magnificence of the ancient Byzantine emperors. More than once he came across one that was empty, without its monk, because it had been expropriated by the state, but there still remained the walls, the rooms, the great icons, silent witnesses of an ancient splendour and of inexorable decay at the present time. He also uncovered the traces of an even more ancient and sacred history in the centres where Christianity had sown her first seeds: Philippi, Thessalonica, Athens, Corinth, places that had been visited by the apostles. In the islands, on the other hand, contact with the faithful and with the problems of a Catholicism which had weathered the storm was more alive. The sea was not always calm. Storms often beat against the rugged coast of the archipelagos which form a crown to the mainland. The people awaited his coming on the promontories, like Santorin, at the end of fourteen turnings where even the mule stumbles as it makes its slow way up the hill.

Above all he had learned to love the men of Greece. He loved them for their virtues, for their innate sense of beauty, for the perspicacity which enabled them to size up a stranger at once, for the devotion they showed to anyone willing to help them. He loved them also for their defects, with their captious and far from sophisticated minds, which seemed at times incapable of logical argument. In particular he loved his bishops and his flock, living isolated lives, exposed to hostility, but dogged, patient, and untiring. At the same time he did not close his eyes to the shortcomings of several of them. The delegate knew that resistance sometimes called for more than courage, and that a little heroism was needed, but he was understanding and forgave them. In Greece more than anywhere there was reason to apply his favourite motto, the one he had taken from Saint Gregory the Great: *omnia videre, multa dissimulare, pauca corrigere* (see everything, hide your feelings about many things, correct a few things). The evils the Church endured in these fragments of an ancient land were not so much caused by the men who lived there at the time as by their ancestors and by a slow process of decay. Catholicism and Orthodoxy lived too far apart to understand each other or even to tolerate each other. Material poverty continued to weigh upon the two faiths, preventing their drawing any benefit from the immense and incalculable store of common treasure. This poverty even aggravated the feeling of mutual antagonism. For this reason it was easier for the Catholics to live in Turkey, in the midst of a nation which had only assimilated a few vague principles of Christianity, than in Greece, which was inhabited by their brothers in the faith. Several years later when he was Patriarch of Venice, he wrote to the Apostolic Delegate in Turkey:

> I look back with sorrow on the moderate results obtained by the movement in favour of union in the East. And yet our duty is to insist always upon it, even against expectation. We are all a little to blame: we Latins—I mean the Eastern Latins—have had, and still have, our share in the responsibility. If we do not give up our comforts and look ahead, our decadence will follow the same rhythm as that of the people of the East, Greeks, Slavs, and Arabs.

The war which had spared Turkey brought about the downfall of Greece in the most tragic fashion in 1940. Hitler, whose plan was to conquer Europe, saw in Greece a possible base for a counter-attack against the Allies; that is why he entrusted to Italy the task of annihilating the potential enemy. Italy began her invasion across the Albanian frontier on October 28, but she met with stout resistance. After six months' fighting the heroic Greek army was still holding out but was exhausted and nearing the end of its resistance. The intervention of the German armoured divisions, after the *coup d'état* in Belgrade and the collapse of Yugoslavia, only accelerated her defeat, and made it inevitable. Metaxas died at the beginning of 1941, struck down by a cardiac seizure.

The long death struggle of Greece was beginning. Once the country had fallen under the domination of the Axis, her former Allies, still masters of the seas, enforced a vigorous blockade to prevent the occupying troops from getting food supplies. As a result the most terrible famine of the war was inflicted on the Greek people, in which

thousands of young children died of hunger. Roncalli was
at Istanbul and these sad events moved him profoundly.
At the same time the Holy See had asked England for help
in its relief work among prisoners of war. Agreement was
impossible, however, for feeling against the Italians was at
its height; even Catholic circles were not exempt from it.
The delegate at once wrote to his faithful private secretary
in Athens, Mgr Martino Biscara, giving him precise
instructions, authorizing him to take any steps, and sending
him more funds so that prisoners of war and the wounded
might receive help. He could no longer rest, but great was
his joy on learning that a Greek military chaplain, Don
Michel Almans, had offered his help and was exercising
his ministry among soldiers of the army which had invaded
his country. He appreciated this gesture greatly, he who,
although an Italian, had on the outbreak of the Greek–
Italian war experienced such a poignant grief and had
trembled for the land entrusted to his pastoral care.
Remembering that time, he wrote later: 'It was then that
I felt how strong was my affection for the sons of that
glorious Hellas with which I had been familiar since the
days of my youth and which later I also came to love
because providence allowed me to appreciate it better.' He
could not go to Greece straightaway. The ambassador,
von Papen, had advised him to wait until the German
troops had withdrawn to make way for the Italian administration, but, as a consequence of the reports he had sent
to the Vatican on the situation in that country, he was
invited to go there with the least possible delay. He obeyed,
although he knew that Greek Catholic circles were displeased at the thought that his coming would annoy their
fellow citizens. Before starting off he wished to take some
more lessons in Greek in order to have all the trump cards
on his side in the accomplishment of such an important
mission.

Roncalli had to go through Sofia. Bulgaria, which up to

that point had kept out of the war, was about to ally herself with the Axis. King Boris welcomed him with exceptional warmth. Queen Joan invited him to come to Vrana to meet her children. He also made contact with members of the government (Kalkov and Popov) and with the Metropolitan, Stephen. Everything passed off discreetly and with dignity, and he was touched to see that after several years his own courtesy and patience had left a lively impression. He reached Athens on July 25 in sweltering weather, and began by visiting the hospitals where the wounded lay. He was moved when the Italian military chaplains unexpectedly pointed out to him several Bergamesque soldiers, and it gave him special joy to bring comfort to them. Among them was one of his nephews, son of his sister Assunta, wounded in the attack on February 5. The country was uneasy. The Greek people were restless and in the numerous concentration camps his visits were more difficult. He wondered whether the prisoners succeeded in drawing a distinction between him as the representative of the Holy See and as an Italian. Moreover the law of retaliation was strictly enforced against partisans and saboteurs. Nevertheless, in Greek circles they already understood, and Roncalli enjoyed the fullest confidence. Before long the delegation became the centre round which public life revolved. Keeping aloof from all political allegiance, far from the hotbeds of discord and hatred, he was so to speak the mediator between two opposing parties. National, religious, and racial discrimination from which the friction and outbursts of cruelty sprang disappeared in the presence of the papal representative. To the invaders he appeared as a moderating influence, to the invaded as their protector. Excesses, almost inevitable where there were suspicion and makeshift decisions, were reduced in severity more than once thanks to him. Respect for the Jewish faith, which was the object of Nazi hatred, gave rise to new ideas every day for ways of escape. Jews were snatched in their hundreds from the clutches of their persecutors, sometimes with the approval of the Italian authorities who were more inclined to pity. His greatest anxiety was over the poverty that existed in the country. The Greek Government had taken refuge, first in Crete and then in Egypt. Under Italian administration the charitable work of the Holy Father was free to develop without causing the slightest opposition. Monetary inflation was increasing at an alarming rate and the sums of money arriving from the Vatican were easily convertible into hundreds of millions. It was the delegate's wish that charity should be completely disinterested, and he asked for nothing at all from the Greeks in return. In no circumstances were they to take advantage of the exceptional facilities offered them by the Italian authorities. Also, he was careful not to take advantage of the monetary weakness of the Greeks: 'Good should be well done', he used to say, repeating Radini's great maxim.

In this work he received the greatest possible help from Mgr Calavassy, the renowned exarch of the Catholics of the Greek Rite, already well known as the saviour of thousands of Greek refugees in Thrace at the time of the exchanges of population after the Treaty of Lausanne. Thanks to him the exchanges had been effected with an organizing ability which is not often met with in Greece, and which had earned him a very high decoration which King George II went out of his way to bestow in person. His knowledge of the Greek people and his aptitude for the work were unique. On the outbreak of hostilities he had placed himself with all his priests and nuns entirely at the disposal of the government for any form of help to the wounded and even to the soldiers at the front. After the collapse of the army he had not hesitated to make contact with the occupying powers, in spite of the risk of being accused of collaboration, in an attempt to obtain concessions and favours for his countrymen. He was, therefore, just the man to work with the delegate and the Greek exarchate. Father Richard Liebl, head of the Capuchin Missions, was in charge of the 'Mount of Abundance', taking advantage of his good relations with the High Command to get himself allocated enormous quantities of food. As for the delegation, it ran the clinic of the 'Good Samaritan' which operated for four years even after the war was over. Thus, by one means or another, a considerable number of Greeks enjoyed the benefit of food, medicine, and care. The relief centres were literally besieged, and the flow of help coming from the Holy See was equally impressive. All that, however, amounted to no more than a drop of oil on a wound which kept spreading. Millions of people suffered hunger or were struck down by disease. They died in such numbers that they had to be buried in groups. The outlook for the future was even more gloomy. Caught unprepared and powerless, the Orthodox clergy found themselves inundated. The one hope of salvation lay in the lifting of the relentless blockade organized by the Greek fleet, which was preventing the arrival of any food. When there was talk in Athens of the possibility of its being raised, the dominant impression was one of scepticism. For that to have happened a pressure on the same scale as events would have been needed and the advancing of much more convincing reasons than the death of thousands of people.

Yet men of spirit were prepared to try, convinced that there was no other means of salvation. It was only after long and difficult discussions that it was decided to turn to the Vatican and make discreet suggestions to the delegate. He rightly judged that a purely personal approach would be too dangerous. He wished to avoid at all costs being accused of paying no attention to the Greek authorities. Although the government was out of the country, he did not wish to appear in any way as the judge of the situation. Nor did he underestimate the appalling difficulties that lay ahead. On the one hand they had to find the funds that were needed to acquire abroad huge quantities of supplies; and on the other, the help that was being provided by the Holy See was not enough. At length it was learned that fortunately the Greek Government had accumulated before the war important capital reserves in Turkey, the United States and Australia. It was merely a question of unfreezing them, and the help of the Vatican would certainly be valuable in this direction.

Another serious difficulty remained to be overcome before the consent of the Allies could be obtained to relaxing the blockade: it was necessary to obtain an assurance that the supplies would not be used by the Axis authorities for their own purposes instead of providing for the needs of the population. The delegate, with the assistance of Mgr Calavassy, who had become the mouthpiece for the needs of the country and who acted as intermediary between him and the authorities, declared himself ready to act, on condition that the leaders of the parties who had stayed behind in Greece together with the vice-regent, who was the Orthodox Archbishop himself, should issue a formal request which could be submitted to the Holy Father. Roncalli went to Rome for the express purpose of rousing the Holy See's interest in the affair. On his return, the delegate accompanied by Calavassy had conversations with Damaskinos himself, and the talks continued in a strained atmosphere, as can well be imagined. The Vatican was negotiating with the Allies while Roncalli was in consultation with the plenipotentiaries of the Axis. The complications of this kind of agreement and the infinite precautions that were taken on all sides can also be imagined. In the end everything worked out all right. The arrival of the first shiploads of supplies marked the loosening of the knot which had been tied tightly round the peninsula for months. At last the delegate could leave for Turkey. As an outward sign of the gratitude of the Greeks he had in his possession a letter of thanks from the signatories of the famous appeal, a letter which overflowed with joyful feelings.

The occupation of Greece lasted four years. Roncalli stayed there from March to Easter 1942, returned again from June to August, but after that the military situation deprived him of all contact with it for almost two years. Fortunately he had obtained from the Vatican a representative directly under his orders, his former secretary in Sofia and Istanbul, Mgr Giacomo Testa, who had in the meantime spent two years in the Secretariat of State. He was therefore easy in his mind, for he knew that he could count on him completely. During those years of separation the intimacy between the former disciple and his master had by no means diminished. The presence of Testa, a most kindly man, was providential for Greece in her great sorrow, and his name is still venerated there. The delegate had to take up the question of Greece once more, towards the middle of 1944. Reoccupied by the Allies who had chased the German troops out, it was subjected to bombardment by both sides. The capital and the surrounding area were subjected to a severe ordeal. Remorselessly the two belligerents set about trampling a dying nation under foot. The existence of Athens, a centre of unique importance in the history of civilization, was threatened.

The indefatigable Calavassy once again approached the delegate with an attractive idea: that of proposing to the belligerents, through the mediation of the Holy See, that the historic importance of the two capitals, Rome and Athens, be respected and that they should be declared open cities. This time the initiative was purely Catholic and the appeal to the Vatican bore the signatures of the two bishops, Latin and Greek, of the Hellenic capital. When the bombardments ceased there were very few who realized to whom this truce was due.

Looking back on his activities in those years, Roncalli was able to write:

By the mercy of God, it seems to me that one is entitled to say that at a terrible time in Greek history the Catholic Church, honourably represented and admirably organized, was not unworthy of its task and of its best traditions. I am happy to make this assertion, at the same time repeating before God and before the Holy Father who inspires, helps, and guides us: *Servi inutiles sumus.*

Chapter Eight

THE FRANCE OF DE GAULLE

DECEMBER 1944. The war was not over, but by now the Allied armies, who would soon bring it to an end, could be seen on the horizon. The German Army, still putting up a dogged resistance, was everywhere in retreat towards its national frontiers. The Allies had landed in Italy and liberating forces were taking over in France. While all this was going on, Roncalli's thoughts were already turning to the traditional Christmas message, which gave him an opportunity of warm spiritual fellowship with his people. For the moment he was on his own in the delegation, those who had been working with him having been posted elsewhere. He was therefore going to have to face quite alone the interminable procession of distinguished visitors bearing good wishes—a custom to which great importance was attached in the East.

Then suddenly a coded telegram from the Vatican arrived. He was not accustomed to the secret code, and it took him some time to decipher the message. To his amazement he learned from it that he had been nominated nuncio in Paris. Three days later came the confirmation of it, bidding him leave at the earliest opportunity. On December 7 the clergy of the cathedral saw, probably for the first time, their bishop looking worried. During the morning procession his step faltered and his face was drawn and preoccupied. He appeared to be ill but it was not until the afternoon that the matter was raised. 'Do you not feel well, Excellency?' Mgr Guillois asked him. 'No' came the reply in a strangely toneless voice which put an end to further questions.

The Franciscans of St. Mary's had arranged a small party for the following day to celebrate the tenth anniversary of his arrival in Turkey. Moved by the warm welcome of his clergy he could keep his secret no longer and in a voice which showed his emotion he made known his imminent departure. There were expressions of regret and congratulation on every side. He had wanted to greet his people, but time was pressing and he did not feel he could stay until Christmas. On December 23 the cathedral clergy were invited to a farewell banquet at which were also present the Armenian Catholic archbishop, Paul Kireciyan, and the Greek Catholic bishop, Denys Varouchas. This time it was not one of those love-feasts which His Excellency knew so well how to enliven with his conversation. He even had to leave before the meal was finished because his departure was timed for immediately afterwards. Getting up from the table he embraced each of his guests and gave them two Swiss golden pieces. With the car containing his luggage waiting outside he went to pray for the last time in his church. Then, accompanied by a little group, he left for the Kadi-Koy quay and thence for the station of Haydar-Pasa where a large number of representatives of the diplomatic corps were waiting to greet him. The train left at six in the evening for Ankara, which he reached the next morning, intending to stay there a few days. He wished to say goodbye to his Catholic flock and to the many friends he had made in the embassies. He even wished to pay a visit to members of the government. Not being an accredited member of the diplomatic corps, there could be no question of his taking official leave of them; he simply wished to make a gesture of respect and gratitude. Menemencoglu was no longer in Ankara. A fortnight before he had gone as ambassador to Paris, and so, without making any attempt to see other members of the government, he left Ankara, convinced that his policy of waiting patiently had not been without effect. The proof of this came a few days later in Paris. It was a very different Menemencoglu upon whom he went to call. Gone was the distant, impassive manner and in its place so many compliments and marks of respect that the nuncio was literally astounded. 'What we could not do for you, Excellency, in Turkey, we do now here in France. My government authorizes me to express to you my deepest respect and my most sincere gratitude.'

Let us return for a moment to the rather depressing day when he left Ankara. The French Government had put at his disposal an old American aircraft which still bore the marks of long service in the war. He took his place in it without fuss on Wednesday evening, December 27, much to the astonishment of ground staff and crew who were expecting more ceremony. And so he left Turkey, and as the lights of Ankara disappeared into the darkness his thoughts were already turning to the future. He was then sixty-three.

He had to stop at Rome. His first visit was naturally to the office of the Secretary of State. On entering Mgr Tardini's room he confined himself to a single greeting and then asked in a sharp tone: 'Whoever had the idea of making me leave Istanbul?' 'I beg of you, Excellency, not to feel angry with me. It was not my idea, but the Holy Father's.' Nor did the visit to Pius XII on December 29 take long either. The Holy Father discussed matters of the greatest urgency with him in a friendly manner and volunteered the information that the nomination had come from him.

Some months later, on March 23, 1945, the nuncio wrote to the Bishop of Bergamo:

> To feel myself seized without any warning like Habbakuk and suddenly transported from Istanbul to Paris seemed to me, too, to be almost an act of magic. It was the last thing I either expected

or wanted. My amazement increased when I learned at the Vatican, where I spent a few hours, that the nomination came from very high up. The Pope told me himself, probably to encourage me: 'It was I, Monsignor, who thought of you and took this decision, no-one else.'

He continued the journey to Paris by plane.

The year 1944 had seen the liberation of Paris and of the greater part of France, but only very few of the great hopes to which the first contact with freedom had given rise had been realized. That winter was perhaps the severest and coldest of any since the declaration of war, and good relations between the old comrades in arms were clearly not easy, since both were at the end of their tether. Besides, the military position could not be regarded as entirely secure. Von Runstedt's December offensive in the Ardennes reminded Frenchmen that they had not yet been completely delivered. As for the government, it was far from feeling secure in the country, and the uncertainty only made it more irritable. The state of isolation in which it had been left by the Allies after the Yalta Conference, to which it had not been invited, seemed to turn it towards Soviet Russia, with which a twenty-year treaty of friendship and mutual assistance had been signed on December 10.

The attitude of the Vatican caused him particular concern. The removal of the previous nuncio had been insistently urged. There was no doubt that the procedure adopted in respect of him, as in respect of the Vichy diplomats, had been irregular to say the least. People were not used to such measures in diplomacy. The unfortunate effect that it had produced was mitigated only by the gesture of General de Gaulle who, receiving the eminent diplomat in audience before his departure, conferred on him the Grand Cross of the Legion of Honour. Neither was it easy, in those confused days, to distinguish between the Vatican and Italy. Everything transalpine invariably finished up by attracting to those two names resentment for all the wrongs and injustices of the past few years. It was even said that the armistice between France and Italy, concluded at the end of the incomprehensible encounter between the two countries in 1940, had been negotiated by the nuncio, Mgr Valeri, to whom certain extremists had the stupidity to attribute part of the responsibility for the excessive claims of the Fascist government of the time.

The new nuncio was certainly going to need patience and prudence. He arrived in Paris without having been specially prepared for his task. Nevertheless his vast learning, his classical and religious training, his friendliness and the understanding which he brought to the study of world events, made him well suited to judge the French situation with penetrating skill. His total surrender to providence gave him, moreover, the tranquillity and confidence he needed to face up to his grave responsibilities.

With their customary sincerity leading Frenchmen did not shrink from analysing the state of the nation. France had fallen into a deep abyss, and she had been profoundly humiliated in front of the whole world. That had been only the last link in a long drawn-out crisis, but she had had time to reflect and understand. She had also prayed to be given the strength for a renewal of spirit and faith. Had not her own revolution been in a sense a kind of religious war? Otherwise, from the political point of view, it would not even have been necessary. All that was needed was for the Allied Powers to liberate France from German occupation and from a regime which, although it was served by the remnants of an army still proud enough to yield only to violence, was nevertheless an unstable one which enjoyed only a specious authority. One thing alone had driven the youth of France, ill-equipped as it was for guerilla warfare, into the arena to fight, and that was a deep-seated spirit of sacrifice, a religious urge, a desire for redemption which indicated a revolt against the stubborn forces of evil, disgust at cruelty and sympathy for the persecuted, a protest in favour of the fundamental freedom of the children of God. The nuncio, therefore, had no difficulty at all in understanding the Resistance movement and it was certainly not by descending to political opportunism that he was able to show France a loyal and friendly disposition. It was not long before the French were able to see in him the signs of a profound and genuine sympathy. He was helped by a thorough understanding of French history and, arising from that, an affection that was none the less genuine for having a religious motive.

He arrived in Paris on December 30 and soon after performed his first official duty. The dean of the diplomatic corps in France was going to convey New Year greetings from himself and from the entire corps to General de Gaulle. The ceremony had been arranged for 10.30 at the church on January 1. The presentation of his credentials to de Gaulle had taken place the evening before. The general received him, flanked on one side by his Foreign Minister, Georges Bidault, and on the other by the chief of protocol. The interview was deliberately confined to the usual courtesies. The atmosphere was charged with suspicion if not with mistrust. Only the nuncio looked at his ease, his face illumined by a respectful smile. The following day ambassadors and ministers plenipotentiary assembled in order of precedence in the great hall of the Elysée palace. The nuncio, whose arrival aroused a lively interest, took his place quietly at the head of the diplomatic corps and began to speak. The utter simplicity of what he had to say immediately became apparent. It certainly surprised those who were expecting to listen to lofty sentiments couched in the language of diplomacy in order to gloss over the critical situation. Absolute honesty and cordiality shone through his every word spoken with perfect clarity: 'In the midst of unavoidable trials and tribulations the year which has just closed has been marked for you by events of the highest importance. Thanks to your labours and political foresight, this dear country has found again her freedom and faith in her destiny.' It was obvious that General de Gaulle was listening carefully. The ideas expressed by the nuncio were the same as those on which he was going to enlarge some hours later in his New Year broadcast to the French people. They were also the same as the ones the French press endeavoured, in language that was at times rather exaggerated, to transmit to the French people. This message of great spiritual force interpreted those ideas in a way that was more detached but also, it might be added, more expressive.

As a result of this experience the nuncio always looked on his inaugural New Year speech as the 'spirit-level' of his diplomatic activity. He took a great deal of trouble over it seeking to transform it from a formal act of courtesy into something spontaneous and sincere. Again in his correspondence we hear the echo of his attempts to infuse into the speech a spiritual element, but only so much and of such a strength as to suit the level of understanding of a mixed audience, in the midst of which he was particularly aware of the presence of diplomatic representatives from countries beyond the Iron Curtain. However, this did not stop him from clearly reaffirming the apostolic and pacifying character of his work. On January 3, 1948, he wrote to a close friend: 'It seems to me that my work, or rather that of the Holy Father, is going as well as possible, in spite of occasional illnesses and storms. My little New Year 'spirit-level', that is to say the exchange of compliments at the Elysée, worked well. I said little, as is the custom, leaving a great deal more unsaid. You know how careful one has to be to avoid incidents.' On January 14 he wrote again:

In my New Year address I was able, without causing offence, to speak of the suppression of liberty in the world, that liberty which is the daughter of God . . . asking God to give us his peace:

Dominus det nobis suam pacem. But that peace will be worth little indeed unless we give it our effective co-operation . . . The person to whom I was addressing my remarks thought fit to revive the memory and the thoughts of that great diplomat and prince of the Church, Cardinal Richelieu. There was no real importance in any of it, and yet what is said there in that atmosphere is quite impressive and pleases everybody.

Finally, on December 31, he had this to say:

I am just back from a visit to the Elysée to present my New Year wishes. I was a little bit afraid of talking to no effect, but President Auriol in his reply was very much of my way of thinking. In any case my thoughts were simple and spontaneous. We are in Paris, I said, not to enjoy ourselves but to fulfil our solemn duty which has become even more difficult these past few weeks. The laws of peace are the laws of civilization, and the laws of civilization come from the Ten Commandments applied on a global and international level. Therefore, God first; honour to the family; then the great precepts of social life: thou shalt not kill, thou shalt not commit adultery, thou shalt not lie, above all thou shalt not lie. To act contrary to these laws means refusing peace, making war, a return to barbarism. The inalienable criterion of sound diplomacy is to fear God and love men. Then, the example of the ancient Romans, according to the praise that history has bestowed on them: *Consilium et patientia.*

His end-of-the-year speech in 1952, on the occasion of the presentation of his New Year wishes, was to be his last. In a letter written before Christmas there are already signs that he was preparing for it. It was at a time of government crisis and the nuncio had taken as his inspiration the last fable of La Fontaine and an inscription engraved on the frontal of the temple at Delphi. From the fable he was to borrow the following lines:

Disturb the water, do you see yourself in it?
Leave it alone,
Then you will see your reflection.
May God grant that this doctrine already summarized in the inscription 'Know thyself' on the frontal of the temple at Delphi and which by its fulness and its nobility of sentiment, rises above any particular application, may be wisely understood and widely

put into practice wherever there is a responsibility to be shouldered in the common cause, and wherever conscience is faced with the gravest problem of the present moment: to save the peace, to save the peace at any price.

The allusions were veiled but they shone through. There could be no finer proof of humanism than this familiarity between a diplomat imbued with the importance of his function in general and his own duty in particular and a French genius so delightfully absent-minded that he once spoke to his son without recognizing him. No-one could have expressed better than he the thoughts of a diplomatic corps composed of such diverse elements. He had been able not only to understand, but to respect the feelings of each one of them. He had achieved edifying thoughts without losing the fascination of simplicity. We can see by the increasing boldness of those addresses the course taken by Roncalli's diplomatic barque through its eight years of hazardous navigation, during which time several French governments came and went.

At the outset of his new career he sought in vain to see beyond the darkened national and international horizons, but he realized that being surrounded by troubled and sensitive groups called for extreme tact and calmness on his part. Besides, he had long ago adopted as a rule of life a remark of Benedict XV to Mgr Ratti, who later became Pius XI, at the time he was leaving for Poland: 'God requires us to be prudent but not to be prophets.' Yet he was surprised to find how quickly he felt at home in the midst of that new world which he understood so well already and even loved.

> I do everything calmly: one step at a time, one advance after another; business, visiting, words, silences, and then patience, waiting in peace and, most important, constant serenity of mind and gentleness.
>
> It is now three months since I left Istanbul and began a new and unexpected life, but I feel as though I had been living in these surroundings for years. I do not know how or why, but the

experience of twice ten years in the East has made me better equipped to look after myself when surrounded by western intrigues. I know what to expect and I am ready for anything. Every time I go out I come across monuments recalling the varying fortunes of men in this city of many faces which offers immense opportunities for every form of human and priestly activity. By the grace of the Lord I manage never to lose sight of my village where my own family works simply and trustingly in the fields, watching the sun which reflects the glory of God.

It is not easy to draw a picture of the activities of a nuncio accredited to a government. The code of canon law is very vague about his duties. It says no more than that he is responsible for fostering relations between the apostolic see and the civil governments. In fact every country presents quite different conditions depending on a variety of factors—the number of Catholics, their strength and influence, the religious history of the country, the policies of the political parties and the composition of the government. Often the ideal of the Holy See is to reach a concordat with the governments of the countries concerned. When that is the case, the activities of the nuncio generally follow a clear pattern and meet few difficulties, for in a concordat a solution has already been found to the great problem raised by a civil and religious society living side by side. In modern times the concordat marks in the religious history of a country a climax which is reached after passing through a period of conflict and tension, and which creates, in matters concerning the relations between the State and the ecclesiastical organization, a kind of *modus vivendi* characterized by mutual trust, respect, understanding or at least tolerance. Naturally those matters on which it has been difficult to reach a compromise give rise to some friction, but this is nearly always smoothed away by loyal adherence to the agreements that have been made.

It is different when the relations between the civil regime of a country and the religious organization are maintained on a day-to-day basis. The problems arising from them are the subject of a constant flow of discussion between the government and parliament on the one hand, and the bishops and the clergy on the other. In actual fact it is the bishops and clergy, and not the nuncio, who play the leading rôles on the national stage in these discussions. But in addition to this dialogue there is another on a plane that is more confidential, more delicate, and more elevated. The Holy See takes part in it in a supra-national capacity, offering wider guarantees. The nuncio carries out a task which is allied to that of the national Church without being identified with it. It does not usually give rise to striking measures, but it does necessitate his presence there all the time, ready with tactful suggestions, patience, discreet protests and congratulations.

The history of diplomatic relations between the Holy See and France during the past fifty years has been rather disturbed. The concordat of Napoleon was unilaterally denounced by the French government in 1905. The Third Republic had brutally secularized charitable institutions, schools, marriages, and the army, and had broken up the religious congregations. The result of this had been the breaking off of diplomatic relations with the Holy See and the inauguration of a regime of separation between State and Church which had been sternly condemned by Pius X in his encyclical *Vehementer Nos* in 1906. New laws had been passed and ecclesiastical property had to submit, for its own security, to regulations which seriously affected the rights of the Church.

Very gradually this situation had improved, thanks to an attempt by both sides to reach understanding, and thanks in particular to the heroism of the French clergy in the first World War, who provided an eloquent demonstration of patriotism surmounting all obstacles. Diplomatic relations were resumed in 1921, although not without setbacks and difficulties. Such relations between Church and State are naturally more precarious when they are not supported by a concordat, and when they are constantly having to adapt themselves they are more subject to the misunderstandings which arise from a fundamental divergence of principle. On the other hand, it can be argued that they also gain in clarity; whenever a fresh question is settled, the two institutions regard each other more frankly. In calling itself lay the State pretends to be unaware of the Church, but in fact it will never have a finer opportunity to get to know her. Diplomats confront each other openly, without sheltering behind convention. Consequently the nunciature in France is not only held by the Vatican to be in the very front rank, it is also considered as a post reserved for eminent men. The colleagues who gather round the nuncio are themselves chosen from among the best candidates for a diplomatic career, and they are sent there in order to broaden their experience. During his time in France, Roncalli often complained of being deprived of the services of colleagues who had been appointed to more important duties. 'I am distressed at having to let my poor O. go off to the Secretariat of State, just when he is changing from the job of auditor to that of councillor. I tried to keep him; but the reply I got was that the nunciature at Paris was a sort of training-ground where those who have been marked out as men of tomorrow and the day after complete their apprenticeship.' That was true, although the explanation was given lightheartedly.

When he arrived in France the separatist regime was an established fact. After his ten years' experience in Turkey he had no difficulty in understanding it and conforming to it. The Catholics themselves, who had at one time opposed it, now considered that this regime offered a freedom and a guarantee of independence which they would not lightly surrender, and so the nuncio adapted himself without any trouble to a situation which had become part of the life of the French people. Thus his activities were from the start restricted and directed. He made no attempt to persuade successive French governments to return to a concordat which would have been out of harmony with the realities of the national situation and which would have encountered too many obstacles. However, he fully realized that the secularization of the State had been brought about in an empirical manner which was not without its ambiguities, and that it was tending to produce a legal and political system almost totally lacking in coherence. Separation from Rome ought not to prevent Catholicism, which was a positive and vigorous force and the most important group in the country, from being recognized by a minimum of legal definitions. It was in this direction and in this direction alone that the nuncio discreetly made his activities felt, in an attempt to get the foundations of a religious policy for France laid down, for the sake of clarity, for the sake of national solidarity and international influence, and for the sake of spiritual unity. This clarification was desired not in order to satisfy the claims of religious administration, not only to secure untroubled relations between the republic and the Church, but in order to ensure that the real value of Catholicism and its constructive support of society were appreciated in France, and to avoid any danger that the lay policy of the State should appear to be reduced to opposing religious institutions or denying the principles of justice and freedom. It was in these terms, at least, that he understood his mission. He saw in it a living witness to the presence of the Church, and nothing else. There was no doubting the nobility of his attitude, his vigorous affirmation of principles and, at the same time, his detachment from anything which bore only indirectly on the matter or which sprang from political passion. As a spectator he was in a good position to observe the major upheavals of those years. He was thus able to remain on dignified and friendly terms with one government after another, preserving his detachment throughout.

The first task to which he devoted himself was that of

establishing peace, not so much in the religious as in the
political sense, in the midst of the divisions which the
liberation of France had only helped to accentuate. The
Resistance set about defending its conquests with a vigour
in which the nuncio was not slow to detect a certain
resentment. To carry their zeal to extremes, to hurl unjust
accusations against their adversaries, to reproach them
with taking up a position which they had only adopted to
save whatever could still be saved, at a time when there
was no other choice, this seemed to him tantamount to
digging a new ditch between the two parties in France, at
a time when the country had need of help from all her
sons. The true unity of France, spiritual unity, could not
be realized without those virtues of self-denial and forbear-
ance which corresponded, after all, to the evangelical spirit
of forgiveness. The nuncio, however, could only suggest this
to those representatives of the government who were
sympathetic to Christianity.

Just how effective and penetrating this patient spreading
of the spirit of gentleness was cannot be gathered from the
documents. Work of that kind is not dependent on official
actions, it rests on personal contact, on the power of friendship, on the appeal of a smile, but more than anything on
spiritual prestige. It was continued later in a variety of
ways. After the May elections in 1946 and the unexpected
resignation of General de Gaulle the work was shown to be
more necessary than ever. At the beginning of January
1948, Cardinal Suhard confided to the nuncio that President Auriol, when he received him at the Elysée, had
spoken with satisfaction of the pacifying influence of the
papal representative, of which there had been growing
recognition in high places and in various spheres of society.
The nuncio looked on internal divisions as a kind of
'Gallic tradition', a homage paid to the memory of
Vercingetorix and Caesar. But those divisions did not
diminish his confidence in the final victory of good sense

and above all they did not make him turn aside from his line of conduct. The fluctuations of political life became very quickly for him a normal condition of his diplomatic activities and for that reason they were accepted without question. They prevented him from establishing long-term programmes, but they did not succeed in disturbing profoundly the life of the nunciature. He calmly adapted his plans to the possibilities of the day. He liked to say that he lived according to the maxim engraved on the front of a palace in Mantua: *sine spe et sine motu*, and he used to compare his destiny to what was written on the scroll of the arms of Paris: *fluctuat nec mergitur*. He wrote:

> There would be cause for grief if we, like Don Abbondio, were destined to end our days in sadness. But to the student of history it is clear that there is nothing new under the sun . . . here one can still catch today the echo of the hosanna of Palm Sunday. But who knows what surprises tomorrow holds in store?
>
> My relations with the members of the government are excellent. As for the parties, we keep ourselves *nec prope nec procul*. The nuncio is harnessed to nobody's chariot. He practises the formula of *omnia probate quod bonum est tenete*, which is a good way of expressing personal regard for everyone . . .
>
> I should add that as my sojourn in this country is prolonged I have come to realize with pleasure that although the French have their faults—that is only human—they belong to an intelligent and distinguished race and even the exuberance they show among themselves contains an element of dignity which should not be overlooked. Certainly the attention I have seen them lavish on this worthy Bergamesque sent to them by the Pope, who has no pretensions of any kind, would tempt me to feel embarrassed if I did not know that it is not worth the trouble. And so we live from week to week, trusting in God for the days of peace as well as for the days of trial, which will not be lacking.

In this spirit of detachment, he was able to appreciate what had been accomplished. He liked to speak of it, albeit in all modesty:

> By God's grace my work goes well; I conduct it calmly and am in touch with all of it; and gradually it falls into place.

I bless the Lord for the help He is lending me, enabling me to avoid complicating simple things but rather to simplify complicated things. At least, that is what they tell me and I listen to them with a smile. I cannot quite explain to my own satisfaction the mystery of official life here: great concern to give a non-clerical appearance to civil institutions in force combined with a respectful and cordial friendliness towards the nuncio on the part of every section that goes to make up this densely populated and variegated collection of humanity which is the capital of France. I am sometimes reminded—*Dominus parcat*—of the miracle of St Januarius at Naples. When the heraldic arms of the saint are placed on the high altar in front of the phial containing his solid, dehydrated blood, the blood begins to liquefy. In my own case there may be some value in my attempt not to lose sight of my native village among all this splendour, nor to forget all the other things that have come to me through the mercy of the Lord.

It was a fact that even in those circles in which non-clerical or even anti-Christian ideas were vigorously supported, there was evidence of a good-natured disposition not to attack the person of the papal representative.

Roncalli never had reason to complain of a disrespectful attitude towards him. In March 1947, the whole of that part of France that was lay and anti-clerical was roused to indignation by the famous 'complot des soutanes'. Reappearing for the first time on March 18 after a four-week strike, the newspapers announced under banner headlines that the police, forcing an entry into a number of religious houses had discovered in them former collaborators who were wanted by the law or who had already been condemned. For eight whole days friends and enemies of the religious spoke of the 'complot des soutanes' as people must have spoken of the Gunpowder Plot in London at the time of James I. Naturally there was no desire to recognize the right of asylum which was constantly being claimed by the Church in favour of persons threatened or afflicted by undeserved or excessive sentences. Father Ricquet, the eloquent lenten preacher at Notre-Dame, addressed to the

Minister of the Interior, who had officially denounced to the public the discoveries made by the police, a note in which he recalled that in times that were still fresh in their memory those same convents had opened their doors to the victims of Nazi persecution, had provided a cloak for the underground resistance movement, and had furnished the concentration camps and the firing squads with an honourable company of martyrs.

Above the general commotion made by the press could be heard the voices of *Humanité* and *Franc-Tireur* claiming to have knowledge of a vast network, the threads of which could be traced back to the Vatican. By reason of his position the nuncio would naturally have been the person most likely to be behind the plot, but no mention was ever made of him, although the attitude he adopted was eloquent proof of his sorrow and disapproval. He took care not to intervene officially, realizing that, behind the discussions concerning the legality of the right of asylum and behind all the violence, the serious problem of the rights of God and of Caesar was at stake. Reasons of state, which are always invoked by totalitarian regimes, could only reject the right of asylum, which is the expression of the mind of God in society and a visible symbol of a justice and mercy superior to that of men. The Socialist Minister of the Fourth Republic was continuing the traditions of Philippe le Bel whose subservient jurists had been the first to legislate against the right of asylum, of Louis XII who had deprived of the right the churches of Notre-Dame and St Jean des Dominicains, the only two churches which had been allowed to retain it, and of Francis I who had declared it illegal, which it has remained ever since.

It was easy for Roncalli to understand the mentality of those who had a different outlook from his own and to see the real reason for discord and divisions. But this ability, instead of alienating him completely from those men, only dissuaded him from making fruitless and naïve attempts at persuasion, and drove him to seek common ground in those spheres of human virtue in which his optimism soon made him discover sources of good. He was able to approach them, not only with great respect, but also with a warm sympathy and friendship that sprang from his innermost qualities. It was his belief that human goodness is also essentially Christian goodness. It was not, therefore, a question of closing his eyes to matters of discord, but of keeping them wide open for those gifts which God has given to everyone.

Among the public figures whose friendship with him occasioned some surprise to those who did not understand the sort of man he was, were the socialist Auriol, President of the Republic, and the radical Herriot, President of the National Assembly. Auriol has left plenty of evidence of this, in recalling the many official occasions on which he met him, and even more the private conversations he had with him. He emphasizes that he invariably fell under the spell of his kindness, of his sensitivity and of his great tolerance. The feeling that Herriot had for him, Herriot the champion of parliamentary battles against the ecclesiastical 'meddlers', was no less astonishing to those who regard diversity of opinions as sufficient reason to divide men completely. But in fact such diversity had given rise in this case to a sort of familiarity which was to have its confirmation during the very days when it was most needed, such as those of the parliamentary debates on the school question in 1951, at a time when their respective positions should officially have appeared contradictory. Sometimes it needed only very little to rouse in Roncalli a feeling of sympathy. It was not always easy to find subjects of interest to discuss with the Russian ambassador, and between him and the nuncio polite relations, which never ceased to exist, remained nonetheless somewhat limited. When in June 1951, M Dumaine, the chief of protocol, left Paris for the Portuguese embassy, Roncalli organized at the nunciature the farewell reception to be attended by accredited diplomats. A brief note informed their excellencies that a presentation would be made to the new ambassador and invited them to send their contribution to Mme Vanier, wife of the Canadian ambassador and herself dean of the diplomatic corps on the women's side. No-one declined this discreet invitation, but the Soviet embassy and its satellites addressed their offerings to 'Mme Vanier, the Apostolic Nunciature', declining to attend the reception and denying themselves the chance of seeing the massive silver tureen in the Empire style, to the purchase of which they had contributed. The nuncio did not expect anything else.

As for his feelings and his impressions, he did not make a secret of them. With a freedom which was in harmony with his uniquely spiritual mission, he expressed his doubts fearlessly, even to his good friends of the *Mouvement Républicain Populaire*. It was known that fairly frequent discussions were held between himself and M Bidault, and that it was the minister who gladly went time after time to the nunciature where he knew that he would find the calm he needed. In contrast, less surprising was his friendship with M Robert Schuman, for a very sincere mutual esteem drew them to each other. The nuncio was genuinely impressed by his profoundly Christian spirit and appreciated his untiring efforts in the cause of European unity. Taken as a whole, however, his relations with the Christian Democrat Party were not close. The members of that party knew perfectly well that open relations with the nunciature would be prejudicial rather than useful, and so they made no attempt to establish them. M Dumaine, the chief of protocol, has left us in his diary a reminder of their critical attitude. There also can be found a shrewd reply by the nuncio: 'Cardinal Ferrata, who was nuncio at the beginning of the century, used to visit the Quai d'Orsay every week. But, whispers Mgr Roncalli, ministers in those days were on the whole hostile to the Church, and the nuncio had to remind them of his existence. I am not in that position. I find myself among friends and do not wish to embarrass them.'*

By making use of the virtues of sincerity and detachment in the service of a profound human sympathy he practised what is usually called the arts of diplomacy. But it may well be asked whether such a description is suitable for an attitude which could not be the product solely of a long apprenticeship in the career of ambassador and which was lacking in anything contrived or studied, let alone false or remote. He himself used to greet with an incredulous smile or, in the case of writing, would follow with a question mark any allusion to his task as a diplomat. In fact he never succeeded in distinguishing between his duties as papal representative and his mission as a priest. Were not both designed to bring about the victory of justice and charity? And were not the conditions of success the same— never to separate the search for justice and truth from the practice of charity? In this connexion he was fond of quoting the saying of St Paul: *Veritatem facientes in caritate*, as a summary of his mission, and he willingly accepted the name 'the good Mgr Roncalli' which had been applied to him by some of his colleagues in the curia who failed to appreciate his interpretation of the diplomatic art and who took him to task for not concealing his intentions sufficiently and not planning his interventions skilfully. He called them 'the other school', and did not envy them their mania for secret meetings and diplomatic notes and protests. It seemed to him that the post of minister of the Gospel imposed on him the duty of acting in accordance with such and such a policy, but at the same time guided by the virtues of simplicity, frankness, and gentleness. Consequently his work seldom became involved. He knew how to wait and to be patient. It was enough for him not to lose contact, and it did not take much to enable him to maintain

* J. Dumaine, *Quai d'Orsay*, Paris, 1955, pp. 62 f.

it: a reception (he never missed one), a meeting round a table, or a message of greeting. He had the gift of making use of opportunities like that in such a way that they lost their conventional character. He believed in the value of small gestures, the effects of which did not show at once, but which one day—he was sure of it—would flourish, like the seed that fell on good ground, and bring forth fruit.

Prominence was given on one occasion to the success of his work of pacification during his stay in Paris, when he was able to indulge the pleasure of inviting to dinner all the successive heads of governments. Thus there were to be seen gathered round his table, in addition to the presidents of the National Assembly in the figures of Herriot, of the French Union, Monnerville, the President of the Council at that time, and René Mayer and his predecessors, the following: Bidault, Gouin, Pléven, Edgar Faure, André Marie, Robert Schuman, Pinay and Fourcade. The atmosphere was wonderfully relaxed, cordial and warmhearted. When the meal was over he had a friendly word to say to each one. Edouard Herriot, ever brusque but profoundly moved, spoke for them all. Briefly he said that the French people would not forget the kindness, the understanding and the marks of friendship he had shown them. He added that he had pondered over the last lesson that had been given by the nuncio at the time of the New Year greetings: namely that the best way to attain the end they were seeking was to get to know each other, and then to go forward in faith, optimism and love.

That lesson had been understood. The nuncio never knew whether he had succeeded in touching the heart of Herriot, the old anti-clerical, but there were many who thought that he had when, shortly afterwards at the time of his death, he was reconciled to the Church.

Chapter Nine

BISHOPS AND SCHOOLS

THE nomination of bishops is one of those matters over which relations between State and Church run into many difficulties. In France this problem has sometimes led to considerable repercussions. For example, after the separation of Church and State and the refusal of the religious organizations to submit to the new lay laws, a large number of episcopal sees had remained vacant. Faced with the impossibility of reaching an agreement, Pius X had, in a notable gesture, personally consecrated in the Basilica of St Peter thirty-two bishops whom he had then sent to live in poverty, without recognition from the government, in the dioceses he entrusted to them. Another incident had occurred after the first World War and the re-establishment of diplomatic relations. It was only under the threat of resignation that the nuncio, Cerretti, had been able to obtain from Edouard Herriot freedom to nominate several bishops in territory previously held by Germany. The government put many obstacles in the way.

The ordeal that awaited Roncalli was no less severe. Between 1939 and 1949 France had been overwhelmed in succession by war, defeat, occupation, resistance and liberation. The whole of society had been affected by these events, the Church as much as any other part. In July 1940, the legality of the Vichy Government had been accepted by the majority of Frenchmen. It was only when Laval set out on the path of collaboration with the Germans that this legality began to be questioned. The ecclesiastical hierarchy had recognized the new regime. It would have been difficult for it to disregard the traditional doctrine of the Church by refusing to obey a legally constituted government, and so relations between the apostolic nuncio, Valeri, and Marshal Pétain had been normal. But public opinion did not stand still. The Resistance movement grew stronger and many young priests and seminarists, won over by a feeling of national pride, became hostile to Pétain. And so, generally speaking, clergy and hierarchy, faced by different responsibilities, had adopted attitudes that were equally different.

An extremely delicate situation took shape as the Resistance began clearly to get the upper hand. While priests and religious could feel completely at ease beside those with whom they had actually fought and with whom they had sacrificed themselves, not to mention supplying numerous martyrs (e.g. Father Louis Favre, Father de Montcheuil, Abbot Vallée), the hierarchy had a good deal to fear from a power which was determined to make no concessions to any group that had dealings with the Vichy Government.

The first signs of intolerance appeared on August 25, 1944, when the Archbishop of Paris, Cardinal Suhard, was prevented by the Liberation authorities from attending the *Te Deum* for victory in Notre-Dame. The case caused a good deal of concern. That eminent prelate, who had succeeded Cardinal Verdier in 1940 at the very moment of defeat, had from the outset been subjected to a brutal investigation and then to numerous affronts. He behaved with the greatest dignity and his frequent appeals on behalf of Jews, internees and hostages, should have won him sympathy. Instead, his silence, his horror of spectacular gestures, and his conciliatory attitude had been misinterpreted and had drawn about him suspicion for which there was absolutely no justification. It was only the dignity with which he suffered adversity, a dignity which made him

reject any thought of self-justification, that later had the
effect of modifying the government's opinion of him.
Nobody among his clergy, let it be said, ever doubted him
for a moment.

A little later came the second ordeal. The government of
General de Gaulle informed the Vatican that new circumstances rendered the presence of the nuncio Valeri in
France almost intolerable. Irresponsible propaganda, in the
pay of the Communist Party, had even gone so far as to
accuse him of collaboration and espionage. The Vatican's
gesture in sacrificing the nuncio must have cost the cause
of appeasement and reconciliation dear. Even so, once the
nuncio had gone the whole hierarchy was left without
protection and in an embarrassing position. This first concession gave heart to the anti-clerical and Communist
forces which had arisen out of the Resistance; they even
went so far as to demand the resignation of a large number
of bishops. Fortunately Bidault, leader of the Christian
Democrat Party and former President of the National
Council of the Resistance, was able to intervene with the
full weight of his authority to put a stop to such a project.
Nevertheless, by virtue of the compromise at which he had
arrived whereby the number of bishops to be sacrificed was
reduced to thirty, he felt morally obliged in parliament to
give a personal guarantee of that number, which was considered as a minimum for the maintenance of the government's prestige.

This was the moment at which Roncalli appeared on the
scene. He had been put in the picture in Rome but only
on the very highest level. In Paris matters were not so
secret, as he was later to find out. The violence of the
accusations made by certain newspapers only increased the
tension in people's minds. His first contact with the
government took place within a few days of his arrival in
Paris, when both sides made their position clear at once.
The nuncio let it be clearly understood that if the accusa-

tions levelled against the bishops arose merely from the fact
that they had in a general way recognized and supported a
legal government, responsible it is true for mistakes later
on which pressure from an occupying power made it
difficult to judge, the Holy See would not agree to removing
on its own initiative one single bishop. In other words, it
would not be right to set in the place of an absolutism
which had been abolished another kind of totalitarianism
which was only too likely to divide France into two: on the
one side all the light and all the goodness, on the other all
the darkness and all the evil. It was not possible to lump
together in one and the same accusation all the deeds and
plans and all the men of Vichy; it was not possible to
compare the attitude of the bishops to that of the collaborators or the informants of the Gestapo. Above all it was
necessary to take into account the grave affront to the
Church in France as a whole, a body which had deserved
so well of its country by virtue of the noble and considerable
contribution it had made to the struggle on the side of the
Resistance. To say all that in the early months of 1945, when
the violence of the purge was still at its height and when
the Catholic press itself hesitated in the face of so much
hatred and abuse of power, required considerable courage.

Afterwards Roncalli took pleasure in looking back on
that first year of his nunciature, in the course of which he
had succeeded or rather, as he put it, 'there had been a
successful attempt to strike out the nought from the number
of 30 episcopal proscriptions.' In an interview which he
gave to *L'Époque* he voiced his feelings, as tactfully as
possible. Negotiations and discussions continued for a year,
but they were kept from the public. The first thing that
struck those who had dealings with him was his perfect
loyalty, which led them to give proof of the same quality
and to be charmed by his firm attitude, made up of clarity,
calmness and patience. As a result, not only were there no
clashes, but gradually, as time passed and minds were freed

from certain obligations imposed by the national resurgence, there grew up between the negotiators a friendship that was absolutely sincere and cordial. Several years later it became clear, looking back on that confused period, that the avoidance of several ill-judged measures had been due to the nuncio's influence. However, he had not hesitated to stand firm in several more difficult instances. On his advice, three bishops handed in their resignations. The Archbishop of Aix-en-Provence had written a pastoral letter in defence of Pétain at the very moment when the general's cause was most compromised. Naturally in the eyes of the Resistance he had gone too far, and so he resigned of his own accord.

At Christmas time in 1945 the feelings of the Church were given prominence, in another direction, by the elevation to cardinal of three French archbishops: Saliège of Toulouse, Roques of Rennes and Petit de Julleville of Rouen, who in different degrees had opposed Nazism and any form of collaboration. Roncalli had undertaken to make known in Rome the views of those who sought the highest dignity for the heroic archbishop of Toulouse and for the other two. Their nomination was so confidently awaited that when it came it only aroused a moderate enthusiasm, as though it were something quite natural. But what was left unsaid and the good that it did were apparent, in spite of some exaggerated remarks written by a layman in 1946 and published in a French Catholic review:

... We had thought that some churchmen had served Caesar before serving God. We feared that a new clericalism might be established in the very heart of the French Church. Nothing of the sort has happened. A bishop, in his pastoral letters, and in the presence of the Christian population, proclaimed himself anti-clerical and this same bishop has just been approved by the successor of Peter. It is really a cause for great rejoicing. Now there is hope for everything. Our French Church will not be the Church of the right-minded egotist, but the religion of Christ and the saints. We are proud to be Christians.

7

Cardinal Saliège's poor state of health did not permit him to go to Rome for the consistory of 1946. The Cardinal's hat was placed on his head by the nuncio at a formal ceremony, which perfectly expressed the fusion of Church and nation in recognition of an achievement about which there could be no argument.

On January 21, 1946, General de Gaulle resigned as head of the provisional government without having been able to bring the work of reorganizing France to a satisfactory conclusion. The first phase of the post-war history of France came to an abrupt end, but there was no denying that a good deal had already been accomplished. The spiritual unity of the French people had begun to be realized, or at least a return to freedom of expression and conscience had been guaranteed. Once the most dangerous source of misunderstanding had thereby been removed, reconciliation between the papacy and the Resistance had followed and from that point on was expressed in friendly relations. The nuncio realized that it was a question of reconciliation not only with the Resistance but also with the whole of France. When in July 1951 Marshal Pétain died on the island of Yeu where he had been exiled, the French cardinals could write quite calmly:

> Standing before the tomb of an old man who has known so much glory and so much humiliation, we think it right to confine ourselves to a few words of peace. Few lives have been more tragic than his. Of the military leaders who distinguished themselves during the first World War he remains in the eyes of his former comrades-in-arms one of the greatest. That brought him in 1940 the dangerous honour of being carried by public opinion, in despair, to the supreme position in the State, in spite of his eighty-four years, and of having to shoulder the gravest responsibilities in face of the invader and the occupation. Since that time his actions have been the subject of bitter discussion. He, however, has always protested the correctness of his intentions, declaring that he would accept the impartial judgement of history. It is, indeed, posterity, who will judge him after God.

The conduct of the nuncio in this sphere continued to be patient and consistent. The nomination of bishops requires on the part of the nuncio an unbroken relationship with the government. The choice made by the Vatican is naturally very often suggested by its diplomatic representative, but as the result of an agreement reached in 1921, the government is invited to say whether it has any objection of a civilian nature to the appointment. It is the nuncio's duty to raise the matter. It is not a question of a right of veto on the part of the State, and the Holy See could override the objections if it considered them unjustified. It is easy to imagine the kind of accusations the government might make: an attitude favourable to Vichy on the part of the bishop in question, a dangerous enthusiasm for the cause of free schools, or his unfriendly attitude towards the constitution or towards the party in power. The inevitably suspicious attitude of the Resistance and even the innocently biased interpretation applied by some excellent Christians in the government to the passages relating to the episcopacy in the epistles of St Peter, were also likely to give rise to awkward objections.

It was the nuncio's business to deal with all these cases. The dossiers of the Holy See in the Foreign Affairs archives which cover that period refer for the most part to just such episcopal nominations. The love Roncalli had for France is shown first and foremost in his constant efforts to give her worthy bishops. In a number of cases in which difficulties were raised, he made his reasons known to the government with incomparable tact and patience. Sometimes he would even give way before the inflexible attitude of the government, for he had the gift of being able to foresee when such an attitude was going to be insuperable. At the beginning of the third year of his *consulatus in gallia*, as he liked to call his stay in France, he wrote:

> I also have had my weeks of trouble. But now I praise God. Patience and constancy have stood me in good stead and the

nomination of the bishops, and good bishops they are, is going
through in the normal way. The announcement of four has been
made, that of three others is imminent. Four or five more are in
course of preparation. And so, in a little more than twenty-four
months the nomination of twenty new bishops has been decided.
And that is not a trifling matter for the apostolic nuncio.

At the end of the third year the Holy See had to its credit
twenty-seven episcopal nominations, 'agreed apparently
without incident, at least as far as good relations with the
authorities were concerned.'

It was whispered in the nuncio's entourage that even on
this subject Bidault had his ideal as an M.R.P. *résistant* and
was determined to uphold it. Yet nobody could afterwards
explain how it was that between the two men there were
unmistakeable signs of mutual esteem and profound respect.

It was not only the question of the bishops that needed
answering during the first year of his nunciature. A few
months after his arrival another difficult problem was
already looming on the horizon. It may surprise anyone
who is not French to find the school problem raised so
quickly, seeing that France had still to find a solution to
many more pressing questions which needed the co-
operation of all her countrymen. The fact is that the
problem of the schools, closely linked with that of religious
liberty once the Gallican regime had come to an end, had
divided Frenchmen into two camps for the past 150 years.
So many and such heated discussions had taken place
between the university, the State citadel of public education, on the one hand, and the protagonists of the private
school on the other, that once the war was over Frenchmen
had felt, after a long period of spiritual upheaval, the need
to get to grips once more with a problem the main points
of which had been thrashed out innumerable times before,
but which had come to represent a sort of family and
national heritage. Once before, after 1918, victorious

France had turned its attention frantically to the problems of scholastic reform. The Third Republic, while recognizing private education, had excluded it from any State grant on the principle of religious neutrality.

After the defeat of 1940 the obvious sympathy shown by the government to the appeals made by the religious authorities had led to a change in State policy. Any private elementary school which could show compliance with the law of 1886 and could prove its financial need became entitled to assistance from the State. This assistance was not shown in a government statement of accounts, for it was distributed, not in the name of national education, but by the Minister of the Interior under the rather vague designation of State participation in the expenses of departments and communes. It was intended that the recognition granted to the schools which educated one fifth of French children should not appear to compromise the unchanging principle of the law of the Republic, in accordance with which neither the State nor its dependent authorities were allowed to subsidize a school that was not a public one. Already in the last year of the German occupation, the difficulties of applying the law had threatened to jeopardize the very principle of official aid for free schools. Later the subsidy was made invariable, and this, with the increase in the cost of living and in the number of children of school age, eventually made that worth very little.

Some time after the liberation, on November 23, 1944, the new Minister of National Education, taking into consideration the exceptional circumstances in which classes had begun again, decided that the grant should continue to be made. On the Catholic side an increased grant was looked for, but this did not take into account the very rapid change in the psychological and political climate. It overlooked the strength of the reaction which was endeavouring to sweep away anything that owed its origin to the Vichy

Government. There began about that time a violent campaign, directed not only against the grants which were declared to be anti-republican, but also against dual education, and therefore favourable to a State monopoly of teaching. Even in western regions, where the private schools had always been in a majority, the violent tone of newspaper articles was remarkable. It was no longer just a question of rivalries, but of a judicial dispute at a national level. Supporters of anti-clericalism claimed that the private school was hindering the re-establishment of French unity, and they thereby implied that they suspected the Catholic Church of being responsible for the mentality of Vichy. Catholic reaction to this was no less lively. They accused their adversaries of intolerance, totalitarianism, and, inevitably, Nazism.

When Roncalli appeared on the scene he had hardly had time to acquaint himself with the situation. The matter had already been raised in the Consultative Assembly, and there, on March 28, a lengthy and dramatic debate ended in the suspension of the grants for private schools. In the language of those who took part in the debate, of journalists and commentators, as well, of course, as in the final vote, the nuncio could clearly read the incredible suspicion in which the Church was held by one part of the nation. Not once, either from the benches of the Right or the Left, had an attempt been made to see in the defence of private schools the expression of an absolute conviction, namely that freedom of education is an essential part of religious liberty. It had been taken to be merely a manœuvre by the Church to obtain, by external pressure, State protection for alleged expansionist ambitions. From December onwards, the campaign had been reinforced by the slogan: 'No more subsidies for religion!' Elsewhere, intemperate language and above all theological doubts abounded, even on the Catholic side. Not many were prepared to face the problem fairly and squarely. Ill-timed interruptions by unqualified

Catholics had the effect of losing the sympathy of a public opinion that was already on edge.

It did not surprise Roncalli to find himself confronted by the schools problem so soon after his arrival. In Bergamo, Sofia, Istanbul and Athens it had followed him everywhere, and he regarded the defence of scholastic freedom as one of his principal tasks and anxieties. He knew from experience how difficult it was to find technical solutions when the true cause of these differences lay in misunderstanding born of two profoundly opposed mentalities. In addition, his personal conviction was that the future of the Church was bound up with the degree of freedom she has to enlighten young people, and it was really for that reason that the problem held the attention of the new nuncio. Apart from its importance at that time, it decided the future of institutions and of society. In his activities in this direction he never lost contact with the hierarchy of the French Church, on whom he lavished help, encouragement, and advice. That was all that was needed, for the French episcopate, fully aware of the situation, managed to imbue its every thought and action with a seriousness, a dignity and a vigour which were beyond all praise. In February 1945, a collective letter from the French cardinals and bishops showed a most timely spirit of conciliation, which eventually developed into a policy to which all Catholics were able to conform.

This then was the position of the nuncio: first and foremost to show the nation that the Catholics were not reactionaries and were quite capable of facing up to such reforms, whether they be of a social, economic, family, or civic nature, as were needed. They did not wish to turn back to a past which was reputed to have been easy for them, but to go forward in a spirit of freedom and with a capacity for adaptation which sprang from the very roots of Christianity. They faced the future without fear, wishing only to safeguard the absolute freedom of the individual and to join, as Christians and Frenchmen, in the permanent reconstruction of the nation. There was to be not so much a conflict about schools, therefore, as a striving after peace and understanding. As for the problems under discussion, the nuncio's opinion was that reasons inspired by common sense were much more effective than strictly legalistic considerations. In a State which was supposed to be neutral in matters of religion, in order the better to defend the liberty of all, it needed only to be understood that the Church had set up schools, not in any spirit of opposition, but simply from a desire for liberty. It should be freely admitted that Catholic schools and State schools were only two expressions, though different certainly, of the same liberty, and not two rivals engaged in combat. Both, therefore, had the right to exist and to go on existing. The reason for the State grant was inspired by the following simple considerations: natural reasons of social justice required that State aid, supplied from a fund to which everyone, including the Catholics, had contributed, should be distributed equitably among the various institutions responsible for public education. The Catholic schools ought not to be reduced to the point where, if they were to survive, they had to fall back on the charity of the faithful. What had been achieved by Christian generosity for the schools constituted a splendid page in her history, which the whole of France must acknowledge, but it had meant a heavy sacrifice which neither could nor should be endured in the future.

The nuncio had access to another sphere in which he could act in favour of the schools: the diplomatic one. In his capacity as representative of the Vatican to the French State, he could raise the voice of prudence so that it could be heard by members of the government, and an even more prudent note among members of parliament and in the country itself. From his observation-post he followed the development of the matter unceasingly and with the closest attention. The agreements reached between the Church and Vichy had, apparently, no need to be broken. To him they represented a minimum of gratitude in recognition of the Church's undeniable achievements in the educational field. As for the series of governments which followed each other after the liberation, and which proclaimed their neutrality in a loud voice, as though to counterbalance Vichy's sympathy towards religious claims, it was only necessary to make them understand that neutrality could not be a negative attitude but that it required the explicit recognition and defence of a whole group of values, values which had rallied Frenchmen of widely different outlook to the common struggle of the Resistance.

The negative vote of March 1945 had been the solitary achievement of the Consultative Assembly. Parliaments formed after the passing of the new constitution in October 1946 were called upon to consider the question at frequent intervals. An improvement in the psychological climate removed some of the obstacles which stood in the way of agreement. Roncalli liked to think that it was not so much necessary to seek to convince one's adversaries as to live according to the Gospel in real and positive friendship with everyone, with an integrity which would show one as an ally and not as a conspirator. Nevertheless the battle was not won without some hard moments. In August 1951, the Bishop of Bergamo was mildly astonished to find that Roncalli, contrary to his usual practice, had put off his holidays. The nuncio replied to him on September 6:

> These good people are engaged in discussing a question which is of capital importance to the interests of the Church in France. How could I leave without seeing it through? At the moment I think I can almost see the end. Last evening they were still very undecided and only one step removed from a crisis. What a pity! In a democracy it is the votes which count. Half of them plus one is enough. Find these votes and the victory of a good cause is assured.

Who would have thought that the aged Herriot would be reduced, at that time of all times, to advising moderation and that, as President of the National Assembly, he would endeavour to pour oil on troubled waters? The nuncio believed, and said as much, that Catholics owed to the Radical leader a part of what they had been able to obtain from this dramatic struggle in parliament. It did not, in fact, amount to very much. The general situation was not likely to be improved much by a concession to the private schools of a modest annual subsidy of 3000 francs for each pupil, the whole of which was earmarked for an increase in pay for the teachers. Nevertheless it was the first step towards educational justice. The nuncio expressed the wish to make known to all those who had had a part in the vote the satisfaction that was felt as the result of an enterprise which marked a memorable date in the religious history of the French nation. In words which bore witness to a sensitive appreciation of their language, and with a friendliness which so well concealed the prudence of the diplomat, he made them aware of the extent to which the struggle that had taken place in France over freedom of education had occupied his attention.

Shortly afterwards at Castelgandolfo, Pius XII had the intricacies of this difficult issue described to him by Frenchmen in private audience.

Chapter Ten

THE CHURCH OF FRANCE

A PAPAL NUNCIO is not only the Holy See's representative *vis-à-vis* the government of a country; he has, in addition, a diplomatic task to perform in relation to the Church of the country to which he is sent. This aspect of his mission also has its difficulties. Common law does not confer upon him any powers of jurisdiction over the local Church and such powers as are granted to him are limited, for they must not in any way restrict that Church's right to self-government, and the independence of the bishops, in relation to the nuncio, is strictly guaranteed. Officially, the rôle of the nuncio is that of informant to the Sovereign Pontiff who alone is competent to make decisions in matters thus brought to his notice. In practice, however, such decisions are very often suggested by the nuncio, so that in fact his functions are considerably more important than those conferred on him by canon law.

The manner in which a nuncio is welcomed by the Church varies from country to country. The very nature of his mission, that of informant, is apt to inspire a certain wariness; in some countries ecclesiastical circles may be led to confuse the duties of the nuncio with those of a kind of inspector. If the nuncio's position is often a delicate one, this is particularly so in France, where special importance attaches to considerations of a legal and even a sentimental nature. Certainly, the Church of France can no longer be accused of Gallicanism; in her relations with the Holy See she no longer manifests a spirit of independence, but she does retain a certain sensitivity. Rome must, therefore, in both word and gesture, proceed with delicacy, showing respect for a religious past in which there has been much suffering and taking account of ancient traditions which are vigorously upheld and which still exert a subconscious influence on the character of the nation, although they may have disappeared from everyday life.

The Gallican doctrine has always regarded the nuncio as an ambassador, no more no less, and each government in turn through the ages has seen to it that he never performed any act of jurisdiction. In actual fact, however, since their return to France in 1921 the nuncios have enlarged the scope of their diplomatic activities, by taking an increasing interest in problems directly affecting the French Church. In doing this they might have been invoking one of Pope Leo XIII's principles. 'The task and the duties of a legate are to interpret the wishes of the Pontiff who has sent him.' It became ever more necessary to do this, for French Catholicism, imbued with a certain particularism—the very expression, 'l'Eglise de France', bears it out—did not possess a single body to represent the authority of its bishops and archbishops; consequently the Church was unable to approach the Holy See through the medium of a representative authorized to speak on behalf of all the dioceses. The nuncio was therefore eventually invested by the Holy See with duties which were strictly outside the scope of his normal activities. It would certainly be an exaggeration to say that this move made the French ecclesiastical hierarchy uneasy. Yet there remained, in this connexion, a certain sensitiveness, although this did not prevent the observance of a perfect courtesy, even in the heat of discussion.

An example of this was seen after Roncalli's departure from Paris when the new nuncio, Marella, had to take up a definite position on the question of the worker-priests. The summoning of the episcopate to Toulouse, Lyon and

Paris, without previous notice being given to the cardinals of the subjects to be discussed, aroused strong feelings in the press, and calm was only restored when *La Croix* intervened to throw some light on the procedure that had been adopted.

Roncalli's lengthy sojourn in the East, where secular susceptibilities are so easily offended, had prepared him for his new duties, so that throughout his nunciature in France he did not once encounter any difficulties of this nature. His attitude towards French Catholicism was always one of most sincere respect, and only rarely did he have any reservations to make. A French intellectual once told us that in his opinion Roncalli had only loved in France the things which reminded him of the deeply religious spirit of his native Bergamo. That judgement is not the whole truth; it may be, for example, that the Vendée district of France was the region with which he felt himself most in harmony, but he was also able to admire and to love the more varied and more turbulent French Catholicism which he encountered every day. He was quick to see in France a land of rebirth and of bold experiment in the field of apostleship, and he was aware that the Church of France was undergoing a unique experience and making the noblest and most courageous efforts to penetrate into a godless society. His personal experience and, above all, his knowledge of history certainly led him, on occasions, to protest against activities which bore obvious signs of being hastily conceived, but it was not in his nature to be mistrustful. His early days in the priesthood had been spent in an atmosphere of such courageous apostolic experiment that he looked with an open mind on almost any attempt to plough new furrows in the field of the Church's thousand years of experience. He realized that the restless effervescence which was characteristic of Catholic life was a natural effect of the terrible upheaval of the war years. A country which was conscious of being reborn and which was moving towards a radical readjustment of its political, social and cultural heritage, needed to be understood in its enthusiasms, its hesitations, and even in its deviations from the accepted path. He was well aware of the characteristic French ability to weather crises with a sort of exasperation. History, however, had taught him that, more often than not, out of this melting-pot there might emerge great institutions such as might provide a stimulus to the Church throughout the world. A saying of Cardinal Pie, Dupanloup's opponent, interpreted exactly, in his opinion, the rôle of France in the Catholic world: 'Italy is St Peter; France is St Paul.' A slightly rhetorical over-simplification, perhaps, but it suggests the reasons for his sympathy and his admiration.

One thing impressed him greatly; that was the great variety of ways in which French Catholicism manifested itself. Everywhere within this nation which was—and which made a point of showing itself to be—dechristianized, Catholicism maintained religious centres whose supporters made up in liveliness and vitality what they lacked in numbers. During Lenten periods after the war, he was positively fascinated by the scene in Notre Dame where men and young people would flock to listen to the sermons of Fr Riquet on such stirring themes of social rebirth as 'Christians and Money', or 'Christians and the Ruins'. Fr Riquet told him that he was constantly having to deal with the objections of those of his audience, and they were many, who were convinced that they were good Christians but who were now discovering to their amazement the inadequacy of their Christianity. This priest's contacts with extremist elements had led to his being denounced in high places, but the nuncio, who understood him well, had no difficulty in defending him.

St Pierre de Chaillot, one of the most beautiful churches in Paris, situated near the nuncio's residence, frequently offered him examples of religious fervour such as one would never have expected in surroundings so typically Parisian. He was careful not to draw from this too optimistic a conclusion; it was of course easy for him to realize the very small percentage of the population that was represented by these crowds of the faithful, for he always had in mind the huge churches of his native Bergamo, vibrating with the impressive sound of countless voices raised in prayer. However, he liked to see in such scenes encouraging signs of a faith which could not be extinguished.

The positive forces of Christianity seemed to him more effective than they had ever been. Movements devoted to thought and study included an intellectual élite which commanded the respect of the whole nation and which professed its faith with pride and courage. In 1947, on mid-Lent Thursday, he was present when Claudel was received into the French Academy by Mauriac, and thus heard two speeches impregnated with Catholic ascetism, philosophy, history and life. Claudel began by recalling the stigma of St Francis and concluded his speech with a reference to the struggle between supernatural grace and nature, as dealt with in *The Imitation of Christ*. The nuncio could not help reflecting that ten years before no one would have dared to utter the name of Christ in the academy.

There were other manifestations which, in his eyes, were more significant than these academic spectacles. He was well aware of the immensity of the work still to be done and of the urgent need for reforms. At a time when world problems were cropping up in such complex forms, and when men, pressed for time, were inclined to be satisfied with over-simplified solutions, precision of thought was no obstacle, but rather a precious guarantee. Of course this did not prevent the nuncio from standing out against the tendency to call profound what was, in fact, mere brilliance of expression; nor did he appreciate the craze for writing which sometimes put before the public ideas which were

out of date, if not actually discredited, and which only
ignorance could have welcomed as new. Confronted with
innumerable publications which should at least have been
subjected to some form of censorship, he would say,
jokingly: 'No priest is happy until he has set the printing
presses groaning with the printing of a book of his own
creation.' He would sometimes, in this connexion, compare
French priests with Italian priests who were afflicted with
an excessive timidity when it came to publication.

It distressed him to realize that the daily routine and
endless interviews did not leave him free to pay closer
attention to other significant religious manifestations. He
therefore turned to certain knowledgeable men. Fr Gabel,
the editor of *La Croix*, often came to see him and helped
him to understand theological 'problem points'—though
the nuncio did not care much for this expression. A young
priest from Bergamo, a student of ethnology at the Sor-
bonne, found himself entrusted, one day, with the task of
reading the university lectures of Fr Teilhard de Chardin.
The most extravagant rumours were circulating at the time
regarding the well-known Jesuit; in particular his university
teaching was criticized as being too daring. It was, however,
difficult to confirm these criticisms, for there was a lack of
written matter and judgement could not be based on what
he had said. Roncalli knew, among other things, that those
who stood up for the priest included Cardinal Saliège, and
that would be enough to prevent his attaching too much
importance to the insinuations which were being made, and
to make him accept the authority of a man who must be
better informed than himself.

He made frequent contact with thinkers and scientists.
Everyone of distinction was invited to the nuncio's residence, but his preference was not so much for official
receptions as for the simpler and more intimate atmosphere
of a lunch or dinner, at which talk flowed smoothly
between men in responsible positions. He had a preference

for university men. University rectors and heads of Catholic institutes were frequently guests at his table, where they mingled with the most celebrated leaders of religious and secular learning and of both classical and scientific studies. His vast erudition, his expert knowledge of ecclesiastical history, his skill in steering the conversation, and his charm, turned those meals into 'the most delightful academic sessions', in the words of one who attended regularly, Professor Le Bras. For the nuncio they also provided the opportunity of listening to the most highly qualified opinions and judgements concerning the trends of modern thought flowing through France.

There was another personality who helped him to a full appreciation of the French mind, a great friend, Mgr Adriano Bernareggi. He was well acquainted with the latest trends, possessing—either by virtue of a natural urge or for the benefit of his apostolic mission—an unflagging appetite for knowledge, and he followed very closely the outpourings of French religious scholarship, finding in it a sensitivity not unlike his own and a courageous broadmindedness such as would enable him to hold his own in the world of Italian intellectuals entrusted to his pastoral care. In this way, there grew up between Paris and Bergamo a regular exchange of impressions, information, reviews and books, the cost of which was usually borne by the nuncio. A fraternal, intellectual conversation began which, although it was more intense during Roncalli's summer holidays, was sustained all the time on a note of intimate warmth by means of regular correspondence. Two characters, fundamentally different, shared the same feelings; what the nuncio knew from his practical experience of men was suggested to the bishop by his reading. Confronted with examples of thought or action which called for certain protests, both men showed the same spirit of broadminded tolerance, although from different motives: in the nuncio's case it arose from a natural kindness and an inexhaustible patience, while the bishop possessed an astonishing gift of sympathy with the difficulties and spiritual travail of others, feeling them as if they were his own.

Roncalli had very much at heart the question of purity of doctrine. He was well aware of certain changes. The theological sciences were undergoing a thorough revision; biblical studies were opening up new horizons which only a few years ago would have made the imagination reel; a more complete knowledge of patristics was restoring to ancient Christian ideas an unexpected depth of meaning; and the liturgy itself was endeavouring, through a renewed eloquence, to get a hearing for its mystical, symbolical language, in order to reach more clearly and with a greater power of persuasion the ears and the hearts of the present-day faithful.

Generally speaking, all this won his admiration. But he thought that doctrine should not advance violently, but should be content to make gradual progress, having particular regard for the feelings of the older generation who would be slow to abandon the atmosphere of personal devotion in which they had been brought up. It should be progress made by the Church as a whole, guided by tradition and by advice from the hierarchy, which was better fitted, by reason of its elevated position, to gauge the strength of any reaction. Above all, such progress would have to be supported by really serious study. Sometimes, the nuncio noticed too much lightheartedness, the lack of a firm basis, a preference for solutions that were attractive simply because they were more acceptable to lazy minds. As usual, he had his own comment to make. This is what he wrote in a letter: 'When people go too far, a little ear-tweaking must be applied.'

Following his natural bent, he took a great interest in new pastoral experiments. In this respect also France was passing through a period of deep crisis and was, in fact, becoming the testing-ground for revolutionary methods which, although they had eventually to be dropped, left a sharper realization throughout the Church of the urgency of missionary problems and indicated forms of apostolic action calling for greater courage. The great Archbishop of Paris, Cardinal Suhard, very much distressed by a situation on which he had meditated for a long time, was now in the act of drawing up plans for missionary activity which was to give fresh impetus to the whole of France. After devoting three whole nights to the study of a memorandum which was later published under the title *France, pays de mission*, in which two of his priests brought to his notice, with great lucidity, the wretched state of Christianity among the members of the French proletariat, he entrusted the evangelization of the working-class masses to a handful of priests, in whom he placed the utmost confidence, granting them unprecedented privileges and powers, and asking in exchange only complete obedience coupled with absolute loyalty. This was the beginning of the *Mission de Paris*.

This book by Godin and Daniel, together with *Problèmes missionnaires de la France rurale* by F. Boulard and *La Paroisse, communauté missionnaire* by G. Michonneau, were among those sent to Bergamo from Paris. The step taken by Cardinal Suhard could not fail to arouse in the nuncio the greatest interest and sympathy. These two men, in any case, seemed to have been made to understand each other: of about the same age, they had both endured in silence periods of great trial and suffering and were ever ready to welcome and to sympathize; they refused to judge by the superficial appearance of things but were always eagerly seeking to find the truth in new ideas; they were both equally opposed to administrative complications and were animated by the same paternal affection. The cardinal was grateful to Roncalli for the firmness with which he had supported the French episcopacy; on his side, the nuncio admired the apostolic zeal, the saintliness and the courage of the Archbishop of Paris. Besides, the latter still needed help. His numerous undertakings were not understood by everybody, nor were they always appreciated as they should have been. The *Mission de Paris*, born of a realization that the parish by itself was not enough, and breaking away from traditional methods, gave many people, clergy as well as faithful, the impression that a new type of Church was being set up, exclusively for humble folk, for the working classes, and scorning that other Church, the Church of the middle classes and well-to-do conservatives.

The new communities to which the mission gave rise drew attention to themselves, and their new methods of apostolic action roused astonishment, causing friction, lack of understanding and even suspicion. The cardinal, indifferent to his own fate, watched these experiments with a passionate interest, guiding, encouraging, and protecting. When he found they were being attacked, he was worried and asked for help, making himself personally responsible for their actions. He invoked, in defence of them, not their present achievement, but the services they would render in the future, the seed they were sowing in the field of the apostolate, and even the concern which they were causing. No argument could be stronger in the eyes of the nuncio, who was himself equally convinced of the need, first of all, to sow the seed. That was why he was quite prepared not to raise objections, appreciating the generosity of heart with which the cardinal was allowing the tares to grow alongside the wheat, and convinced, in his own mind, that it was worth while showing a little tolerance in order to avoid discouraging people of goodwill and running the risk of stifling part of the seed. But the difficulties were only beginning. The *Mission de Paris* was already turning towards more ambitious programmes of drawing closer to the working classes, which were soon to give rise to the worker-

priest movement. The idea of the extra-parochial community was giving way to that of a campaign in the
factories.

In 1946 there were not more than half-a-dozen worker-
priests in Paris, and a few more were working in Lyons. A
team was being assembled in Limoges and others were soon
to be formed in Montceau-les-Mines, Bordeaux, Toulouse,
Saint-Étienne, Nice, Le Havre, in the northern region, in
the Lorraine basin, on the dam-building sites in the Alps
and elsewhere. The number of priests, about fifty in all,
and most of them secular, had increased by 1951 to about
one hundred. The problems raised by this new form of
apostolate caught the Church unawares. In order to
penetrate deeply into the heart of the dechristianized
working classes these noble priests were ready to submit to
becoming 'naturalized' workers; this meant emerging from
the ecclesiastical framework within which a priest's life
normally develops. They believed that they would be
accepted by the workers—an essential condition of their
being able to carry out a really efficient apostolate—only if
they abandoned all priestly attitudes, joining in the everyday life of the worker and being therefore bound by his
social, political and trade union obligations. Exhaustion
after a long day's work, living together in furnished
apartments, in short this whole new way of life, soon
showed up the dangers of casting off all semblance of the
priestly calling—or at least of spiritual under-nourishment
which could not fail in the long run to be fatal. Membership
of unions based on Communist Party ideals and system-
atically opposed to the Church, raised many doubts
concerning the presence of members of the clergy and their
witness, in spite of endless precautions.

This situation made it necessary to recruit only exceptional individuals and to establish a seminary that would
offer a completely new form of training designed to supply
theological and devotional nourishment suitable to the

requirements of an apostolate in daily contact with new and unfamiliar realities. The fact that in France they had the courage to envisage such a programme proves the existence in that country of a Christian vitality which very few nations could claim to possess. It was, however, such a bold programme that it did not receive the approval of all the bishops. Roncalli watched with sympathy and confidence the beginnings of this new undertaking, but the form taken by this missionary project did not really fit in with his own predilections, which lay more in the direction of a regular and disciplined personal life, based on the practice of piety and following the liturgy of the Church, and of a continual manifestation of the supernatural. This other way of life, outside all the wise defences and safeguards of the ecclesiastical state, exposed to all the miasmas of a corrupt world, called for a degree of resistance that was very difficult to acquire. He thought that even in the most favourable cases results would not be achieved without a wear and tear of the spirit, likely to compromise seriously the enthusiasm for, and even the possibility of carrying out, an effective missionary activity. A few regrettable cases did not, however, unduly dismay him; for he knew that some went into the movement as they would into a kind of Foreign Legion, in order to avoid the control of their bishops, and that a few—very few, it is true—finished up by deserting and by renouncing their priestly ideals. A few weak characters always manage to penetrate into movements started up by generous spirits.

For Roncalli the chief problem was to find out whether the experiment had any real chance of success and whether it ought to be allowed to spread, or whether, on the contrary, it would not be necessary to think of an absolutely new method, designed to contain the movement within well-defined limits. The Church could adopt one of three attitudes: she could disapprove, approve, or keep close watch without committing herself. For as long as he was

nuncio in Paris he favoured the third solution. Such
behaviour needed defending, especially against those who
were allergic to changes of any kind. Responsible persons
who, in the years to come, had to go to the Vatican to deal
with matters connected with the worker-priests invariably
found the atmosphere there disturbed by protests, hostile
reports and denunciations emanating from inside France.
Roncalli preferred to wait. It was one of his principles that
'without a touch of sanctified madness, the Church cannot
grow.' Besides, the movement was trying to put into
practice the central master plan of Cardinal Suhard's life.
A man of such high spiritual calibre should at least be
given the chance to try out a system without interference.
The last of the cardinal's admirable pastoral letters, *The
Priest in the City*, which he completed just before his death
on May 30, 1949, constituted for his diocese a sort of last
will and testament in which he asked that his work should
be regarded with understanding and patience. The last
churchman to visit him on his deathbed was the nuncio
himself, to whom he entrusted a message for the Pope,
which was a profession of love and fidelity, as well as a plea
to be understood.

Unfortunately, the movement was later to cause the
nuncio more serious worry. Towards the end of 1947 a
'Union of Progressive Christians' had been founded which,
after the Resistance front had broken down and the
Communists had been thrown back into opposition,
declared its intention not only of refusing to support any
anti-Communist campaign, but of marching alongside the
Communist Party, without being affiliated to it, in order to
encourage the chances of a victory which alone could
ensure social progress. The nuncio knew that they were in
fact receiving help from the Cominform and obtaining
funds from the same source as the Communists. On the
dissolution of this union, progressive action was continued
by the *Jeunesse de l'Eglise* movement, whose mouthpiece,

Fr Montuclard, revealed such dubious theological trends that his book was later condemned by the Holy Office. Furthermore, certain worker-priests thought they could see in the ideas of Christian progressives the theory for which they were still looking and which justified their actions and the way they were developing their priestly rôle. They thought that they could fight the same battle as Communism, uniting their efforts with those of the Communists, their decision being based on the assumption that there was no connexion between politics and the Church. They did not hesitate to identify themselves with the struggles of the Party, even when these were directed against workers' movements which were Catholic-inspired. According to them, ecclesiastical opinion had to make itself heard on the political and social level, and no longer in the fields of doctrine and evangelization, where hitherto only a religion adapted to middle-class thought and feeling had found expression. This indicated a permeation of Marxist principles which could no longer be tolerated. It was obvious that something would have to be done, but the question was what form it should take. Would not total suppression of the movement, as demanded by certain French circles, threaten to stifle not only the unhealthy offshoots, but also the parent branch which appeared to contain life-giving sap? Were the deviations really a symptom of trouble at the root of the movement, or were they merely the consequence of inexperience or a lack of perspicacity on the part of the leaders? Roncalli thought it would be better to wait a little longer and set up some form of supervision, but at the same time avoid striking at the inspiring principles which formed the basis of the working-class apostolate.

In the meantime, however, distrust and suspicion in Rome had become more pronounced, especially in the offices in charge of discipline and the teaching of the clergy. In Rome everyone agreed that French innovations in this missionary field were a proof of clear thinking and of vigorous youth, but it was also felt that the doctrinal attitude of French Catholics could not fail to promote a gradual slipping towards compromise and a serious deviation from apostolic methods. It was not long before warning signs began to appear. First of all, the recruiting of worker-priests was forbidden; the provisional statute granted by the Holy See to Cardinal Suhard, two days before his death, for the purpose of building the *Mission de France* seminary, was not enforced until much later and, after a three-year trial, was not renewed. Feltin, Cardinal Suhard's successor, who had already encouraged the few worker-priests in his archidiocese of Bordeaux in accordance with Roncalli's ideas, was to further Cardinal Suhard's ideals at the same time tempering them with a greater measure of prudence and discipline. Every effort was made by the French episcopate to prevent a catastrophe. The nunciature let it be clearly understood that the movement was undergoing a final scrutiny and that the position was extremely delicate. As an experiment, changes were made on the staff of the more important bodies; in particular, the missionary apostolate was placed under the more direct control of an episcopal committee. Did Roncalli still believe in the possibility of salvation *in extremis*?

On August 24, 1953, the nunciature published the Vatican decision to close the *Mission de France* seminary provisionally, and, in September, informed the bishops that the worker-priests experiment was about to come to an end. Roncalli had already left Paris several months before and the new nuncio had received very strict orders.

The task of a nuncio, in relation to the Church of the country to which he is sent, cannot be accomplished if he is content to remain in the capital. The richness of religious life and activities, the variety of spiritual conditions, can only be properly appreciated if direct contact with all the provincial regions is maintained. Roncalli lost no time in making a pilgrimage through the whole of France. The desire to get to know, and to form a personal opinion about, things and people provided the chief motive of his numerous journeys. He also frankly admitted that he was animated by a spirit of adventure; discovering new things was, for him, an ever-fresh source of joy. Then, too, in France, his journeys provided him with almost the only opportunity to exercise in some measure that pastoral activity which was still the dream of his life. During the great liturgical ceremonies—now that he was no longer a diocesan bishop —his thoughts would dwell, in spite of himself, on his cathedral at Istanbul and, even more often, on the cathedral at Bergamo, the scene of his early years in the priesthood. He admitted as much, with apologies, to the Bishop of Bergamo: 'I notice that I too am getting very old, for I recall more readily the events of my early youth that those of my maturity.'

The French episcopal secretariat has managed to draw up an almost complete schedule of the visits paid by Roncalli during his eight years as nuncio. Most of the French dioceses were visited by him, some of them more than once. His journeys began towards the end of March 1945.

1945:

Le Mans:	Traditional Palm Sunday ceremony.
Toulouse:	Social week.
Besançon:	Feast of the Immaculate Conception; also at Luxeuil and Faverney.
Le Puy:	Pilgrimage of repatriated prisoners of war.
Orléans:	Celebrations in honour of St Joan of Arc: translation of the relics of St Benedict to Fleury-sur-Loire.
Tours:	Informing Canon Robin of his nomination to the bishopric of Blois.
Clermont:	Visit to Mgr Piguet upon his return from deportation.

1946:
    Angers: Unity Congress.
    Quimper: Funeral of Mgr Duparc.
    Valence: Blessing of the church of St Theresa.
    Clermont: Feast of Notre-Dame-du-Port.
    Marseille: Feast of the Sacred Heart.
    Viviers: Crowning of Notre-Dame-de-la-Mure, pil-
                 grimage to La Louvesc; opening of the canal
                 and dam at Bollène.
    Bourges: Feast of St Ursin.
    Rennes: Consecration of Mgr Perrin (Bishop of Arras)
                 and of Mgr Coupel (Bishop of Saint-Brieuc).
    Toulouse: Celebrations in honour of Cardinal Saliège.
    Further visits to Bordeaux, Moulins, Coutances, Vézelay,
    etc.

1949:
    Nancy: Eucharistic Congress.
    Luçon: Festival of the Sea, at Sables d'Olonne and
                 visit to the seminary at Les Herbiers.
    Autun: Raising of the Saint-Lazare cathedral to the
                 rank of a basilica.
    Belley: Celebrations in honour of St Jean-Marie
                 Vianney, at Ars.
    Versailles: Vocations congress.
    Rheims: Feast of St Rémy.
    Amiens: Ecclesiastical congress.
    Soissons: Eighth centenary of the consecration of the
                 cathedral.
    Vannes: Local processions in honour of St Anne.
    Rouen: Thirteenth centenary of the Saint-Wandrille
                 Abbey.
    Le Mans: Feast of St Julian.

The journeys usually took place, by car, in the summer
and always coincided with some religious occasion which

was peculiar to France: Eucharistic or Marian congresses (at Nancy in 1949, at Saint-Claude and Rennes in 1950, at Nîmes in 1951); 'social weeks' (at Toulouse in 1945, at Nantes in 1950, at Montpellier in 1951, at Dijon in 1952); celebrations in honour of bishops, centenary celebrations (nineteenth centenary of the evangelization of the Provence region at Aix; fourteenth centenary of St Colomban at Luxeuil; sixth centenary of the death of Pope Clement VI at Le Puy and at Toul; ninth centenary of the church of La Trinité at Vendôme; fiftieth anniversary of the 'Three Ave Maria Society' at Blois; third centenary of the birth of St Jean-Baptiste de la Salle at Reims; centenary of the consecration of Algeria to the Sacred Heart; fifth centenary of the birth of Leonardo da Vinci at Amboise). Lourdes was the object of a yearly pilgrimage. His tender devotion led him to believe that providence had assigned to France the task of making known to the entire world, through Lourdes, the Immaculate Virgin and her graces.

These journeys were a source of perpetual joy to the nuncio. He would prepare for them in the winter, when his normal activities kept him in Paris. The Pope's representative arouses the interest of the crowds in France much more than in Italy. Frequently, even in Communist districts, he would come across public squares and churches where tens of thousands of people were waiting to welcome him with genuine enthusiasm. The lively accounts of his journeys in letters to friends are overflowing with emotion and optimism. He felt that he was in touch with the deeply religious heart of France which was putting up a desperate resistance in all the spiritual crises and against the erosion caused by secularization. On June 26, 1948, he wrote:

> Much good has been done in France. After a spell in Paris, lasting more than six months, I have made two or three different trips. A month ago I went to Provence. At Les Saintes-Maries I blessed the sea; there were a good 50,000 people present. At the ancient city of Arles I was able to visit the

magnificent ruins alone. On the other hand, the St Trophime cathedral where I said Low Mass was filled to overflowing; the civic authorities were there in full force. Afterwards, I was invited to the town hall where the entire town council gave me a warm welcome.* In Marseille, on the evening of the day on which the new archbishop was nominated—before that he had been bishop—a huge crowd was gathered in the vast cathedral; in the afternoon, the nuncio had been received at the prefecture. Twenty days later I was in Brittany. At Nantes, the evening I arrived, a repetition of Marseille in the cathedral; the next day, at the Pontchâteau Calvary, in honour of St Louis-Marie Grignion de Montfort, nearly two hundred thousand of the faithful were assembled in the open air, overflowing with religious fervour. Just the same as in Bergamo, on certain occasions.

Nineteen-fifty was the year of his journey to Africa. Invited by Leynaud to celebrate the centenary of the consecration of Algeria to the Sacred Heart, and by the Bishop of Constantine to commemorate the fiftieth anniversary of the consecration of the Basilica of St Augustine at Hippo, the nuncio wanted to take his time in getting to know Algeria and the religious situation there. He therefore set out to travel all over the country. By reference to the *Semaine Religieuse* of Algiers, it is possible to retrace, step by step, this long journey which lasted about forty days. But the best account is to be found in the letter he wrote on May 1, 1950:

As for me, thanks partly to my temperament and partly to being accustomed to self-discipline, which has been strengthened, these days, by age and experience, I am able to remain calm in the midst of storms and also physically fit.

Well, there you have it. In thirty-eight days of travel, I have done 10,000 km. by car, following in the tracks of the Arab invasion, from Tunisia, right through Algeria and Morocco, as far as the Pillars of Hercules, then into Spain and from there to Poitiers where Charles Martel stopped the invaders. I had to make—especially in Algeria and in Tunisia—about fifty un-

---

* The council was almost exclusively composed of Communists.

rehearsed speeches or short addresses. Not once was I unwell, except for a cold which I caught visiting the Escurial. A day of rest and fasting at the nuncio's residence in Madrid put me on my feet again.

After this trip, the chauffeur who had driven him everywhere without a hitch, found that, like Scipio of old, he had earned the title of 'African'. Wherever he went, the graciousness and friendliness of the nuncio became proverbial. He himself enjoyed the receptions all the more when they were simple and spontaneous. He could appreciate the real meaning behind a little girl's greeting when she presented him with a bunch of flowers, just as well as he appreciated the noise of bugles and drums; he knew that this enthusiasm would, later on, during the religious ceremony, be transformed into an intense feeling of faith. He gave the impression of never being in a hurry and of always having time to spare. Genuine admiration found expression in a series of short addresses, in which he apologized for not knowing enough French to be able to express his feelings fully.

In churches, in historic abbeys and in convents, he was attracted by the many artistic and historical treasures; his fund of knowledge would then bring to mind a thousand historical associations which surprised and charmed those round him. Shown a painting on leather of the Holy Face, kept in the Abbey of Corbie, he revealed a deep knowledge of relics brought back from the East—the painting came from Constantinople—at the time of the Fourth Crusade, and he added, smilingly, that crusaders, like all conquerors, left behind them in the East quite a reputation as robbers.

Replying once to the after-dinner speeches of the archbishop and the Minister of Justice at a Dagermann reception held in Rheims, he spoke of the delight which he had experienced in seeing the artistic treasures of that city. He added that he would not even attempt to praise the cathedral, for its beauty was above mere words to describe.

But in addition to the cathedral, Rheims had the glory of possessing another artistic jewel, the basilica of Saint Remi. And in this connexion the nuncio gave proof of a degree of erudition at which his audience could not but marvel: he spoke of Robert de Lenoncourt who restored the porch of the side entrance, of the statues of the peers which adorn the tomb of the saint, of the chandelier with its ninety-six lamps, a reminder of the years lived by Saint Remi and a symbol of the perpetual youth of the Church.

He was constantly trying to express his feeling of confidence, his faith in the eternal vitality of the Church and, at the same time, in its glorious tradition. His fund of personal recollections was immense. Forty years in the priesthood, from the time of his first meetings with the ecclesiastics and prelates of France, at Radini's house in Rome, at Bergamo and elsewhere had enriched his memory with innumerable incidents which he knew well how to recall at the appropriate moment. At Annecy he announced that it was not his first visit to the town: he was, in fact, there in 1911 as secretary to the Bishop of Bergamo, at the translation of the relics of St Francis de Sales and St Jeanne de Chantal. The bishops went by car, while he followed along the dusty road on foot, in the wake of the endless procession. He reminded his audience that in 1905, a few months after being present in Rome at the beatification of St John Vianney, he had already been to Ars where, as a young unknown priest, he bowed before the glorious relic of the humble parish priest, who in his opinion furnished the finest possible example of the priestly life. As for St Martin of Tours, he declared that he had known and loved him ever since he was a child. The son of simple peasant folk, he grew up in a little village near Bergamo in whose church the apostle of the Gauls is venerated. Ever since those days, he had always carried in his heart the vision of Jesus who appeared to St Martin disguised as a poor man.

His contacts with ordinary people were frequent. He liked talking with them, listening to them, blessing them. While on a visit to Amiens, where he was accompanied by Mgr Guillois, who had previously been his secretary at Istanbul, he suddenly left the officials by whom he was surrounded and went over to a group of peasants standing in a nearby yard. Joining in their conversation, he said: 'You are country people, aren't you? I, too, was brought up in the country, you know . . .' In seminaries or in episcopal residences he showed himself no less cordial, however serious the problems to be dealt with and however great the study he was obliged to devote to getting acquainted with those who belonged to the hierarchy or who might do so later. The bishops and clergy of France had won a place in his heart and they showed him a respect and an affection which amazed and, at the same time, moved him intensely.

Returning to Paris after his journeys, his heart would be filled with joy. He was happy at the thought of having taken to far-off places proof of the kindness and goodwill of the Holy Father, whose ardent desires he had also made known. He had been present, too, at many demonstrations of faith, had spread serenity and courage wherever he went, and had made new friends. Once again, he had sown the seed, discreetly and with understanding. He only expected modest results but with these he was prepared to be satisfied. Not far from Toul, in Lorraine, he had noticed the tomb, built in the Renaissance style, of a distinguished bishop who lived at the beginning of the sixteenth century, Hugues des Hazards. The stone bore the inscription: *Nasci, Laborare, Mori*, followed by other words, forming a sort of maxim: *Moderata durant*. This was also his own motto. In Paris he resumed his secluded life. He even had to give up the short walks which for some years had been a daily habit of his. Instructions had reached him from Rome, giving him to understand that the Pope wished for his regular presence at the nuncio's residence. The fact was that Pope Pius XII noticed everything and preferred that things should be done in the same way as when he himself was nuncio in Berlin, where his sole recreation was a long ride on horseback on Saturday afternoons.

Chapter Eleven

THE LAND OF ST MARK

I T was many years since Pius XII had created a cardinal.
During the summer holidays of 1952 which Roncalli
spent at Bergamo, this formed one of the topics of conversation raised by his friends to sound his feelings on the subject
and also to express discreetly their own wishes. The nuncio
faced up to the question.

> It is the customary fate of nuncios to France, provided nothing
> goes wrong. To me it would come as a complete upheaval. At
> the moment there are no clouds on the horizon. If one should
> appear, I am convinced that it would leave my little bark
> floating peacefully on the Seine. I would like to give ten years to
> France also, that is to say the same length of time that I gave to
> Bulgaria and to Turkey. I would then have reached the age of
> 74, the same age at which Mgr Furietti, well known for his
> archaeological studies, and later as secretary of the council, was
> made cardinal by Clement XIII in 1759.

He had returned to Paris after a lengthy tour: Milan (two
days), Luino, Sesto Calende, Venegono, Novara, Alexan-
dria, Savona, Bordighera, Bussana, Nice and the Alpes-
Maritimes, Digne and Gap, Thorenc, Antibes, Cannes and
Grasse, Fréjus, Aix, Avignon, Viviers, a trip up the Rhône
for the opening of the Donzère-Mondragon canals, and
finally Paris. There, after a brief pause at Meaux to take
part in the celebrations in honour of Bossuet, the round of
audiences and the long evenings filled with work had begun
again.

On resuming his post, he had found nothing new awaiting him except an invitation to be passed on to one or two prelates not to be in any hurry over their *ad limina* visits. He felt that this indicated something unusual but was not sure what. He was at the time reading *L'âme embrassé du Saint Bernard* by Canon Despinay, and he was preparing his report to send to Milan, for the inquiry into the virtues of Cardinal Ferrari. November had not run its course when Mgr Martini informed him that his name was on the list of new cardinals. He had learnt long ago to receive with humility even satisfactions such as this. But his joy was short lived. Within a few hours came the news that his sister Ancilla was seriously ill, afflicted with a disease which gave little or no hope of recovery, a complaint of the stomach. This sister was the favourite of the whole family, and he was greatly distressed. He foresaw that promotion and the celebrations that followed it would end in a great grief. So he prepared himself more for the sacrifice than for the celebration by reading again the third book of *The Imitation of Christ*.

Everyone who knew him was thrilled by the news of his nomination. The French episcopate surpassed itself in honouring the nuncio, to whom it was particularly grateful for what he had done in bringing peace to people's hearts. The French Government did not mean to be outdone. President Auriol informed him that he would be very happy to be the one to invest him with the biretta (cardinal's hat), according to tradition and as a mark of his affectionate esteem, in the name of the whole of France. It brought to the nuncio's mind a saying of Father Talpa, a disciple of Saint Philip, which had been read to him in the seminary: 'When they speak ill of you—it is true. When they pay you compliments—they are joking.'

Before Christmas he set out again for Sotto il Monte to be with his sister, who seemed to be nearing the end without suffering. After an absence of thirty winters he had the pleasure of once again seeing snow on the hillsides. His visit was very brief and he went straight back to Paris to prepare himself for the 'final initiation' which had been fixed for January 15. 'It is neither a sacrament nor a sacramental', he wrote. 'And yet it is a kind of sign that providence has responsibilities in store for me which will require me to give a serious account of myself.'

Little did he know how prophetic those words were. However, he did know shortly afterwards that the Pope was thinking of entrusting him with the Patriarchate of Venice. He was allowed time to reflect. He reflected, and taking the view, as usual, that in this manifestation of the divine purpose he really counted for nothing, he decided to place himself entirely in the hands of the Holy Father. 'I came in the end to the conviction that it is also a grace for which I should bless the Lord and which will earn for me some other grace', he wrote again. For a long time the image of the funeral gondola cleaving the waters of the lagoon as it bore the body of the late Patriarch of Venice to the island of Cyprus remained before his eyes. This vision had struck him forcibly. It helped him, as ecclesiastical honours were bestowed upon him, to scorn the things of the world: *terrena despicere*. But later, to give himself courage, he reflected that in 1852, just a century ago, Pius IX had sent as Patriarch of Venice another Bergamesque, Aurelio Mutti di Borgo di Terzo. He was sixty-six and he lived another six years, leaving behind eight volumes of his works. From that moment he pushed on with his preparations to leave Paris. The Pope was pressing him to wind up any important matters without delay. As he did not have to go to Rome for the ceremony of receiving the hat, he devoted his last days to quiet work and to making contacts which, although they were no longer of interest to him, had a very real interest for the Church.

The ceremony took place in the Elysée on January 15. It was clear that President Auriol was deeply moved; there was still ringing in his ears the last speech of January 1. Immediately after the presentation of the biretta, the new cardinal made a brief speech. Once again he drew inspiration from the words which 'his' bishop Radini had spoken on July 6, 1893, in Paris, whither he had been sent to place the biretta on the head of Cardinal Bourret, accompanied in his capacity as secretary by Achilles Ratti, the future Pius XI. He closed with these words: 'I hope that you will say of me: he was a loyal and peace-loving priest, always and in every circumstance the sincere, unwavering friend of France.'

Several of those present recalled the presentation of the cap to Cardinal Maglione by President Lebrun in 1939. It was a strictly formal ceremony, one that kept closely to etiquette and at which only a few officials were present. No photographers were present, and no guests other than the most important ones. The French Republic, jealous of its secular prestige, had observed a rigid diplomatic politeness. But for Roncalli protocol was ignored and a humble priest from his native countryside took his place beside ambassadors, then sat at the table of the President of the Republic. Anything with which the nuncio was connected invited a display of cordiality. The atmosphere was quite different from that of an earlier occasion. It was a magnificent send-off, the very hallmark of dignity, but at the same time a real farewell between friends. President Auriol's emotion was such that he was seen at one point to wipe away a tear.

The new cardinal had already given thought to the models he would imitate. There were so many to choose from among his predecessors. He knew Cardinal La Fontaine who had once invited him to stay to lunch, and who became Pius X; but his thoughts turned especially to a picture adorning the altar of our Lady of Sorrows in the cathedral of Bergamo, representing the first Patriarch of Venice, St Laurence Justinian. He left Paris on February

23 and went straight to Rome. From there the journey to
Venice became a sort of pilgrimage. He spent three days at
Bergamo where he was enthusiastically welcomed, and
then stopped at the abbey at Praglia (where Matti had
been abbot) for a retreat lasting three days. At Padua he
said Mass at the altar of Bd Gregory Barbarigo, former
Bishop of Bergamo, and on March 15 he made his ceremonial entry into Venice. At that very first encounter
on the Grand Canal he discovered the heart of Venice. The
spontaneity and the sincerity of the welcome moved him
profoundly. For their part the Venetians could not conceal
their emotions as they listened to his address. He had not
written it out in full, but merely made notes of the beginning of it on three small sheets of paper:

I want to talk to you with the utmost frankness. You have
eagerly awaited my arrival. You have heard and read things
about me which are more than I deserve. Let me introduce
myself humbly to you.

Like any other man on this earth, I come from a particular
family and region. I enjoy, thanks be to God, very good health,
and have a certain amount of commonsense which enables me
to see things clearly and quickly. Well disposed in love towards
my fellow men, I abide by the law of the Gospel, respecting my
own rights and those of others. This prevents my doing ill to any
man and encourages me to do good to all.

I come from a humble family and have been accustomed to a
state of poverty, which demands little and helps to develop
those noble virtues which equip men to overcome the biggest
obstacles in life.

Providence drew me from my native village and led me to
travel the world from east to west, bringing me into contact with
people of varying religions and ideologies. I have been confronted with social problems as distressing as they were urgent,
but the same providence granted me the necessary degree of
calmness and balance to enable me to deal with these things.
During all this time I have been careful, mindful of moral
principles and of the Catholic faith, to concentrate not on those
factors which separate and cause conflict, but on those which
unite.

At the end of this long experience, here I am in Venice, with its land and sea that were familiar to my ancestors for more than four centuries; Venice, the object of my studies and of my personal sympathies. No, I have not the courage to apply to my person the words that Petrarch, a friend of Venice, spoke of himself, nor have I stories to recount to you as did Marco Polo on his return to his people. But I am certainly bound by strong ties to Venice. I was born in Bergamo, the land of St Mark, the birthplace of Bartolomeo Colleoni; at the back of the hill there lies Somasco where is to be found the grotto of St Jerome Emilien. This will give you some idea of the modesty of the claims I make.

The task which is entrusted to me in Venice is a great one and falls to me quite unmerited. But I would like to commend first and foremost to your kindness one who wishes to be simply your brother, loving, approachable, understanding. I am firmly resolved to remain faithful to an honourable past which itself has perhaps prepared me for finding in Venice a population especially responsive to a man who will speak from the heart, who does not hide the simplicity of his life, and who wishes to preserve in all his relationships a loyalty beyond reproach and one able to withstand any trial.

This is the man, this newly arrived citizen of Venice whom you have been kind enough to welcome today with such splendour and such solemnity.

For the cardinal there was beginning once again—and he certainly thought it was for the last time—a new life. And yet it was not altogether new. Some people in Venice were wondering rather anxiously how the new patriarch would behave after thirty years of diplomatic life. The hazards of diplomacy are very different from those of the pastoral life. A seasoned diplomat is someone quite different from a shepherd of souls. If he becomes a shepherd, perhaps he will be too preoccupied and lacking in warmth. Besides, in the history of Cardinal Roncalli, there were precedents that were quite different from those in the lives of other Venetian patriarchs. A certain curiosity was therefore understandable in respect of the pastoral leadership of a man who was so well versed in diplomacy. But Roncalli had never really felt himself to be a true diplomat, for ever since his ordination to the priesthood he had never ceased to feel and to act as a priest and as an apostle first and foremost. Consequently, the Venetians were surprised by the assurance and the ease with which he entered into his new mode of life. They did not yet know from which 'episcopal' school he had emerged, and they had forgotten that in Istanbul he had already shown himself to be first and foremost a bishop. Actually, he had no adjustments to make. He had only to apply the few simple but fundamental rules which he had set himself to follow on that day, long ago, when he was consecrated bishop: namely to govern like a father, with a heart open to everyone, to act without undue haste always allowing events time to develop, to have confidence in men, to put up with a great deal, taking no notice of slights but meeting them with the utmost courtesy. In addition, he did not propose to spend his time in feverish activity; not much action, but such as there was, deliberate and significant. Above all he pledged himself to stimulate and support the actions of his colleagues.

The cardinal insisted on carrying out alone the first round of confirmation visits in the parishes of his diocese. This afforded him an excellent opportunity for getting to know the hearts of the faithful. When in August Mgr Augusto Gianfranceschi, at that time Bishop of Cesena, was attached to him as assistant, he could truly say: 'I am happy about this appointment; especially happy in the knowledge that once again I have had no hand in the matter.'

The spheres of activity of a bishop in modern times are many and varied: the clergy, seminaries, Catholic Action, religious education, the press, the workers, hospitals, welfare, emigration, the cinema . . . A vast field of action, by means of which the Church seeks to permeate society, is subject to his jurisdiction and control. The previous

patriarch, Agostini, had been a valiant worker and had
died of exhaustion soon after his sixty-fifth birthday on
December 2, 1952. It would have needed at least fifteen
years to bring his programme to completion, but what had
been accomplished by him in four brief years was enough
to earn him high praise for his prodigious energy. He had
set up parishes, built churches, acquired sites for others,
started numerous buildings and finished the construction
of 'his' little seminary at Fietta. He had toured his diocese
several times and knew it thoroughly. He had a passion
for prompt action. His impatience often revealed itself in
his facial expression; he had the look and the gestures of a
man who, seeking to overcome a natural shyness, does not
always succeed in being gentle and sometimes even
appears a little brusque.

The first thing the Venetians noticed was a marked
difference between Cardinal Roncalli and his predecessor.
They were struck by the extreme warmth of his humanity,
by his manner, which was at once paternal, noble, restrained, and impressive. He had a way of behaving which
excluded any harshness but which did not allow anyone to
take advantage of his kindness. He could judge men
without the slightest trace of prejudice or partiality. There
was something mysterious about his method of getting to
know a person, and he formed a firm bond with those he
had chosen. He put perfect confidence in them and pro-
tected them with the full weight of his authority against
criticism from anyone else, but, in return, he required of
them absolute integrity devoid of any pretence or deceit.
He straightway forbade any enterprise which could only
achieve its end by having recourse to cunning or at the
price of lack of charity. His closest colleagues were vividly
impressed when, in spite of being exhausted by a sleepless
night of worry over some problem, he would not show the
slightest sign of bad temper or ill-will. They simply could
not understand in what depths he buried certain sorrows

or in what inner recesses of his heart he hid this power of universal love. He always carried out his activities calmly, in a spirit of complete surrender to providence, ready to change direction the moment obstacles appeared insurmountable, but not on that account giving up his ultimate aim which he pursued with fearless determination. It was almost as though his behaviour were the result of native innocence which, being unaware of the malice in men, approached them with a tranquil mind and succeeded by some secret means in disarming them. His activity was bound by rigid rules; it took a variety of forms but it was incessant.

Looking through the papers of his predecessor he noticed that Cardinal La Fontaine had maintained contact with his flock not by means of weighty documents but by brief and frequent letters. He proposed to follow this example, amplifying his thoughts and words whenever he deemed it necessary. His eloquence was gentle, persuasive and dignified. It was certainly not remarkable for its ardour or its dialectics, nor was it scathing. Without losing anything of its pastoral tone, it was particularly inspired by theology and the Bible. His feeling for the Old Testament led him to make frequent use of quotations from the Psalms and from the books of Wisdom. The grandeur of St John Chrysostom harmonized perfectly with the simplicity of St Ambrose. Episodes drawn from his long experience and his wealth of culture enabled him to adorn a speech with vivid illustrations and with remarkable adroitness. His skill was reminiscent of that of the French orators at the time of Louis XIV: the same full, balanced, and sweetly reasonable style. He knew how to develop the subtlest themes in words that were so clear and direct that everybody, scholar and simple follower alike, drew sustenance from them.

For all these reasons and many more—his characteristic gait, his imposing air, his piety at once profound and tender —Venice had no difficulty in discovering in Cardinal

Roncalli something of Cardinal La Fontaine, which was a pleasant surprise. Outwardly all bishops tend to resemble each other. They have certain traits in common and almost the same deportment. Episcopal behaviour has over the centuries become stereotyped in a way which blurs individual peculiarities, their movements and their words, and reduces them to a kind of common denominator. And yet the new patriarch could hardly be likened to the others. Apart from Cardinal La Fontaine, he recalled in his good fellowship and cordial manner Cardinal Sarto. But he was, in addition, a humanist in the full sense of the word. He loved the Latin classics and quoted from them, pursued historical studies, was endowed with impeccable taste, and appreciated art and artists. He had profound respect for mankind and confidence, apart from his belief in the infinite possibilities of divine action, in the astonishing potentialities which abound in the heart of man.

So it was that Venice and the patriarch came to love each other. Among other things Venice reminded him of the East. He saw in that city with its tombs of the saints, of the Fathers of the Church, doctors, and eremites, with its wonderful relics of the Passion, and the suggestive melody of its patriarchal chant, a sort of bridge, as in the glorious days of the republic, between the East and the West. And so he did not fail to let the Venetians know how much he was preoccupied with the problem of the Eastern Churches. Each year the octave of prayer for the reunion of the Churches provided him with the opportunity to voice his great apostolic concern in the matter. In January 1954 he himself gave a series of lectures on the subject in the hall of St Basso. The Venetians were surprised to hear words, the vital, convincing, and touching quality of which revealed a very personal interest in this problem and an extraordinary grasp of it.

'The road to unity between the different Christian creeds is love, so little practised on either side', he had the courage

to say in the course of one of those gatherings. He stressed
the need to study pure Christian doctrine, in which, he
said, so many common points of contact could be found.
He brought his third lecture to an end by reminding his
listeners of the biblical figure of Joseph who, raised to a
position of great power by mysterious means, was unable
to contain his emotion on meeting his brothers who had
betrayed him and would not recognize him, and who
exclaimed with a great gesture of forgiveness: 'I am Joseph,
your brother.' The patriarch added: 'My heart is big
enough to wish to encompass all mankind.'

The new patriarch entered fully into the life of Venice.
In a previous will he had expressed the desire that on his
death his body should be taken to the little cemetery at
Sotto il Monte to lie with his beloved parents, but soon
after his arrival in Venice he changed his mind and
preferred that his body should lie in the crypt of St Mark
with the other patriarchs. Everything about the city
interested him, its religious and civic life, as well as its
history, its traditions, its festivals, its saints and its devotions. He was full of enthusiasm for the beauty of the town,
and St Mark's moved him profoundly. He applied to the
basilica what was said of Dante's work: heaven and earth
have had a hand in it. It was he, the man who was not a
Venetian, who drew the attention of its people to the figure
of the most Venetian of patriarchs, St Laurence Justinian.
In 1956 the fifth centenary of the saint's death was celebrated. Great was his astonishment when he came to
realize that the most illustrious occupant of the Chair of
St Mark, although still living in sculpture and painting,
was more or less forgotten: his example, his writings and
cult interested only a handful. He himself had read his
works and found them full of mature wisdom, and so he
organized a veritable *peregrinatio Laurentiana*. The body of
the saint was borne in procession through the sixty-seven
parishes of the coastal region, through the island and the

inland territory, and was brought back to the city for the
final ceremonies which took place at the beginning of 1956.
The centenary celebrations had the effect in the end of
moving the patriarch himself much more deeply than he
had originally expected. He was filled with a strange,
intense fervour, for he had discovered in this glorious son
of Venice a secret harmony of apostleship and contemplation which delighted him. The pastoral letter which he
wrote for Easter 1956 reveals his admiration for this
eminent doctor of the Church.

It was he again who, at the end of 1956, on the occasion
of the death of Lorenzo Perosi, drew a magnificent portrait
of that priest and artist. Again, in September 1957 he
commemorated the fourth centenary of the death of
Giovanni Gabrieli. He saw in the Venetians a splendid
example of the faithful. The sincerity of their religious
feelings reminded him of Bergamo. He would often apply
to them the words with which St Augustine praised his
followers: *Tales inveni quales desideravi.* (I found them as I
would wish them to be.) He spoke of them to everybody.
He loved the very appearance of his diocese, a diocese rich
in children because family life is still thriving there and
marriage ties are strong. But steps had to be taken to help
them and to enable them to grow up in good conditions,
and so he intervened on their behalf. Roncalli liked to be
surrounded by children and to hear them call him simply
'Father', as in the early days of his priesthood. A number
of hospitals surrounded the great city, a reminder to the
thoughtless of the reality of suffering. He often visited them
as a work of mercy. 'In the making of a good bishop', he
used to say, 'the fourteen corporal and spiritual works of
mercy are very effective.'

There were also numerous groups of workers. A great
concentration of them had grown up at Marghera and at
Mestre at the gateway to Venice, but many were only
workers in name owing to the scourge of unemployment.

The patriarch had understood the meaning and importance
of the sudden appearance of this congested city on the
mainland. For some centuries now Venice has been showing signs of decadence because of its separation from the
vital flow of sea-borne trade and because of its isolation.
The future of Venice lies in the bridgehead it has established
on the continent to which the younger people are now
moving. The patriarch's first visit outside the city was none
other than to visit the petroleum workers of Agip who were
celebrating Easter in the industrial port. The chapel was
small and the faithful crowded round in the open air.

It was also his first contact with the problem of building
new churches. In 1915, at the beginning of the episcopacy
of Cardinal La Fontaine, the diocese consisted of fewer
than two hundred thousand souls. Forty years later the
population had nearly doubled. The newly built-up areas
lacked any centre for religious worship: no churches, no
church schools. Building projects were under consideration
which would require thousands of millions of lira, enter-
prises of a size to daunt anyone, and yet absolutely
essential. The patriarch humbly took to begging. He did
so—as he had done for other causes—with a moving
dignity. In the early days of 1957 when he instituted the
annual two days 'for the building of churches', he had
already put his signature to a decree for the erection of
fifteen new parish churches and thirteen chapels of ease,
not to mention another thirty cases waiting their turn. He
was kept equally busy with the social welfare of the
workers. He approached employers in the frankest manner,
even to the extent of writing open letters, if he thought he
could ask them for a greater effort of charity and justice in
favour of the working class. Here, again, thanks to his
natural diplomacy, he never overstepped the bounds of
discretion. He did not set himself up as an expert on
technical problems and did not suggest solutions which
were the province of specialists. Leaving all such questions

to those competent to deal with them, he repeatedly
stimulated people's goodwill and interceded like a father
for his children.

Venice is also characterized by certain moral problems.
Throughout the year, but especially in summer, its charms
attract enormous crowds of tourists. The danger of vice is
an obvious one and caused the pastor a good deal of
anxiety. True to his personal inclinations and to principle
based on experience, he never descended to details in order
to draw attention to certain repugnant realities. Rather
than describe the various forms of vice and their provoca-
tion, he preferred to uplift people's souls towards the
beauty, dignity, and courage of virtue. To this end he
remonstrated on several occasions, sometimes in his official
capacity. One such remonstrance, in the summer of 1956,
had repercussions outside Italy.

In April, 1957, he expressed his alarm on learning that
the communal administration was proposing to move the
Lido casino into the town. The plan was entirely contrary
to the spirit of Venice whose history contains many
examples of prohibitions issued by the ancient Senate of
the republic itself, expressing its concern over the evils
arising from the abuse of gambling. Cardinal La Fontaine
had succeeded during his lifetime in preventing the
execution of the plan for the casino, but Cardinal Piazza
had been obliged to yield, although he did manage to
insist that the building should not be set up inside the city
itself but should be relegated to a site beside the sea. And
now once again the mirage of the profits to be made from
it brought the plan to life again. It was proposed to set up
the casino in the Justinian Palace itself, formerly the
residence of the Patriarch of Venice, opposite the Church
of the Salvation, not far from St Mark's Square, from the
historical and religious point of view the most sacred spot
in Venice.

The patriarch hesitated a long time before intervening,

but when the situation appeared to him to be really serious he made his complaint, perhaps the saddest and the most deeply felt that was heard during the whole of his ministry of peace and love in Venice. He succeeded, as Cardinal La Fontaine had done, in having the execution of the plan suspended. It was only after he had left Venice that the authorities took up the matter again, and the casino was put up in the town but near the railway station.

There were many other problems of a similar nature with which he had to concern himself. Venice is the city of festivals, of biennial gatherings and of a great many other artistic and cultural events, worldly in tone and of no great merit. The attitude of the Church towards them can only be one full of reservations. It therefore fell to Roncalli to issue a sanction in connexion with the biennial festival of painting in 1954. Certain pictures in the exhibition were really indecent and offended religious feelings. He acted with extreme delicacy. He did not like the idea of intervening and making use of his episcopal prerogatives to obtain something which was strictly not within his sphere of influence, but he did not allow that to stop him. Something had to be said to those in charge of civic life who were responsible for this kind of event. Simply by using a good deal of tact and moderation he managed to obtain his ends. In 1956 the representatives of the various nations taking part in the festival were received by the patriarch in the great hall of his palace, and they felt rather than heard his desire for the observance of decency. The international exhibition which found in Venice the historical and artistic background best suited to increase its development and prestige, thus came face to face with the religious world. The new departure was well received and, even on the level of art, had certain advantages. The prohibition which since the days of Cardinal Sarto prevented priests from visiting the exhibition was thereby rescinded.

Famous in the annals of Venice was the question of the

iconostasis in St Mark's, the marble screen cutting off the high altar and the sanctuary of the church and preventing the public from following and watching the ceremonies. The question had been raised as early as the beginning of 1954. It had been the great concern of every patriarch since the time when the basilica, shortly before the end of the Venetian Republic, had been raised from the status of a ducal chapel to that of a cathedral and the official seat of the patriarchate. The question had also deeply concerned Roncalli's two immediate predecessors. The patriarch Agostini had tried out a kind of platform in front of the iconostasis to be used for the celebration of the divine mysteries at the time of the great festivals. This enabled the people to follow the ceremonies and to take part in them, but it disfigured the famous sanctuary and reduced the amount of space. It was not a success, as the cardinal realized.

The same drawbacks were at once apparent to Roncalli but he certainly could not dream of removing the iconostasis, a marvellous work of art which delights the eye of every visitor. The statues of the twelve apostles, of the Blessed Virgin and of St Mark, the work of Jacobello and of Pietro Paolo delle Masegne, are real masterpieces. The architrave is supported on columns of eastern and African marble and the spaces between these columns are filled by six marble plaques. The whole presents a harmonious appearance in its florid Venetian Gothic style. Above, the silver crucifix of Jacopo Bennato dominates the whole and worshippers focus their attention upon it. All the same, the sublime rites of the liturgy and the marvellous sparkle of the ciborium and of the gold chalice-cover, together with the mosaics of the dome, could only be seen by a very small number, standing in the presbytery and in an adjoining chapel. If in olden times this precious piece of workmanship was intended to separate the ducal authorities and members of the diplomatic corps from the rest of the people, it had become anachronistic now that a very large part of the faithful found themselves shut off by it from the solemn ceremonies.

The patriarch was only concerned with the religious aspect. He was aware of the delicate aesthetic problems involved—it was in fact a matter affecting the whole of that great religious monument, St Mark's—but he did not appreciate the hesitation of certain circles in the town to accept the principle that the cathedral's first duty was to be used for the faithful and for religious practices, and that the altar was a real centre of human fraternity and unity. The risk—invoked with alarm by those circles, with how much sincerity it was hard to say—of seeing the sanctuary turned into an object of curiosity for Orthodox, Protestant, Moslem, and Catholic tourists, all armed with cameras, and thus of seeing it subjected to some kind of profanity, did not worry him at all. Our Lord could very well turn the most unlikely means to the glory of His name.

The change he suggested was not a big one: it was purely and simply the removal of the six marble plaques which obstructed the view of the ceremonies between the pillars of the monumental marble partition. The essential structure of the iconostasis would be respected and would be set free from the encumbering parts which in his opinion spoiled the appearance of the Dalle Mesegne transept, a Gothic addition superimposed on the very light primitive Byzantine pattern of the basilica. He put forward his proposal in the same way that he used to in his diplomatic days. He took good care not to allow it to come as a surprise or to impose his ideas by other means than those of persuasion. From the beginning of his stay in Venice he spoke about it openly to everybody: to all those in authority, religious, civil, or in the government. He remained absolutely calm even when the opposition exaggerated things by talking of arbitrary action compromising the very stability of the structure, the nobility and beauty of its architectural and ornamental detail. The liveliness of the reaction and the inconsistency of the opinions surprised and pained him, but he showed to what lengths self-control can be carried. He proclaimed his principle clearly: 'I am not going to make this an occasion for polemics, even though I am convinced of the soundness of my proposition. If I were told that to make a success of it I had only to kill a single ant, I would not kill it.' He waited a long time, getting the press to give the proposal an airing from time to time. He was still waiting when he had to leave for the conclave. The opinions of others were sacred to him, whatever position they held. He was a prince of the Church and yet not one gesture, not one word was permitted that might make others think that he considered himself superior.

The people of Venice are very kind-hearted, but the fact that the patriarch was even more kind-hearted roused their admiration. Accustomed to look on the patriarchate as a sort of inaccessible royal palace, they could hardly contain their enthusiasm when they realized that it was now inhabited by a man who went out accompanied only by a secretary, who took part in the historical regattas on the first Sunday in September, stopped to chat with gondoliers and tried to talk their dialect, and made pleasant conversation with those who were employed by the Church. Above all they sensed that this gentle condescension did not arise from his manner or from a pose, but simply from the warmth of his heart. Writing of Radini, the Bishop of Bergamo, his young secretary once said that that prelate and his diocese seemed to be destined to meet and to complete each other. Much the same could be said of Cardinal Roncalli in Venice.

It was therefore easy to understand that the patriarch's heart should be opened, simply and without fuss, to his priests and his flock. This is the criterion by which the work of a pastor should be primarily judged. If he remains isolated and does not mark the life of the diocese with the imprint of his mind, he merely becomes a temporary presence in a movement which carries on apart from him. The atmosphere of Venice was, on the contrary, just what he liked. The few small clouds on the patriarchal horizon soon dispersed, blown away by the gentle wind of charity. Several of his colleagues felt that they were in the presence of a new type of man whom they had to understand by penetrating below the surface, for beneath a great simplicity were hidden unsuspected depths. Venice let no opportunity pass without giving the patriarch proof of its affectionate veneration. Each year, on the anniversary of his nomination, there reached him the faithful echo of the love of his sons. The Venetians participated with the utmost sincerity in the losses which he suffered during those years: the death of his sisters, Ancilla and Maria, and of his brother, Giovanni. They also shared in his joys: the jubilee of his ordination on August 10, 1954, and the thirtieth anniversary of his episcopate on March 19, 1955. There were two other dates which brought untold joy to his heart.

The first was that of the mission preached in the city from March 20 to April 3, 1955. The cardinal preceded this with a pastoral letter, one of the finest written during his stay in Venice, devoted to the question of spiritual rebirth. This theme of the need for continual rejuvenation was one of his favourites. A week earlier he broadcast an appeal to the faithful on Radio Venice. At the end of the mission his voice, usually strong and sonorous, had become hoarse through speaking. The triumphant closing ceremony, first in the basilica of St Mark where during a lengthy evening service he found himself surrounded by a throng of men and young people, and then beneath the sky in the magnificent square decorated as on feast days, roused in him untold admiration and emotion. That Sunday evening, April 3, in spite of the exhaustion that had overtaken him, he could not go to rest without expressing to the people of Venice his heartfelt praises.

The other occasion was that of the diocesan synod which took place in November 1957, and which was the crowning event of the pastoral visitation. As a gesture of high esteem for his predecessor he had begun the visitation in the very year of his arrival at the very point where the prelate had left it when he died. He was careful to use all the material that had already been gathered, but here again, he had his own methods, and gave evidence of rare tactfulness. He was not sparing in his praise, feeling sure that people of goodwill would take care to correct those things of which he might have shown disapproval. In addition to his relationship with his priests he sought to establish contact with the people, with the children whom he went to see in their schools, and with the sick whose houses he visited. The synod left him with the impression that he had reached an objective, which he felt was a great blessing. The feelings he had experienced at the time of the solemn synod held in the early days at Bergamo by Radini returned to him. The devotion of his clergy, assembled round him in the golden basilica, gave him the feeling of fatherly satisfaction. Everyone was aware of his being imbued with a tenderness and joy which conveyed a particularly persuasive note to his words and to the remarkable addresses that he gave. It was, indeed, the ultimate fusion of the patriarch with his Venetian clergy.

It was natural to expect that Cardinal Roncalli, with his wide experience and knowledge of men, would turn his attention to the scene beyond Venice and show interest in the events which at that time were unfolding elsewhere in Italy. His name was more than once mentioned in Italian newspapers in connexion with events of national importance about which he thought it his duty to express an opinion. Judgement is hardly the word to express this form of intervention. To pronounce judgement implies too proud an attitude of mind to give a true description of the actions of the Patriarch of Venice. His self-detachment, the simplicity with which he carried out his actions, gave him an air of modesty, almost of shyness. Those who were closest to him also knew the extreme prudence with which he prepared for such action, a prudence that was characteristic of any move he made, so that each step was taken only after the ground had been carefully tested and found absolutely safe.

February 11, 1954, was the twenty-fifth anniversary of the conciliation. The patriarch celebrated this event at St Mark's where, in spite of bad weather, the people turned up in force. The address he delivered on that occasion brought joy and surprise to the whole of Italy. Recalling the atmosphere of relief which that event had spread throughout Italy and the world, and reminding them briefly but authoritatively of the facts of the question which had divided the Italian people for so many years, he went on to speak of the two men who had presided at the agreement: Pius XI and Mussolini. It was still quite risky to mention the name of the Fascist leader in spite of the years that had elapsed since the terrible end of the man and of his regime. At a time when many, even in the Catholic ranks, were beginning to doubt the timeliness of that agreement and were seized with a feeling of apprehension whenever they spoke of it, he did not hesitate to say that the Lateran Pacts 'formed a milestone in the history of Italy and of the Catholic Church in the eyes of the whole world.' Facing up to the crucial point of the question, he resolved it with a loyalty which roused the admiration of all.

This was the man whom providence brought face to face with Pius XI . . . He later became an object of great sadness for the Italian people. Yet it is human and it is Christian not to deny him at least this claim to honour after his immense misfortune, namely the effective and decisive part he played in preparing and concluding the Lateran agreements; and after his humiliation to commend his soul to the mystery of the divine mercy of our Lord who, in the realization of His design, is in the habit of choosing the most appropriate vessels and who, once the work has been accomplished, breaks them as if they had not been prepared for that. My brothers and sons, I know that you can understand how I feel. Let us also respect the fragments of the broken vessel and let us turn to good effect the lessons they teach.

Roncalli thought his own comment on the great event much too simple and he was almost embarrassed by it. And so he was much surprised at the stir that it caused and the approval which reached him from every side.

Another of his interventions, in February 1957, was less fortunate. This was a crowded month for Venice. The magistrature had chosen the city as the seat of a discussion for a lawsuit which had been grossly exaggerated by the press employing all the resources of the technique of scandal. The attitude of the city on this occasion was simple and noble: in the midst of the general agitation it preserved an eloquent calm and looked on at the exposure of shabby trivialities in this case with a detachment which was a lesson to all. The conduct of the clergy and of the Catholic press—at a word from the patriarch—was perfect and struck the only happy note in the midst of all that excitement.

That same month there met in Venice, in the middle of an important crisis, the national congress of the Italian Socialist Party. It came at a very awkward moment in the political life of Italy, right in the middle, too, of the controversy, started among Catholics, over the possibility of an overture to the Left. The Italian episcopate had given its views many times on this subject, and Roncalli had also voiced his opinion in August, 1956, in a document which had roused considerable attention, concerning the problems of the modern humanist trend and Catholic discipline, with special reference to the different 'overtures'.

On this ground the cardinal was particularly anxious to

defend his own people, not only against an inferiority complex but also against the danger of too much aggressiveness. The attempts to make overtures, in particular in the direction of those who were 'to the left', were inspired by the false idea that the forces of Catholicism were not large enough, vigorous enough or sufficiently strong-willed for a social movement of real rejuvenation, and also by the fact that an undeserved credit was attached to other movements. Such a faint-hearted and imprudent attitude could cost them dear. Besides, the cardinal did not like bitter polemics either between Catholics themselves or between them and those who held different opinions. 'You put a little too much salt into it', he said on a note of light reproach to the editor of the Catholic weekly. At the moment when the Socialist Congress was about to meet, he decided to address a few words of welcome to them. It was certainly an action of rare courage, carried out only after deep reflection and after consulting the authorities. The interpretations that were subsequently placed on it did not take account of the spirit which inspired it nor for that matter of the text of the message itself. After having said a word or two about the lawsuit mentioned above, the patriarch added:

And now another conference, on a bigger scale if not equal in depth, will assemble in the next few days at Venice, with representatives from every region of the peninsula: the congress of the Italian Socialist Party.

The fact that I myself am addressing a few words to you, with respect and serenity as a good Venetian who has a high regard for hospitality, in accordance with the Pauline precept by virtue of which the bishop ought to show himself *hospitalis et benignas*, should make it clear to you how much I appreciate the exceptional importance which this event has for the immediate future of our country.

It is certainly inspired, or so I would like to believe, by the desire to promote a system of mutual understanding which should lead to the improvement of living conditions and to social prosperity.

It is always a matter of embarrassment, sometimes of acute embarrassment, for a shepherd of souls to have to state that a number of honest and highly intelligent people remain unresponsive and silent as though worshipping empty skies either ignorant of, or pretending to forget, the fundamental principles of the divine message. In spite of the weakness of man and of the times he lives in, that message has inspired twenty centuries of history, of science and of art, to the great honour of the European nations. It is also painful to observe that it is thought possible to reconstruct the economic, civil, and social order in accordance with ideologies which do not have their origin in the Gospel of Christ. But when that much has been said, as it must be in order to define clearly the spiritual position, and as is becoming between courteous friends, it remains for me to wish with all my heart that the sons of Venice, welcoming and friendly as they have always been, will play their part in making this assembly of so many brothers from all parts of Italy, a profitable one, having in view a general uplifting towards the ideals of truth, goodness, justice and peace.

This message made a considerable impression on the editor of the Catholic weekly to which it was sent. His hasty reading of it put a meaning into it which the text did not contain. A telephone call was made to the patriarch to ask him if they might follow it with a brief comment. Permission was readily granted and the comment approved. It is clear from reading this note, which struck a slightly anxious tone and which took a little time to appear, that the editor had only partly understood the meaning of the cardinal's gesture.

The hopes of the Church, which form the lifeblood of our Most Eminent Pastor, have been published within the last few days in a document. Is that any cause for astonishment? Should we look for hidden meanings or suspect condescensions in regard to doctrines far removed from those of Christ and opposed to them? No.

Human malice, party interest, the inability to appreciate fully the meaning of a noble gesture should not be allowed to obscure the true light: the light of Christian hope emanating from the soul of a venerable Father of the Church and which

seeks to illuminate the souls of others, in particular those in
which the divine grace is extinguished.

In the midst of so much agitation by politicians, seeking to
win the Socialists over to democracy, is it surprising that a
bishop should try to win them over to Christ?

The comment seems a little unfair, even though it may be
fundamentally true. In the mind of the patriarch the
gesture must have been less calculated and more disinterested than was suggested. He wished only to set an
example of kindness, courtesy, and above all, of charity.
The points of difference were clearly stated, but that did
not prevent the author, in his kindness, from expressing an
ardent desire for peace and unity between all men. He was
hardly surprised, therefore, when he learnt that his action
had given rise to protests. A few days later he himself
hinted at the correct interpretation of his words, in a
panegyric devoted to two noble bishops of Treviso, but
which included also a magnificent conception of the
episcopal ministry:

The episcopal mystery achieves its highest summit of perfection by seeking after the truth: *Veritatem facere*, against all the
weakness and the deviations of human faith, drawn towards
ideologies in disagreement with or in opposition to the teaching
of Christ and of the Church. Faced with the purity of this
teaching, it is quite impossible to admit hazardous variations
and uncertain interpretations.

But alongside purity of doctrine there open up fields and
horizons for the exercise of charity, a charity of devotion and
sacrifice, a charity which begins with those forms of respect and
courtesy which are the charm of human society, and which
aspires magnificently to the prodigious and heroic demonstration
of pastoral service.

Chapter Twelve

THE CHAIR OF PETER

IN 1958 a journey to Lourdes for the centenary of the apparitions and the consecration of the underground basilica brought great comfort to Roncalli. At Venice the religious ceremonies commemorating this centenary had been followed with fervour, and the cardinal had decided to journey outside his diocese to Caorle, Faenza, Verona, Lodi, and Padua, where he alternated sermons and conversations—as he put it—on this theme that was so dear to his heart.

The beginning of October was spent in making a few pastoral visitations. But then suddenly on the first Sunday of the month the news got round in Venice that the distinguished doctor, Antonio Gasparrini, who had come to Venice for a consultation, had been urgently called to the Vatican. The patriarch, who was getting ready to leave for Iesolo, was deeply distressed when he learned the news. In the past few years the Pope's health had caused him concern, and he wasted no time in inviting the faithful to join their prayers with his for the Pope's recovery. The Venetians realized the filial affection which bound him to Pius XII, to whom he owed personally the last honours of his ecclesiastical 'career'. On October 6 the newspapers announced that the Pope was very seriously ill and it was soon understood that all hope of a cure was lost. The Pope, who had remained so courageously at his post until the last moment, was rapidly dying. His last few dramatic hours were followed with great anxiety by Roncalli.

On October 11, two days after the death of Pius XII, a service was conducted at St Mark's which reminded the patriarch of the one that he had celebrated many years before at Istanbul at the time of the death of Pius XI. As on that occasion it was the cardinal's wish that the great sorrow of the hour should be linked with a resounding proclamation of faith in the indestructibility of the Church. After a moving eulogy of the Pope, to whom the cardinal applied very aptly the words concerning Jesus: *Bene omnia fecit, et surdos fecit audire et mutos loqui*, the precentor of St Mark's intoned triumphantly the *Tu es Petrus*.

The entire Church, plunged into mourning, united its thoughts in prayer to the Holy Spirit for the new Pope. From all corners of the earth the cardinals were getting ready to travel to Rome. The patriarch also made his arrangements for the journey which would enable him to exercise a power that was the most delicate and responsible of his functions as a cardinal. With his customary calm he put his affairs in order and packed his bags. He made sure that nothing had been forgotten, that everything had been made ready for the third 'adoration' of the new Pope and for the receptions that were bound to follow. But his Bible remained in its usual place since the visit was to be a very short one. He also left in the drawers of his desk important personal documents which he was keeping until he got back.

Even so a certain fear could be read in his face and he was more contemplative than usual: the words of a man who realized that he was known to half the world, who enjoyed the esteem of so many of his colleagues in the cardinalate, could not always conceal a certain apprehension. During his stay in Venice a dozen cardinals had come to visit him and he had made the acquaintance of as many more in the course of his journeys through Italy and abroad. Before embarking in the motor boat which was to take him to the station he wished to visit the basilica again, where he gazed once more at its treasures of faith and love.

This rapid tour of the basilica seemed to those present like a farewell.

All the way along the Grand Canal he was cheered by the crowds. They wished him a good journey and a successful mission; their unfinished sentences left the rest to the imagination. When he reached the station he climbed into his reserved compartment and stood in the doorway where he remained, moved but smiling, until the time came to leave. It was with the same smile, the same look that conveyed so much that he had won the hearts of the Venetians and had given them a rule, a principle of life. Above the tightly packed crowd which had accompanied him to the station, and indeed above the patriarch himself, there hovered the memory of another departure fifty years ago, in 1903, that of another Patriarch of Venice, Cardinal Giuseppe Sarto, leaving for Rome to take part in the conclave. On that occasion also a crowd of Venetians had thronged the station and there had been cries of 'Eminence, come back; do not leave us!' And the future Pius X, profoundly moved, had replied: 'Dead or alive, I shall return.'

The conclave had been fixed for October 25 and during the days of waiting Roncalli lived in the *Domus Mariae* in the shadow of the Vatican on the Via Aurelia. The story of those days would certainly be very interesting if it did not refer to a time too recent and too delicate to be told. Those who were present at the time to hear the words and to see the gestures and the meetings prefer to keep their memories to themselves. It was quite natural that a discreet veil should be drawn over everything that concerned the cardinals at a time when the journalists of the entire world were indulging in absurd comments on every movement and were unable to find in the minds of the electors anything except human or political preoccupations.

About certain aspects of this story, however, there can be no doubt. In the first place as the days passed Roncalli had the strong impression that several of his colleagues were showing a more than passing interest in him. If, on leaving Venice his fears had been only vaguely defined, on the eve of the conclave his heart was already experiencing serious misgivings. That day he wrote to several of his dearest friends, those whom he might expect to pray for him. Those pages reveal his apprehension that the responsibility might ultimately be his. They constitute a document which should be read by all those who spoke at the time of manœuvres carried out by the cardinals under the impulse of personal ambition or political inclinations. To the Bishop of Bergamo he wrote:

> Just a line as I go into conclave. It is in the nature of an appeal which I address, through the voice of the bishop, to all that is dearest to my heart as a good Bergamesque. As I think of so many venerated and beloved images of the Blessed Virgin, scattered throughout the diocese, as I recall our patron saints, bishops, and illustrious and holy priests, monks and nuns of outstanding piety, my soul thus comforted looks forward to the new Pentecost, which shall give to the Holy Church by the renewal of its head and by the reconstruction of the ecclesiastical body, a new vigour leading on to a victory for truth, goodness, and peace. It matters little whether the new Pope be Bergamesque or not. Combined prayers should ensure that he be a wise and gentle man, and that he be a holy man and one who spreads holiness. You will understand me. I send you greetings and affection. My blessing to all your people.

On the evening of Sunday the 25th the heavy doors of the conclave closed behind the cardinals and the handful of people who were allowed to help and serve them. Among the names of the cardinals likely to be elected, that of the Patriarch of Venice kept recurring in the press. At the moment, of course, they were only vague rumours, but many people were impressed by them. One cardinal, as he went into the conclave, was heard to remark: 'I can think of no-one except Roncalli: he has the most sympathy and understanding and the widest experience.' From that moment on the only person who could approach the cardinal, apart from his valet, was his secretary, Mgr Loris Capovilla who had come with him from Venice.

In the wing of the apostolic palace reserved for *garde-nobles* the members of the conclave formed a splendid family. In the same apartment with the patriarch were the Cardinal Archbishops of Saragossa, Palermo, Quito, and Buenos Aires, and the Prefect of Rites and Religions, with their secretaries and servants. From this wing, one of the least comfortable in the palace, they made their way to the Sistine Chapel where, in the very strictest secrecy, the ballots took place. The only sign that could give any indication as to what was going on beneath that marvellous vault painted by Michaelangelo was the impression that could be gained by studying the faces of the cardinals as they returned to their apartments. The Patriarch of Venice often appeared absorbed and moved. He was more silent than usual and looked anxious, signs which did not escape the perceptive mind of his secretary. The attention with which the other cardinals surrounded him appeared to his secretary to indicate a discreet silence at the moment when a grave and solemn decision was about to be taken. It was as though they desired, by the warmth of their devotion and by the promise of a filial loyalty, to strengthen him for all the hours of joy and suffering that lay ahead.

Outside, the crowd thronged the huge square of St Peter's, watching the columns of smoke which were the only indication of the progress of the ballot. It was as though these columns were intended to increase the nervous tension as the crowd and the Christian world waited. Even on television their colour varied from white to dark, raising hopes and dashing them again. The traditional white smoke, indicating the final ballot, did not appear until October 28, at about a quarter to five in the evening, and even then for some moments it took on a neutral colour.

The cardinals had prevailed over the will of him who had been elected. In a flash the immediate approaches to the Sistine Chapel, the ducal hall, and the royal hall were deserted. The members of the conclave with their secretaries and servants were now free to go into the Ladies' Gallery, but the secretary and the servant of the Patriarch of Venice had to stay behind waiting patiently near the closed door of the ducal hall. Half an hour passed without anyone coming out. When at last a door was opened a little way, the secretary could not resist making himself known and saying the name of his cardinal. It had been arranged that the first to be admitted into the Sistine Chapel should be the secretary of the one who had been chosen, and he was allowed to go in at once. In that wonderful chapel the sight that met his eyes was unbelievable. The cardinals were in their places, smiling, seated on the low seats of their thrones. Only the throne of the one who had been elected, as yet unoccupied, was raised up, and under the canopy there could be seen in big letters the inscription: Card. Angelo Gius. Roncalli.

John XXIII had already made known the name which revealed at one stroke to the world his new status, a name which summed up his tenderness of affection, piety of feeling, and depth of culture. He could be seen in the little sacristy, already clothed in white, having found again his calm and his smile. Once again he began to spread round him a great serenity. Already the world had learnt the news from the lips of Cardinal Carrali, who was himself much moved. The enthusiasm of the Bergamesques and the Venetians knew no bounds. In the humble house at Sotto il Monte the family of the newly elected Pope could not contain its emotion and its tears. His brothers, just back from the fields, looked at their rough hands and wondered whether they could really believe what had happened to 'him'. All those who had known him well—in Bergamo, Venice, Rome, France, Turkey, and Greece, and in many other countries—could hardly believe the news. None of them would have dared to think of this happening, so simple, familiar, friendly and human had been their relations with this man, on whom had fallen the high dignity of the Vicar of Christ and whose office would now oblige them to keep at a respectful distance.

The author of these pages, who was in Rome at the time with some close friends, standing in front of the statue of St Térèsa Bernini, remembered then a letter written some years before by the new Pope to a friend:

> Live from day to day. Nothing is lost, even when one feels one's life slipping by. Bossuet in his *Elévations sur les Mystères*, devoted twenty-two chapters to the presentation of Jesus in the temple. A piece of sublime teaching. In the last chapter he says: 'Simeon has sacrificed love of life and allows it, so to speak, to expire at God's feet in pure loss.' What mystery there is in this breathing out of life before God, in pure loss! He did not in any way lose it. All the time he was doing nothing he was being prepared to present Christ the Saviour to the world. At the moment I must say that my poor life continues to pour itself out, as you know; and on my loins the hair-shirt which is so dear to me.

And so the man who had at that time the impression of pouring out his life in pure loss had really been destined to present Christ to the world, and more especially to represent Him. On the following day, October 29, after the unexpected prolongation of the conclave, John XXIII appeared on the balcony of St Peter's, from where he leant forward towards the people and embraced them in a symbolic gesture of joy and universal peace. The spontaneity and tenderness of this action revealed at once something of his heart. All those who have approached him since his elevation to the papacy bear witness that he has preserved his customary simplicity and modesty.

Chapter Thirteen

PORTRAIT OF A PONTIFICATE

I T might be thought that the passage of time since John XXIII's coronation on December 8, 1960 is too short to enable a biographer to make an appraisal, however humble, of the stately activities of a head of the Church. One could with even better reason suppose that the interval is too brief to allow this same head of the Church, faced with the vast problems raised by the strenuous and many-sided life of the Church, to outline his programme, let alone elaborate a complete one. But that is not necessarily true of Pope John.

He evidently lost no time after his election in forming an idea of the task which providence wishes him to fulfil. Out of a whole lifetime's experience he has come to understand, simply and quickly, the significance of his new vocation. He has been guided by God in his journeyings in East and West so that his vision of the Church might be universal and he might develop the missionary aspirations of one acquainted with that world which is outside the Christian community, and with the divisions inside it. A powerful force has given his heart renewed strength and he has been consumed with a desire to make contact with the Church as a whole, not only the gradual contact of chance meetings but also a unique, complete, and formal contact which would bear impressive witness to the greatness of the Church. And so it was that within a few months of his election to the pontificate he announced to the world, in a way that was entirely personal and spontaneous, the Second Ecumenical Vatican Council.

Some have read into this grand gesture a sign of haste, a desire to push ahead and to concentrate into one great event all the activities that time could not normally be expected to allow to a Pope on the threshold of his eighties. Such a desire would certainly be understandable, but it is not sufficient explanation of the work he has undertaken. It is reasonable to look farther afield. Pope John is very much interested in the history and the theology of the Church. His training and his convictions have made him attach great importance to ecclesiastical institutions which, even though they have not enjoyed much prominence in recent years, have at least been a credit to the Church and have considerably enriched its life throughout the centuries. Of the twenty ecumenical councils which have been held by the Church only two have taken place within the last five centuries: the Council of Trent (1545–63) and the First Vatican Council. It could not be said that conditions in the Church made them unnecessary. It may be that, as the organization of ecclesiastical government became more powerful and more centralized, less importance was attached to them, or perhaps a feeling of fear overtook those whose duty it would have been to prepare for such a vast movement of men and ideas. In any case the First Vatican Council, with its definition of papal infallibility, provided such a firm instrument of doctrinal guidance that it seemed to render superfluous any other means of realizing the necessary ecclesiastical unity.

In actual fact such councils are of vital importance to the Church. No doubt they have in the person of the Pope a leader who represents Christ and who possesses an authority received from Christ and made lawful by him. Nevertheless, this authority is exercised not only over the Church but for the Church and with the Church. The privilege of doctrinal infallibility is retained by the Pope and by the bishops bound to the Pope. The power of binding and loosing was conferred by Christ not only on Peter but on the entire Church in its living and ordered unity.

John's feeling is that the Church cannot limit itself to receiving passively from the Pope the word that Christ addresses through him to the Church and to the world. That word must be sought also by the Church in order that it may be better expressed and translated into action. The more the Church thinks, talks, and seeks, the greater its vitality and activity. Personal contact, exchange of ideas, investigations, self-examination—an ecumenical council can achieve all this with the help of the Holy Spirit and under the guidance of the Pope. That is the splendid prospect that John wished to open up for the Church.

The announcement caused surprise. Nothing that has happened in the last twenty or thirty years, nothing that has been undertaken by the eminent popes of recent decades could have led to the forecast of such an event. Profound crises like those of modernism, the gradual de-christianization of the great majority of ordinary people, or the disappearance of whole nations from the Christian community; grave new dangers such as the rise of tyrannical and anti-religious powers and the menacing advance of Communism; problems such as research into new ways of spreading the Gospel and into a modern theological and liturgical language—these are some of the factors and tendencies which have brought drama to the life of the Church since the beginning of the century. The government of the Church has taken timely action in connexion with these problems. Popes have sent out an increasing flow of messages and encyclicals, some of which have left a profound impression on the Christian conscience. The Roman offices have issued orders which have been all the more effective for having emanated from observation and command posts that are better informed and more powerful than they used to be, but such orders have always come from above and been dictated by a small group. The Church has not been called upon to take part in a plenary assembly or in formal consultation. That can only be achieved through a council.

John XXIII's belief is that the entire Church should be grouped round him in such a grave, and at times tragic, period of its history. It is not an abdication of papal authority but a better exercise of it. He wishes not only to define, but to act in such a way that his definition shall give real meaning to unity and universality. The official announcement of his intention to summon the council appeared in the first encyclical letter *Ad Petri Cathedram* addressed to the Church on June 29, 1959, the feast of Peter and Paul. But the Christian world already knew of the Pope's intention as early as January 25, the closing day of the octave of prayer for the unity of the Church. In a formal address delivered to the cardinals alone after pontifical Mass had been celebrated in the basilica of St Paul, Pope John started to disclose his great project.

The first reaction, not only throughout the world but in Rome and in ecclesiastical circles, was astonishment, all the more so since the Pope's words were taken to mean that the council was to initiate a movement towards the unity of the Church: 'a light, a subject of edification and joy for all Christian people and, for the separated communities, a fresh invitation to pursue meekly with us the search for unity and grace which are so heartily desired by people all over the world.'* With this disconcerting simplicity and serenity an historic event of immense scope was decided on by a man who after the conclave had been represented by some as a 'caretaker' Pope. At one stroke the Church found itself embarked on an enterprise which called for the employment of all its energies and the

* Address to the diocesan presidents of the Italian Catholic Action *Osservatore Romano*, August 10–11, 1959.

mobilization of its whole resources. The general surmise was borne out later by the Pope when he said that the idea of the council had not matured in him 'like the fruit of a prolonged meditation but like the flower of an unlooked-for spring.' He had merely applied his spiritual rule of 'absolute simplicity in the acceptance of divine inspiration and prompt submission to the apostolic requirements of the hour.'* If the first announcement concerning the council had bordered on timidity, it was followed by an unceasing flow of papal exhortation. The determination to show that this was not just wishful thinking became clear at once. No-one was to be dismayed by the tremendous difficulties, the problems that needed solving, by doubts or unpreparedness. Gently but firmly the delicate and complex machinery which was intended to control this immense upsurge of the spirit was assembled and set in motion.

John XXIII's frequent allusions to the council in his speeches have made it possible to understand more clearly the objective he had in mind. A mistaken interpretation of the wording of the first announcement had given the impression that the invitation to the council would also be extended to all the Churches separated from Rome, Eastern and Protestant alike. In fact the invitation that was sent to the separated communities 'for this seeking after unity and grace' could not be considered as an invitation to take an active part in the council itself. The divisions between the Christian Churches are unfortunately too deep to allow such a project to be entertained at present. The council clearly had to be limited to the one Catholic Church. Above all it is a great act of inward renewal by Catholicism, without imitating the councils of the past which were chiefly concerned with matters of doctrinal clarification and with the need to relate certain important

* Address to the seminarists of Bergamo, *Osservatore Romano*, August 15, 1959. Compare also the message addressed to the Venetian clergy on the occasion of the translation of the body of Saint Pius X.

points of dogma and discipline to the sources of revelation
and tradition. The Second Vatican Council is devoting
itself to an equal extent to the internal problems of the
Church. It is seeking to find a more complete affirmation
of the life of the Church today; in other words, it is endeavouring in the words of Pope John 'to give dazzling
effect to the essence of human and Christian thought and
life, of which the Church has down the centuries been the
trustee and mistress.' In fact the aim of the council is not
strictly ecumenical.

Yet there can be no doubt that the Pope means the
council to bear in mind the unity of the Church. The
separated brethren are not yet called upon to take an
active part in it, but their presence in the spirit is keenly
desired. They are detached but important onlookers at a
council which may have for them the significance of an
example, a silent but at the same time eloquent appeal.
In taking this line the Church attacks nobody, and its
attitude will not be polemical as has sometimes been the
case in the past. Nor is the Church setting out to give an
appearance of greatness or supremacy which would make
for false pride and might intimidate others. On the contrary, the council is to pursue its course in an atmosphere
of purity both of purpose and thought, in a profound and
humble aspiration to that 'fullness of Christ' (Eph. iv. 13)
which no-one can imagine has been attained yet.

The inspiration behind this council was born in Pope
John out of his deep concern for unity. At the time of his
first announcement he was constantly meditating on the
poignant invitation of Christ to make the unity of the
Church a reality.* One month earlier his Christmas
message had rung out sounding a fervent appeal for a
meeting in Christ of all those who believed in Him, and
his sincerity had roused a favourable echo in the non-
Catholic world. He stretched out his arms to the separated

* As, e.g., in the address printed in *Osservatore Romano*, 10–11 August, 1959.

brethren, driven by a desire which perhaps outstripped the possibilities of the moment. The world press which drew over-optimistic pictures and talked of a 'Council of Church unity' certainly got the matter out of perspective, but it rightly guessed that in the soul of the Pope there lay an aspiration in this direction, even if a limited one. There were some who thought that he hesitated for a time between two different conceptions of the aims of the council: one limiting it to Catholics, the other contemplating some form of invitation to the other Churches, but in fact these two conceptions were not contradictory and they have grown closer together in his thoughts. In the numerous statements he has made about the council he has seldom spoken of it without evoking at the same time the vision of Christian unity. Even the prayer which he composed with the council in mind asks for the gifts of the Holy Spirit for the bishops and clergy and faithful as well as for 'the sheep who are no longer in the one fold of Christ.' Unless the papal idea of the council is seen against the background of these two conceptions the full splendour of it will not be appreciated.

This basic conception of the council made the actual form in which the admission of non-Catholics to the work of the council could be envisaged a less urgent question in the early preparation stages. The utmost prudence and reticence were called for. However, the form of the council allows, parallel with the committees who share the real burden of the groundwork, a secretariat whose special task is to deal with requests for information from the other Churches and to work out the outlines of a theological doctrine which will take particular account of ecumenical problems. This means that the members of the separated Churches can only follow the work of the council indirectly. That is in accordance with the express wishes of the Pope: the Church must withdraw as one entity into itself before attempting to make contact with other

Christians.* Such contacts, though premature at the present time, represent the dearest hopes of John XXIII for the future. The real, direct appeal will perhaps come later. 'When we have completed this immense task of removing anything which, from a human standpoint, might prevent us from freely opening up the way, we shall present the Church in all its splendour, *sine macula et ruga*, and we shall say to all those others who are separated from us, Orthodox, Protestant, and so on . . .: Come, brothers, here is the Church; we have striven to remain faithful to her . . .'†

The council has already, without waiting for that day, taken on a profound ecumenical meaning and has therefore, by implication, the force of an appeal to the separated Christians. As an historical and theological fact it can make a strong impression on their religious sensibilities. Once papal infallibility had been defined, Protestants often insinuated that the Pope would no longer have any need to convoke a council because he could decide everything himself. This council can provide just the proof that is needed to show that Catholicism still attaches great importance to the doctrine—so dear also to the hearts of some separated Churches—of the authority of the episcopal body. Papal authority neither absorbs nor supersedes the universal function of the bishops.

But there is another theological conception at the root of the Pope's thinking. It is that the deeper Christianity goes the more radiant it is, and the more it recovers its original purity and splendour the greater will be its power to permeate and prevail. Now the Pope is not by nature a

* Those who, without sharing absolutely in the profession of the Catholic faith desire in a spirit of loyalty and trust to be informed of the work of the council will not find unreasonable or lacking in courtesy our invitation to them to wait until the Fathers and their advisers . . . have finished their work and everything is arranged and in order . . . for contacts on the higher level of the mind, heart, and supernatural understanding . . .' (Address on the opening of the preparatory stage of the council. *Osservatore Romano*, November 15, 1960).

† Speech reproduced in the *Osservatore Romano* on August 10–11, 1959.

pessimist and he does not join in the chorus of those who believe that Catholicism is doomed to gradual decay; but at the same time he is too well aware of the circumstances in which the Church finds itself not to admit that it is threatened by serious dangers, both within and without. The convocation of the council is at once a courageous recognition of the state of the Church and a great act of faith in the divine forces which still lie concealed within it, forces which the grace of God and honest research cannot fail to bring to light. Thanks to his personal experience, Pope John is not blind to the fact that Christianity loses its strength once it demeans itself or when, through apathy or pusillanimity, it allows itself to be contaminated by ideas or influences which insidiously compromise its spiritual purity. The ardent desire of the Church to realize fully the Christian ideal is in itself an important and favourable guarantee for the council, and exercises a powerful and mysterious magnetism on men's minds.

If the announcement of a council stirred world feeling as it is known to have done, it is precisely because the Pope's long-term ecumenical purpose has been understood. It is only a first step; we are still a long way from the meetings which will prepare the way for union, but it is a step of considerable importance. At a time when other Churches are engaged in discussion and do not always know what they represent or what they want, the Catholic Church is withdrawing into itself for a frank self-examination, from which it will emerge rejuvenated and better prepared. For the same reason the other Churches have received the Catholic initiative with sympathy or at least with respect. We should remember, by way of contrast, the hostile reception given by non-Catholic communities to the announcement by Pius IX of the First Vatican Council. It can therefore be said that the step the Pope has taken allays the anxieties of those in the modern world who aspire to Christian unity. No generation has suffered more than ours from the appalling division of Christianity, and no age has spent more time trying to abolish the scandal. Through the dialogues of theologians and exegetes, through the feeling of solidarity which has been strengthened by the anti-religious dictatorships of our day, through common worship, through sacrifice, and through faith in God, Jesus Christ, and the Church—through all these things Christians today have come to understand the full meaning of their brotherhood. It was this feeling that gave rise to the universal joy which was expressed when Rome, growing tired of equivocation, came out resolutely in favour of the ecumenical movement. It is perhaps the first time since the Reformation that such a definite step in that direction has been taken. And Rome will not stop there.*

An elaborate machinery was set in motion to prepare the way for the council. Two stages were planned to guide the Church along the path towards the event itself: a pre-preparatory phase and a preparatory phase proper. The first began on May 17, 1958, with the nomination of a committee under the presidency of Cardinal Tardini. More than two thousand seven hundred letters were sent out to bishops, abbots, representatives of the Holy See, heads of communities and rectors of theological colleges, inviting their suggestions and opinions on questions that would be dealt with in the council. The replies were analysed, classified, made the object of coordinated reports designed to underline national and general trends and to draw attention to subjects of particular interest to the bishops. Secrecy still envelops the findings of this vast 'exploration'— as the Pope was pleased to call it—but it is known that it

---

* 'If one considers the most luminous aspects of the whole of history, one can feel sure that the Ecumenical Council . . . has already roused in the hearts of bishops and clergy the ardent desire and the determination to broaden the frontiers of Christian love . . .' (Extract from John XXIII's letter to the Venetian clergy, dated April 24, 1959.)

has brought to light in an extraordinarily fresh and vivid manner the present-day needs of Catholicism.

The second stage began on June 5, 1960, at Whitsuntide, with the nomination of ten committees charged with the study of the findings of the pre-preparatory inquiry in the various spheres, before submitting them to the council. One glance at the special terms of reference of these committees is enough to give one an idea of the magnitude of the questions which the council faces: theology and morality, bishops and diocesan government, discipline of the clergy, religous orders and congregations, sacraments, liturgy, seminaries, eastern Churches, missions, the lay apostolate. The list of presidents, advisers and secretaries of each one of the ten committees was drawn up on a strictly international basis. The members were chosen with a breadth of vision beyond anything that could have been hoped for. Two secretariats were added to the committees, one responsible for the press and propaganda, the other for relations with the separated Churches. The second was the express wish of John XXIII and has a clearly defined aim: 'In order the better to show our love and good feeling towards those who are honoured by the name Christian but who are separated from the Apostolic See, and in order that they may follow more easily the work of the council, and the more easily find the way towards that unity which Christ asked of our Heavenly Father in a fervent prayer.'

The work of those committees, although only preparatory, must have an almost decisive bearing on the council because the assembly is on too vast a scale to allow prolonged discussion, and must inevitably make decisions in the light of this preliminary study. And so it is true to say that the preliminary stage of study and detailed research is a delicate and crucial one. It is a stage which has not been overlooked by the Pope and the bishops in their wisdom, but of which, on the contrary, they must, and expect to, make use.

How long would this phase last? It was difficult to predict, but conservative estimates put it as high as two years. One thing was certain. Pope John was a constant encouragement and stimulus to those round him. The rhythm of work for those who were called in to collaborate with him was very intense and has been marked by a sense of urgency which the Pope never ceased to foster. He himself closely followed the inquiries of the pre-preparatory committee and personally examined the proposals put forward by the bishops, the Roman Curia, and the universities. The papal documents relating to the council are comprised in one monumental edition containing anything bearing on the preparation of this, the greatest gathering of the Church in a thousand years of its history. The Pope appears not only as the inspiration behind all this but, during the preliminary stage, he clearly directed the work. Everyone has been struck by the insistence with which he has returned, both in formal statements and in private conversation, to the great enterprise with which he feels that providence has entrusted him.

If the nature of his pontificate is to be properly understood it is important that the other activities of Pope John should be considered in the light of this ecumenical event. By February, 1962, he had already created more than fifty-two new cardinals, so that the number of members of the Sacred College, which was fixed at seventy at the end of the sixteenth century, has been raised to eighty-seven. The reduction in numbers and in importance of the members of the supreme Senate of the Church remains one of the facts of the last years of Pius XII and one of the greatest enigmas of his pontificate. Foreseeing, perhaps, a complete transformation in the structure of this institution, Pius XII had not concerned himself with filling the gaps left at the centre of it, and on his death he left a body of cardinals only about fifty strong to nominate his successor. John XXIII's idea is not only to give back to the Sacred

College its traditional importance, but also to restore its prestige. Apart from the increase in numbers, a feature of the new nominations is a broad feeling of universality in the choice of persons; Italians are still numerous, if not a majority, because of the high proportion of places they retain in the Vatican's diplomatic staff, but the number of foreign cardinals has increased to such an extent that the Sacred College has taken on an undeniably international look. This fact is not only explained by the needs of the moment, but it has an obvious bearing on the ecumenical council. John XXIII wishes on this solemn occasion to have round him well-qualified representatives of Catholicism as a whole, 'in order to bring to the decisions of the council an awareness of and a response to the vast requirements and to secure the adherence of all, not only through the authority of the Holy See but through the assent of such an eminent world senate.'* The increased number of cardinals also had the effect of imparting fresh zest to all levels of the Roman Curia by making possible a more equitable division of responsibilities.

This pontificate has been marked by another fact which has an ecumenical bearing, that is, the regularity with which John XXIII proclaims the pre-eminence of charity. For various historical reasons the papacy has sometimes been obliged to adopt an attitude or exert an authority inspired by principles not deriving from the Gospel. The evangelical conception of authority is nevertheless that of service, of devotion to one's brothers out of love for Christ. It has a profoundly human and profoundly theological meaning, the quality which for centuries the Pope has attributed to himself: *Servus servorum Dei*, 'servant of the servants of God.'

It is as though the Pope wished to make that quality

---

* Compare the address given on March 28, 1960, at the time of the secret consistory for the nomination of new cardinals. (*Acta Apost. Sedis* of May 7, 1960.)

incarnate in his person, thereby removing from the popular conception of the papacy any idea of an overbearing power beset with privileges and jealous of its rights. Stronger in him than awareness of his authority is a sense of mission, and in his devotion to it he is liable to act upon instinct, adopting attitudes and performing actions which sometimes sweep away established protocol in order to make individual contact with men. The unhappy consequences of the split between the Church and the Italian State after 1870 had condemned the Popes to a solitude which was too easily interpreted as a sacrosanct attribute of the papacy. John XXIII has had no difficulty in tearing down every barrier. His visits to hospitals, hostels and prisons in Rome, participation in the sacred rites in ancient basilicas and new churches, all this has earned him the nickname among the common people, without the least lack of respect, of 'John Without-the-Walls', an allusion to the basilica of that name outside the boundaries of the ancient city. These are touching episodes but above all they show that he is interpreting the papacy as an apostolate and as a ministry of love. His contacts with the crowds, at the many audiences he has held, have a familiar, almost intimate, flavour. One is conscious in his extempore speeches—which are sometimes reminiscent of the homilies of St Gregory the Great—of a conversation, as though he were trying to draw a veil over the greatness of the speaker in order to allow love and nothing else to shine through. Even when he is denouncing mistakes and errors, one has the feeling that he is never speaking to enemies. He is capable of loving men as they are, sinful, wandering and blind. The persecutors of the Church themselves provoke in him a deep sorrow, but they, too, are souls to be won.

As for the faithful of the separated Churches, they are true 'brothers' to him. The terms in which he praised the great Christian heritage of the Eastern Churches in his first Christmas message made a deep impression: 'They carry on their forehead the name of Christ, they read His Holy Gospel and they are not insensitive to the inspiration of religious piety and charity.' In his first encyclical, *Ad Petri Cathedram*, he was careful to make a respectful reference to the World Council of Churches, and very moving was the prayer addressed to the members of the separated communities in which he asked to be allowed to call them 'brothers' and 'sons'.*

The same encyclical recalls the great principle which has always inspired his pastoral activity: *in necessariis unitas, in dubiis libertas, in omnibus charitas* (unity in essentials, liberty in matters of doubt, charity in all things). It was addressed as an important appeal to all Christians, Catholics as well as non-Catholics. Of Catholics he required that they should avoid zeal based on jealousy, the dispute of the 'disciples'; to non-Catholics he said that they need have no fear of finding in the Church of Rome a rigidity of thought that was indifferent to what was sound and good in their religious traditions. Unity is not the same as uniformity. Unity leaves room for a large variety of religious customs, liturgical rites, schools of theology, within the orbit of the same faith. Unity seeks by prayer the new ways into which Christ is leading His people and is guided by a love which smooths away difficulties, removes prejudices, goes beyond conventional methods, and which creates and innovates. The terrible secular obstacles which bar the road to unity will only be surmounted by discussion and encounter if a wind of charity has first of all swept away all egotism and prejudices, and ushered in a new era of mutual understanding. In emphasizing the pre-eminence of charity, what the Pope has really been endeavouring to achieve is a change of climate in relations between Christians and between the Churches.

* One of the most interesting aspects of the public audiences given by the Pope is the number of Christians of other creeds who attend and the genuineness of their enthusiasm.

In the period since he became Pope the effects of this new climate have already been felt. In one event of great importance he himself was the prime mover: the visit to the Vatican of Lord Fisher, at that time Archbishop of Canterbury. The simple fact of this meeting is significant, let alone the benefits that may accrue from it. Two years earlier it would have been unthinkable. Outwardly nothing transpired, for there was no time to raise matters of importance. Everything points to the probability that the two personalities involved simply sought to make a first contact and wanted to accomplish nothing more than a symbolic gesture. But everyone understood that it was a gesture of profound significance, one which marks an advance along the road towards a new era in the relations between the Christian Churches.*

Both John XXIII and the previous Archbishop of Canterbury have been credited with the intention of trying to prepare the way for unity through some form of religious federation or practical collaboration between the Churches. Without becoming involved for the moment in theological discussions, Christians could begin by unifying their action in the domain of charity by pursuing numerous common ideals. It is probable that Lord Fisher cherished just such an interesting proposal; declarations to this effect were attributed to him by authorized newspapers. As for the Pope, there is not sufficient evidence for us to form a judgement.

The objection has been raised that Pius XI in the encyclical *Mortalium animos*, one of the basic texts for Catholic ecumenism, declares himself to be opposed to any form of practical and federative pan-Christianity. But the position has been misunderstood. It is not a question of reducing the unity of the Church to some form of common action,

* Lord Fisher had already announced, at the time of his famous visit to Rome, his intention to retire as head of the Anglican Church. His retirement came into effect on January 19, 1961. His successor, Dr Ramsay, has already made known his readiness to meet the Pope.

but rather of completing one stage in the long road which leads to union. It will certainly be necessary to work together on tasks much more supernatural and profound than a simple rapprochement on the level of human activities. And yet the Church is many-sided: what is involved is not only a question of truth, but also of holiness, of prayer, and of the Church's mission. First there must be a confrontation, out of which will grow both a spirit of unity and of emulation.*

The Church cannot afford to delay. The present situation in the world makes it all the more urgent for Christianity, if it is not to perish, to proclaim its ageless principles with vigour. New nations are continually appearing on the world scene, with the result that at great international conferences and even at the United Nations itself there has been a shift of power away from the Christian countries who once used to dominate the whole world. The time may come when the great power-blocs into which the world is divided will hurl themselves against each other in defence of the great principles of their civilization rather than over the fleeting problems of the moment. Already Communism constitutes the most terrible threat of our times, not as an economic and political theory but as a materialist doctrine. Elsewhere there are signs of an attempt to draw together the Moslem populations on the basis of their Arab civilization. The keenest rivalry in the future will be that between ideas. Everything points to the need for the Christian world to re-establish its lost unity and close its ranks round the glorious inheritance left it by its Lord. Problems of peace and war, help for under-privileged countries, the right to personal and religious freedom, colonialism, education and culture, social welfare, State affairs—on these salient points there is among

---

* The idea of emulation in prayer between the Churches appears in the encyclical *Ad Petri Cathedram* itself. It is an idea dear to the modern theologians of ecumenism, including Catholics.

Christians a substantial and creative identity of views. It would be a fact of inestimable value for nations and for the individual of today, bewildered by a multiplicity of messages, if all Christian bodies declared their willingness to unite in defence of the common heritage of the Gospel. It is a sad fact that the large-scale missionary movement which has been at work in Asia and Africa for centuries has had very little effect, and today is not only powerless to influence the grave crisis which threatens these continents, but may be all too easily swept away, probably because of the divisions within Christianity and worse still because of the frequent subjection of Christian ideas to material interests or to national ambitions.

It is not a question of building unity by an attempt on the part of the Churches to combine over practical issues. Nevertheless, it would be unwise to ignore the infinite possibilities which co-operation in love would even today offer to Christians in combating the grave dangers which threaten the world. We are wrong if we believe that John XXIII, who suffered so much and still suffers today from the consequences of Christian divisions, would not look sympathetically on any enterprise which tended to unite all the Churches in a closer bond.

Meanwhile, in whatever manner Christians may come together, one thing is certain: charity has already begun to operate. Since the accession of Pope John the unity of the Church has become the great aspiration of Catholicism. The ecumenical problem is no longer merely a subject of study for some theologians left to their own devices. Something very important has happened, something of which it is still difficult to grasp all the practical implications because so little time has elapsed and the ultimate aim is too delicate to describe in detail, but it is something that will not stop. The problem of division is taken seriously, it is regarded as a terrible but undeniable fact, but one to which Christians can no longer resign themselves and which will no longer brook delay. The situation is being faced in a realistic manner, for it is only by doing so that a solution can be reached. Non-Catholics are regarded with greater humility and more respect. For everyone the period of preparation for the council has been a time of prayer and meditation which makes us understand implicitly that we have need of clear thinking and wisdom, of a more complete possession of the 'unfathomable riches of Christ', and of purification also. The Catholic conscience has now been roused and is on the move. It is no longer content to wait and pray, it feels its responsibility, it is searching and it is taking action. This is a prelude to that Pentecost which John XXIII ardently desires to see realized in the Church by means of the present Council. This in itself is one of the fruits of charity.*

Another interesting characteristic of the pontificate of John XXIII is what he has done as Bishop of Rome. The Pope is the Vicar of Christ for the universal Church in his capacity as successor to St Peter in the See of Rome, of which city he is consequently the bishop. This historic basis for the papacy is not without importance for Pope John and perhaps explains why he misses no opportunity to underline its episcopal powers. It is one more proof of his love for anything connected with the ancient history and tradition of the Church. It would be necessary to go

---

* The Berlin Catholic newspaper, *Petrus Blatt* (April 21, 1960), observed in connexion with the eucharistic World Congress at Munich: 'Among the special characteristics arising out of Munich must be counted the fact that the faithful have everywhere begun to listen extremely attentively to the appeal for Christian unity by our Pope, John XXIII, which has already made itself heard in so many different ways. This represents the profound link which leads from the Eucharistic Congress to the next Ecumenical Council.' There is no doubt that the crowds literally rushed to the lectures on ecumenism which, in themselves, were something new at an event of this kind. The Archbishop of Paderborn, Mgr Jaeger, was host during the congress to the Lutheran Bishop of Munich. An official representative of the German Evangelical Church was present at the main functions. Professor Sucker, head of the Institute of Protestant Studies, examining the different religious creeds, has expressed the view that every effort was made at the congress to bring to the fore the universality of Roman Catholicism. (cf. *Echo der Zeit*, April 21, 1960.)

back a very long way in the history of the popes to find one who was able to give so much attention to his Roman diocese. Even before the conquest of Rome by the Italian State in 1870 had shut the Pope up in his enclave in the Vatican, the increasingly complex functions that fell to the pastor of the universal Church had already completely absorbed the attention of the popes. The responsibility for the diocese of Rome was almost entirely entrusted to the cardinal-vicar who was helped by an assistant bishop.

John XXIII wished to find time to be Bishop of Rome as well. From the beginning his visits to parishes, hospitals, prisons, institutions, and seminaries in the capital, his participation in liturgical ceremonies and in festivals which were especially timed for his convenience, were very real innovations in his pastoral ministry. Nowadays Rome is no longer surprised to see the papal car with a very much reduced suite in attendance, speeding through the streets taking the Pope, smiling and giving his blessing, to some church.

The most tangible sign of the concern that the Pope has for his diocese is the synod which was held from January 24–31, 1960. The announcement of the synod had come at the same time as that of the ecumenical council on January 25 of the previous year, and was not the least of the surprises of that famous speech. A real synod, that is to say a consultative assembly of the clergy setting out to determine the pastoral rules of religious life in the diocese, had never been held in Rome before, and there were those who expected the Pope to encounter serious obstacles to the realization of his project. If there were any obstacles they were easily surmounted by the persistent gentleness of John XXIII. In one single year the synodal committee, as a result of the work of conferences and sub-committees, prepared a text of synodal statutes comprising more than seven hundred articles dealing with different aspects of pastoral life in the diocese of Rome.

The Pope himself presided over the Synodal Assembly in the course of which more than three hundred ecclesiastics listened to and were handed the text of the constitutions. He delivered several addresses, written entirely by himself. They represent a vigorous and very individual commentary on the spirit of the synodal articles and at the same time a fervent appeal for the two principal requirements of the priestly life: on the one hand, dignity, austerity, the obligation to pray and study; on the other hand, apostolic zeal in all functions, even administrative ones.

The religious needs of Rome are immense. A town which, forty years ago, consisted of fewer than 700,000 inhabitants divided into sixty-two parishes, has now more than two million inhabitants distributed among 190 parishes. The priests, secular and regular, who serve in this area number little more than five hundred. There is need for at least twice that number; an increase of at least fifty every year is required, whereas in 1960 only fifteen new priests were ordained. The growth of the Italian capital especially after the last world war has completely disorganized the already weakened machinery of religious administration. Both the means and the methods of evangelistic activity have therefore remained inadequate: Catholic Action has progressed rather unsteadily, the liturgical movement has hardly got under way, there is almost complete ignorance of the new methods of religious education, and participation in working-class movements hardly goes beyond a polite and paternal acquaintance. There are, it is true, a number of parishes in which bold evangelistic experiments have been made with good results, but in general, the evidence of religious fervour in the Holy City, the seat of the papacy, would certainly not edify the pilgrims who gather there from all parts of the world.

The Synod of Rome was meant to be the first stage in the

reorganization of the entire apostolic movement. Pope John was not content to remind the Roman clergy of the duties attaching to their vocation; he appealed to a number of young Italian and foreign priests, who happened to be studying in the capital, to help their Roman brethren in the parishes. It was his wish that any priest in an ecclesiastical administrative office, in a convent, seminary, or religious house, should be at the disposal of the vicariate for apostolic purposes every Sunday. He even appealed to the lay brothers for help. Seminarists in dioceses where recruitment is strong were offered the opportunity of pursuing their studies free in Rome and of staying on afterwards in the service of the city's vicariate. The pastoral government of the diocese was to be divided into four areas, each having an assistant bishop at its head. Liturgy, religious training, Catholic Action for youth and for adults, study circles and schools were singled out as the surest ways of exercising a lasting influence, and a big expansion of these departments was urged.

What struck the Roman clergy most on the occasion of the synod was the Pope's care for his flock and the real interest he took in the problems of the ministry. His long diplomatic career and now the weight of great responsibilities have failed to extinguish in him the old ideals or his aspiration to be the pastor who knows his sheep intimately. In the tradition of his great model, Radini, he proclaims to the world the ideal which animated the prelate's life and which has also inspired all his own speeches from Sofia to Istanbul and Venice. It is with this same ideal that he has continued to stand before the world after his election as Pope. But because it might be felt that his image as the universal pastor and the high duties of his office would make him remote from the pressing needs of his flock, it has been his wish to fulfil the humbler function of looking after a small flock as a diocesan bishop, as a complement to his more august function. In this way he can more easily maintain close touch with his people and find many opportunities for individual contacts and for sharing worship, for private conversations and mutual encouragement.

And yet, in analysing this zeal which attracts Pope John to his people, one should not overlook another aspect of his episcopal ministry as he sees it. By laying emphasis on his office of bishop he is adopting a standpoint from which he can more easily talk to the members of the separated Eastern Churches, who do not recognize the Pope's jurisdiction over the universal Church but have great respect for the ancient privileges and authority of the episcopal See of Rome. To present himself to them as Bishop of Rome, in a rôle which is familiar to them and recognized by them, without jeopardizing his powers as Pope, shows him to be inspired by a charity capable of bridging gaps and making discussion easier.

In order to complete this impression of the first years of the pontificate of Pope John it is necessary to take a look at his spiritual make-up and at his work as chief pastor of the Church. An immense responsibility weighs upon the shoulders of a man who is elected Pope at the age of 78, but it has not disturbed his serenity or his joy. This serene and smiling confidence is perhaps the element in his character that has created the most favourable impression on the outside world. The unexpected break with his previous activities, his entry upon a new and imposing way of life with its solitude and pomp, and the separation from his friends—these changes roused in him a certain uneasiness, which was increased by the prospect of his new duties and sovereign powers.

Every Pope has had to pass through this trial, by submitting to God whose will it is that he should occupy that office. But in John XXIII a willing obedience was the true and only secret of his acceptance of the call to take this great step and the source of his peace of mind. During the early months the visits paid to the Vatican by those who had been his childhood friends and his companions during his career were so numerous that they seriously embarrassed the master of ceremonies who was responsible for regulating the flow of the audiences. If now and then one of his close friends, in particular a contemporary of his young priesthood days, stayed too long at the interview, a message would reach him by some means or other which was at once an invitation and a gentle reproach. At these meetings, the new Pope gave proof to everyone of his tranquil spirit, his courage, and his trust in God.

Work started at once and became increasingly absorbing. He did not have to search for long; he found the path along which he had to travel without difficulty, yielding to the certainty of being carried by God, recognizing with a readiness which was at times disconcerting the heavenly 'inspiration' which was guiding him in the execution of his plans. Thus his task is simplified by his habit of obedience and the enthusiasm with which he seeks to carry out God's will for His Church. The divine will is not always easily followed, it may even strike out along new and unexpected paths. When this happens some anxiety and reluctance is inevitable, but the Pope is able to overcome difficulties easily, without haste, with a persuasiveness that may appear timid but which is in fact strong and with a love which communicates and calls forth loyalty at the same time.

There is no attempt to conceal difficulties, and he relies on people without being too much of an optimist. He knows them as it were intuitively, distinguishing their virtues from their defects, but only for the purpose of giving strength and effect to the virtues. He knows that men are guided by God, and that even if they oppose Him they still contribute in some mysterious way to the realization of His plans. He relies therefore first and foremost on God, whose providence always surrounds our lives. It is not difficult to see the hand of God in the history that surrounds us; the Pope's faith sees in every new event not an obstacle but a constant reassurance. He himself feels that he is borne along by God, that it is not his own steps that lead him forward. 'It sometimes seems to me as though I were an empty sack', he recently told an old friend, 'into which the Holy Spirit suddenly pours redoubled strength.'

It has been remarked how many times in his speeches, and not only in his extempore ones, he relates stories of his own life and returns to the theme of the 'many people' he has met and the 'numerous countries' he has visited, and it is with a quiet emotion that he refers to them. It has a poetic effect because it springs from detachment, and detachment is a primary element of poetry; but even more it arises from religious contemplation of the way in which providence has ordered his life. Every phase of his life, every moment of it, is set in a framework which speaks of the divine goodness. The religious inspiration of Catholic Bergamo, the sufferings of the Bulgarian Church, the invigorating experiences in Turkey, the refined spirit of the Greek world, the bold vigour of the French mind and of French Catholicism, the warm and loyal sympathy of Venice, these and a host of memories are still for him a source of unfailing joy.

People enjoy his company and would like to prolong an audience which leaves an unforgettable impression. The main impression that visitors take away with them is of that spiritual tranquillity which he considers it his apostolic duty to communicate to those around him. His strong personality attracts and compels. His powers of sympathy and understanding are such that those who are received by him wonder if they can really be the object of it. He is incapable of indifference or envy.

His pontificate has revealed the widest possible interest in humanity and in human values. He believes that goodness, wherever it is found, comes from God. This principle is the source of his strength and gives him peace of mind in his work of guiding the Church and guarding its liberty. The world offers the spectacle of a constant conflict between different ideologies and powers, of formidable clashes between spiritual and material interests. But the Church pursues its path, leaving politics, science, finance, and technology to others. Its message can thus be expressed in terms of the Gospel and has no need to be tied to any earthly power. It judges human trends, by approving or condemning them, but it intends to remain independent and free.

Pope John loves a freedom of spirit which, while enabling him to show his sympathy for any form of true goodness, allows him at the same time to remain completely faithful to himself. The principle which inspires his government of the Church is still that of the Gospel: 'Be wise as serpents and innocent as doves.' One would expect him personally to prefer the symbol of the dove. He is not afraid —and never has been—of that conflict within the Church in which the confident and almost prophetic boldness of some is opposed to the cautious restraint of others experienced in the subtle calculation of human relations.* He does not fear, indeed he considers as creative, the eternal dialectic between existing institutions and new experiences. In the heart of the Church, side by side with tradition, there is the activity of the Holy Spirit which 'blows where it wills.'

He prefers to encourage rather than to restrain. It is less dangerous, in a world which moves fast, to keep moving even if it means feeling one's way. The important thing is to keep going forward without resting on old set customs, to go in search of new contacts so that Christ may be

---

* Compare the words reported by the *Osservatore Romano*, July 13-14, 1959: 'Divine providence is about to throw light on one of the great mysteries of all time, the mystery of the mercy of the Lord towards all people'—an allusion to the ecumenical council and in particular the present dangers that face the Church.

proclaimed and acknowledged in all manner of ways.*
Those with only a superficial knowledge of the way in
which he had developed expected him to make a break
with the past. There is no doubt that he loves the past:
often when he speaks he insists on the need to return to
family traditions.† He himself has lived according to them
and has experienced their gentle warmth and their constructive strength. He respects religious tradition and the
imprint it has left on the life of the Church in matters of
piety, liturgy, and theology, but he thinks of it as a past
to be judged in the light of events and with the sensibility
of an apostle. Very few have grasped as he has the grandeur
and humanity of the Church. Very few have been aware
as he has of the strength and weaknesses of the ecclesiastical
organization. It is perhaps this perception which has given,
and still gives, to his life its rare moments of anxiety. It
certainly keeps his zeal fresh. The idea, sponsored by him,
of the reform of canon law will appear bold to those who
are acquainted with the problems relating to ecclesiastical
laws. In the vexed question of the use of modern languages
in the liturgy, the first steps taken by the Pope, although
they form only a beginning, reveal a great breadth of
view.† His exhortations to read and study the Bible are
frequent; they are in keeping with the vast biblical movement which has had such a beneficial effect on the internal
life of Catholics and which contains the seeds of a rapprochement with the members of the Protestant Churches.
Concerning the problem of missions the encyclical

---

* Compare the speech during the general audience at St Peter's, March 20,
1960 (*Osservatore Romano*, March 25, 1960).

† In a letter dated September 9, 1960, addressed to the Catholic Melchite
Patriarch of Antioch, the Pope took the very unusual step of annulling a
decision of the Holy Office forbidding the use of the vernacular (English in this
case) in the celebration of Mass according to the Oriental Rite. Also well
known is the fact that in an impromptu speech delivered to Santa Maria del
Soccorso, a parish on the outskirts of Rome, the Pope said that he hoped to see
the vernacular occupy a more important place in the liturgy. Published in
several newspapers, these words were not confirmed by the *Osservatore Romano*.

Princeps Pastorum gives directives which show an awareness of the most recent events. The Pope wishes the training of the native clergy to be adapted 'to take account of special local conditions peculiar to the different localities and countries.' Finally he lays emphasis on instruction in missiology which must be in accord with the sound teaching and tradition of the Church. It should also be aimed at sharpening the students' minds so that they may be able to form a true estimate of the cultural traditions of their own homelands, especially in matters of philosophy and theology, and to discern the special points of contact between them and the Christian religion. This clearly involves criteria which are valid for all countries.

Of particular significance is the recommendation addressed by the Pope to Catholics, and especially to the clergy, concerning serious study. The pastoral experience of his whole life, and now the deeper knowledge he has formed of the demands of evangelization, have convinced him of the importance of Catholic culture. Equally important, however, in his eyes is the aim of culture. Purely scientific work, although necessary, is not an end in itself for the priest, but it should serve to enlighten the mind further and to prepare it for a more thorough and effective ministry. The intellectuals must be inspired by the apostolic motive, especially the scholars who celebrated on January 17 at the Vatican, in the presence of the Pope, the fiftieth anniversary of the setting up of the Biblical Institute. He expressed his mind to them quite plainly.

In addition to study, Pope John also urges the importance of holiness upon his priests. Not only in the encyclical *Sacerdotii nostri primordia* but also in dozens of addresses he tackled the theme of the inner life of the priest. He persistently recalls the need for prayer, but perhaps the words which issue most spontaneously from his heart are those extolling certain virtues such as gentleness, modesty and obedience, of which he himself provides such a magnificent example. In the following passages he unintentionally traces his own portrait:

> Gentleness and humility constitute another precious ornament of the priestly life. The Son of God, who came on earth to teach men, puts forward no instruction that is more clear or precise than this one: humility of spirit, of thought, word and deed. Often this humility is expressed by silence, and the gentleness may appear as weakness. On the contrary it is strength of character and adds dignity to life; it is the guarantee of real worth in the sense that it makes easier relations between men. Success is always assured and granted to the meek in heart. He who is not meek in heart, he who yields to the temptation of presumptuous pride must look forward to days of bitterness, to finding himself suddenly empty-handed and to experiencing years of profound discouragement.*
>
> Seeking after wealth, distinctions, honours and personal gain is not in harmony with *Christum sequi*; it is in flagrant contradiction with the *reliquimus omnia* which is the starting-point of the journey to the authentic greatness and glory of Christianity, the Church and the priesthood for all time. On this subject, permit your bishop and Father to express a keen regret which often causes him to pray in anguish.†

We may place alongside these words the fatherly confidence which the Pope uttered to a group of Japanese pilgrims as he spoke to them informally. He admitted that for him it was each day a real sacrifice to allow himself to be carried on the *sedia gestatoria*. He accepted this outwardly pompous exaltation only because it enabled him to greet and bless his people more extensively.‡ On another occasion he confided to his friends that the *sedia gestatoria* symbolized very well the will of God which bore him along and to which he surrendered himself in quiet obedience. His constant motto is: *Obedientia et pax*. It is indeed the first

* Speech to the students of the Propaganda, *Osservatore Romano*, December 1–2, 1958.

† Speech to the Roman clergy, November 25, 1960, *Osservatore Romano* of the same date.

‡ *Osservatore Romano*, April 6, 1960.

and last characteristic of the figure of John XXIII. He
himself constantly returns to it:

> It is really, if we study it closely, a mysterious and powerful
> expression which strengthens the spirit and remains all the time
> a precise and magnificent motto, even if it involves sacrifices—
> which, it must be said, are made tolerable and not burdensome
> by it. Great peace of mind is the unfailing consequence of it.
> With this treasure in one's heart, even the heaviest weight
> becomes acceptable, and one goes forward without fear,
> whatever the judgement of the world may be, sustained by
> divine omnipotence.*

* Speech to the members of the Secretariat of State. *Osservatore Romano*,
November 19, 1958.

INDEX